Study Guide

Financial Accounting
Seventh Edition

Belverd E. Needles, Jr.
DePaul University

Marian Powers
Northwestern University

CONTRIBUTING EDITOR
Edward H. Julius
California Lutheran University

Houghton Mifflin Company   **Boston**   **New York**

Senior Sponsoring Editor: Bonnie Binkert
Associate Sponsoring Editor: Margaret E. Monahan
Associate Editor: Bernadette Walsh
Marketing Manager: Melissa Russell
Senior Manufacturing Coordinator: Priscilla Bailey

Printed in the U.S.A.

ISBN: 0-618-02339-9

23456789—CRS—04 03 02 01 00

Contents

Appendix

To the Student

This self-study guide is designed to help you improve your performance in your first accounting course. You should use it in your study of *Financial Accounting,* Seventh Edition, by Needles and Powers.

Reviewing the Chapter

This section of each chapter summarizes in a concise but thorough manner the essential points related to the chapter's learning objectives. Each integrated learning objective is restated and all key terms are covered in this section. Where applicable, a summary of journal entries introduced in the chapter also is presented.

Self-Test

The Self-Test within each chapter reviews the basic concepts taught in the chapter and helps you to prepare for the examination your teacher will give based on the learning objectives assigned and taught in class.

Testing Your Knowledge

Each chapter contains a matching quiz of key terms, a short-answer section, true-false statements, and multiple-choice questions to test your understanding of the learning objectives and vocabulary in the chapter. This Study Guide also contains eight crossword puzzles to test your knowledge of key terms.

Applying Your Knowledge

An important goal in learning accounting is the ability to work exercises and problems. In this section of each chapter, you can test your ability to apply two or three of the new principles introduced in the chapter to "real-life" accounting situations.

Answers

The Study Guide concludes with answers to all questions, exercises, problems, and crossword puzzles. All answers are cross-referenced to the learning objectives in the chapter.

B.E.N.
M.P.
E.H.J.

CHAPTER 1 USES OF ACCOUNTING INFORMATION AND THE FINANCIAL STATEMENTS

REVIEWING THE CHAPTER

Objective 1: Define *accounting,* **identify business goals and activities, and describe the role of accounting in making informed decisions.**

1. **Accounting** is an information system that measures, processes, and communicates financial information about an identifiable economic entity. It provides information that is essential for decision making. **Bookkeeping,** a small but important aspect of accounting, is the mechanical and repetitive recordkeeping process.

2. A **business** is an economic unit that sells goods and services at prices that will provide an adequate return to its owners. For a business to survive, management must make satisfactory earnings to hold investment capital (called **profitability**) and must keep sufficient cash on hand to pay debts as they fall due (called **liquidity**). The company also has other goals, such as improving its products and expanding operations. It is management that directs the company toward these goals by making decisions.

3. Businesses pursue their goals by engaging in financing, investing, and operating activities.
   a. **Financing activities** are needed to obtain funding for the business, and include such activities as issuing stocks and bonds and repaying creditors.
   b. **Investing activities** consist of spending the funds raised, and include activities such as buying and selling land, buildings, and equipment.

   c. **Operating activities** involve the everyday sale of goods and services as well as the related everyday activities.

4. **Performance measures** indicate the extent to which management is achieving its business goals and is managing business activities. Accordingly, performance measures often serve as the basis for the evaluation of managers. Examples of performance measures are cash flow (for liquidity), net income or loss (for profitability), and the ratio of expenses to revenue (for operating activities).

5. A distinction is usually made between **management accounting,** which focuses on information for internal users, and **financial accounting,** which involves the preparation, reporting, analysis, and interpretation of accounting information in reports for external users. These reports are called **financial statements.**

6. The **computer** is an electronic tool that rapidly collects, organizes, and communicates vast amounts of information. The computer does not take the place of the accountant. However, the accountant must understand how the computer operates because it is an integral part of the accounting information system.

7. A **management information system (MIS)** is an information network that takes in all major functions (called *subsystems*) of a business. The accounting information system is the financial hub of the management information system.

Objective 2: Identify the many users of accounting information in society.

8. There are basically three groups that use accounting information: management, outsiders with a direct financial interest, and outsiders with an indirect financial interest.

   a. As already stated, **management** steers a business toward its goals by making the business's important decisions. Specifically, it must ensure that the business is adequately financed, productive assets are obtained, goods and services are produced and marketed, employees are managed, and pertinent information is provided to decision makers.

   b. Present or potential investors and present or potential creditors are considered outside users with a direct financial interest in a business. Most businesses publish financial statements that report their profitability and financial position. Investors use these financial statements to assess the strength or weakness of the company, whereas creditors examine the financial statement to determine the company's ability to repay debts on time.

   c. Society as a whole, through government officials and public groups, can be viewed as an accounting information user with an indirect financial interest in a business. Specifically, such users include tax authorities, regulatory agencies, and other groups (such as labor unions, economic planners, and financial analysts).

9. The **Securities and Exchange Commission (SEC)** is an agency of the federal government set up by the U.S. Congress to protect the investing public by regulating the issuing, buying, and selling of stocks.

10. Managers within government and within not-for-profit organizations such as hospitals, universities, professional organizations, and charities also make extensive use of financial information.

Objective 3: Explain the importance of business transactions, money measure, and separate entity to accounting measurement.

11. To make an accounting measurement, the accountant must answer the following basic questions:
    a. What is measured?
    b. When should the measurement be made?
    c. What value should be placed on what is measured?
    d. How should what is measured be classified?

12. Accounting is concerned with measuring transactions of specific business entities in terms of money.

    a. **Business transactions** are economic events that affect the financial position of a business. Business transactions can involve an exchange of value (for example, sales, borrowings, and purchases) or a nonexchange (for example, the physical wear and tear on machinery, and losses due to fire or theft).

    b. The **money measure** concept states that business transactions should be measured in terms of money. Financial statements are normally prepared in terms of the monetary unit of the business's country (dollars, pesos, etc.). When transactions occur between countries with differing monetary units, the amounts must be translated from one currency to another, using the appropriate **exchange rate**.

    c. For accounting purposes, a business is treated as a **separate entity**, distinct from its owners, creditors, and customers.

Objective 4: Describe the corporate form of business organization.

13. The three basic forms of business organization are sole proprietorships, partnerships, and corporations. Accountants recognize each form as an economic unit separate from its owners. A **sole proprietorship** is an unincorporated business owned by one person. A **partnership** is much like a sole proprietorship, except that it is owned by two or more persons. A **corporation,** unlike a sole proprietorship or partnership, is a business granted a charter from the state and legally separate from its owners (the stockholders).

14. The corporation is the dominant form of American business because it makes possible the accumulation of large quantities of capital. The stockholders of a corporation are at risk only to the extent of their investment, and ownership (evidenced by **shares of stock**) can be transferred without affecting operations.

    a. Before a corporation may do business, it must apply for and obtain a charter from the state. The state must approve the **articles of incorporation,** which describe the basic purpose and structure of the proposed corporation.

    b. Management of a corporation consists of the board of directors, who determine corporate policy and appoint managers, who carry on the daily operations. The board is elected by the stockholders, and the officers are appointed by the board.

c. Some specific duties of the board of directors are to (a) declare dividends, (b) authorize contracts, (c) determine executive salaries, (d) arrange major loans with banks, and (e) appoint an **audit committee** to serve as a channel of communication between the corporation and the independent auditors. Management's primary means of reporting the corporation's financial position and results of operations is its annual report.

Objective 5: Define *financial position,* **state the accounting equation, and show how they are affected by simple transactions.**

15. Every business transaction affects a firm's financial position. **Financial position** is shown by a balance sheet, so called because the two sides or parts of the balance sheet must always equal each other. In a sense, the balance sheet presents two ways of viewing the same business: the left side shows the assets (resources) of the business, whereas the right side shows who provided the assets. Providers consist of owners (listed under "owners' equity") and creditors (represented by the listing of "liabilities"). Therefore, it is logical that the total dollar amount of assets must equal the total dollar amount of liabilities and owners' equity. This is the **accounting equation**. It is formally stated as

$$\text{Assets} = \text{Liabilities} + \text{Owners' Equity}$$

Other correct forms are

$$\text{Assets} - \text{Liabilities} = \text{Owners' Equity}$$

$$\text{Assets} - \text{Owners' Equity} = \text{Liabilities}$$

16. **Assets** are the economic resources of a business. Examples of assets are cash, accounts receivable, inventory, buildings, equipment, patents, and copyrights.

17. **Liabilities** are debts of the business. Examples of liabilities are money owed to banks, amounts owed to creditors for goods bought on credit, and taxes owed to the government.

18. **Owners' equity** represents the claims by the owners of a business to the assets of the business. It equals the residual interest in assets after deducting the liabilities. Because it is equal to assets minus liabilities, owners' equity is said to equal the **net assets** of the business.

19. The owners' equity of a corporation is called **stockholders' equity** and consists of contributed capital and retained earnings. **Contributed capital** represents the amount invested by the owners, whereas **retained earnings** (broadly) represent the accumulation of the profits and losses of a company since its inception, less total dividends declared. **Dividends** are distributions of assets to stockholders from past earnings; they appear as a reduction in the statement of retained earnings.

20. Retained earnings are affected by three types of transactions. **Revenues,** which result when services have been provided, increase retained earnings. **Expenses,** which represent costs of doing business, decrease retained earnings. When revenues exceed expenses, a **net income** results. When expenses exceed revenues, however, a **net loss** has been suffered.

21. Every business transaction changes the balance sheet in some way. In practice, companies do not prepare a new balance sheet after each transaction. However, it is important for accounting students to understand the effect of each transaction on the parts of the balance sheet.

22. Although every transaction changes the balance sheet, the accounting equation always remains in balance. In other words, dollar amounts may change, but assets must always equal liabilities plus owners' equity.

23. **Accounts** are used by accountants to accumulate amounts produced from like transactions.

Objective 6: Identify the four financial statements.

24. Accountants communicate information through financial statements. The four principal statements are the income statement, statement of retained earnings, balance sheet, and statement of cash flows.

25. Every financial statement has a three-line heading. The first line gives the name of the company. The second line gives the name of the statement. The third line gives the relevant dates (the date of the balance sheet or the period of time covered by the other three statements).

26. The **income statement,** whose components are revenues and expenses, is perhaps the most important financial statement. Its purpose is to measure the business's success or failure in achieving its goal for profitability.

27. The **statement of retained earnings** is a labeled calculation of the changes in retained earnings (defined in paragraph 19) during the accounting period. Retained earnings at the beginning of the period is the first item on the statement, followed by an addition for net income or a deduction for net loss and a deduction for dividends declared.

The ending retained earnings figure that results is transferred to the stockholders' equity section of the balance sheet.

28. The **balance sheet** shows the financial position of a business as of a certain date. The resources owned by the business are called assets; debts of the business are called liabilities; and the owners' financial interest in the business is called stockholders' equity. The balance sheet is also known as the *statement of financial position.*

29. The **statement of cash flows** focuses on the business's liquidity goal, and shows much information that is not found in the other three financial statements. **Cash flows** refer to the business's cash inflows and cash outflows. *Net* cash flows represent the difference between these inflows and outflows.

30. The statement of cash flows discloses all the business's operating, investing, and financing activities during the accounting period. As discussed, in part, in paragraph 3, operating activities consist mainly of receipts from customers and payments to suppliers and others in the ordinary course of business. Investing activities might include selling a building or investing in stock. Financing activities might include issuing stock or paying dividends. The statement will indicate the net increase or decrease in cash produced during the period.

Objective 7: State the relationship of generally accepted accounting principles (GAAP) to financial statements and the independent CPA's report, and identify the organizations that influence GAAP.

31. Accounting theory provides the reasoning behind and framework for accounting practice. **Generally accepted accounting principles (GAAP)** are the set of guidelines and procedures that constitute acceptable accounting practice at a given time. The set of GAAP changes continually as business conditions change and practices improve.

32. The financial statements of publicly held corporations are audited by licensed professionals, called **certified public accountants (CPAs),** to ensure the quality of those statements. Before an **audit** can take place, however, the CPA must be independent of the client (without financial or other ties). On completion of the audit, the CPA reports on whether or not the audited statements "present fairly, in all material respects" and are "in conformity with generally accepted accounting principles."

33. The **Financial Accounting Standards Board (FASB)** is the authoritative body for development of GAAP. This group is separate from the AICPA and issues *Statements of Financial Accounting Standards.*

34. The **American Institute of Certified Public Accountants (AICPA)** is the professional association of CPAs. Its senior technical committees help influence accounting practice.

35. The Securities and Exchange Commission (SEC) is an agency of the federal government. It has the legal power to set and enforce accounting practices for companies whose securities are traded by the general public.

36. The **Governmental Accounting Standards Board (GASB)** was established in 1984 and is responsible for issuing accounting standards for state and local governments.

37. The **International Accounting Standards Committee (IASC)** is responsible for developing worldwide accounting standards. To date, it has approved more than thirty such standards, which have been translated into six languages.

38. The **Internal Revenue Service (IRS)** enforces and interprets the set of rules that govern the assessment and collection of federal income taxes.

Objective 8: Define *ethics* and describe the ethical responsibilities of accountants.

39. **Ethics** is a code of conduct that applies to everyday life. **Professional ethics** is the application of a code of conduct to the practice of a profession. The accounting profession has developed such a code, intended to guide the accountant in carrying out his or her responsibilities to the public. In short, the accountant must act with integrity, objectivity, independence, and due care.
    a. **Integrity** means that the accountant is honest, regardless of consequences.
    b. **Objectivity** means that the accountant is impartial in performing his or her job.
    c. **Independence** is the avoidance of all relationships that could impair the objectivity of the accountant, such as owning stock in a company he or she is auditing.
    d. **Due care** means carrying out one's responsibilities with competence and diligence.

40. The **Institute of Management Accountants (IMA)** has adopted a code of professional conduct of competence, confidentiality, integrity, and objectivity for management accountants.

SELF-TEST

Test your knowledge of the chapter by choosing the best answer for each of the following items.

1. Which of the following is an important reason for studying accounting?
   a. Accounting information is useful in making economic decisions.
   b. Accounting plays an important role in society.
   c. The study of accounting can lead to a challenging career.
   d. All of the above are important reasons for studying accounting.

2. Which of the following groups uses accounting information for planning a company's profitability and liquidity?
   a. Management
   b. Investors
   c. Creditors
   d. Economic planners

3. Economic events that affect the financial position of a business are called
   a. separate entities.
   b. business transactions.
   c. money measures.
   d. financial actions.

4. For legal purposes, which of the following forms of business organization is (are) treated as a separate economic unit from its owner(s)?
   a. Sole proprietorship
   b. Corporation
   c. Partnership
   d. All of the above

5. If a company has liabilities of $19,000 and owners' equity of $57,000, its assets are
   a. $38,000.
   b. $76,000.
   c. $57,000.
   d. $19,000.

6. The payment of a liability
   a. increases both assets and liabilities.
   b. increases assets and decreases liabilities.
   c. decreases assets and increases liabilities.
   d. decreases both assets and liabilities.

7. Investments by stockholders will
   a. increase both total assets and total owners' equity.
   b. increase both total assets and total liabilities.
   c. increase total assets and decrease total owners' equity.
   d. have no effect on total assets, liabilities, or owners' equity.

8. Expenses and dividends appear, respectively, on the
   a. balance sheet and income statement.
   b. income statement and balance sheet.
   c. statement of retained earnings and balance sheet.
   d. income statement and statement of retained earnings.

9. Generally accepted accounting principles
   a. define accounting practice at a point in time.
   b. are similar in nature to the principles of chemistry or physics.
   c. rarely change.
   d. are not affected by changes in the ways businesses operate.

10. Independence is an important characteristic of the following in performing audits of financial statements:
    a. Government accountants
    b. Certified management accountants
    c. Certified public accountants
    d. Accounting educators

TESTING YOUR KNOWLEDGE

Matching*

Match each term with its definition by writing the appropriate letter in the blank.

_____ 1. Accounting

_____ 2. Bookkeeping

_____ 3. Computer

_____ 4. Management information system (MIS)

_____ 5. Management accounting

_____ 6. Financial accounting

_____ 7. Accounting equation

_____ 8. Dividend

_____ 9. Certified public accountant (CPA)

_____ 10. Sole proprietorship

_____ 11. Partnership

_____ 12. Corporation

_____ 13. Generally accepted accounting principles (GAAP)

_____ 14. Balance sheet

_____ 15. Income statement

_____ 16. Statement of retained earnings

_____ 17. Statement of cash flows

_____ 18. Separate entity

_____ 19. Money measure

_____ 20. Asset

_____ 21. Liability

_____ 22. Owners' equity

_____ 23. Contributed capital

a. A debt of a business

b. A business owned by stockholders but managed by a board of directors

c. A distribution of earnings to stockholders

d. The standard that all business transactions should be measured in terms of money

e. The statement that shows the financial position of a company on a certain date

f. The repetitive recordkeeping process

g. An economic resource of a business

h. An information system that measures, processes, and communicates economic information

i. A business owned and managed by two or more persons

j. An expert accountant licensed by the state

k. Representation on the balance sheet of stockholders' investments in a corporation

l. The statement that shows a company's profit or loss over a certain period of time

m. The statement that discloses the operating, investing, and financing activities during the period

n. The branch of accounting concerned with providing external users with financial information needed to make decisions

o. An electronic tool that processes information rapidly

p. The balance sheet section that represents the owners' economic interest in a company

q. The statement that shows the changes in the Retained Earnings account during the period

r. The information network that links a company's functions together

s. Assets = Liabilities + Owners' Equity

t. The accounting concept that treats a business as distinct from its owners, creditors, and customers

u. The guidelines that define acceptable accounting practice at a given point in time

v. A business owned and managed by one person

w. The branch of accounting concerned with providing managers with financial information needed to make decisions

---

*Note to student: The matching quiz might be completed more efficiently by starting with the definition and searching for the corresponding term.

Chapter 1

Short Answer

Use the lines provided to answer each item.

1. On the lines that follow, insert the correct heading for the annual income statement of Zeno Corporation on June 30, 20xx.

   _____

   _____

   _____

2. Briefly distinguish between bookkeeping and accounting.

   _____

   _____

   _____

3. Briefly define the terms below, all of which relate to the accountant's Code of Professional Conduct.

   a. Integrity _____

   _____

   b. Objectivity _____

   _____

   c. Independence _____

   _____

   d. Due care _____

   _____

4. What three broad groups use accounting information?

   _____

   _____

   _____

5. What two objectives must be met for a company to survive?

   _____

   _____

6. List the four principal financial statements and state briefly the purpose of each.

   Statement

   a. _____

   _____

   b. _____

   _____

   c. _____

   _____

   d. _____

   _____

   Purpose

   a. _____

   _____

   b. _____

   _____

   c. _____

   _____

   d. _____

   _____

Circle T if the statement is true, F if it is false. Please provide explanations for false answers, using the blank lines at the end of the section.

T F **1.** Financial position can best be determined by referring to the income statement.

T F **2.** The IRS is responsible for interpreting and enforcing GAAP.

T F **3.** One form of the accounting equation is Assets – Liabilities = Owners' Equity.

T F **4.** Revenues have the effect of increasing owners' equity.

T F **5.** The existence of Accounts Receivable on the balance sheet indicates that the company has one or more creditors.

T F **6.** When expenses exceed revenues, a company has suffered a net loss.

T F **7.** The measurement stage of accounting involves preparation of the financial statements.

T F **8.** Dividends appear as a deduction on the income statement.

T F **9.** The current authoritative body dictating accounting practice is the FASB.

T F **10.** A sole proprietor is personally liable for all debts of the business.

T F **11.** The statement of cash flows would disclose whether or not land was purchased for cash during the period.

T F **12.** The statement of retained earnings links a company's income statement to its balance sheet.

T F **13.** The IASC is responsible for setting guidelines for state and local governments.

T F **14.** A corporation is managed directly by its stockholders.

T F **15.** Generally accepted accounting principles are not like laws of math and science; they are guidelines that define correct accounting practice at a given point in time.

T F **16.** Net assets equal assets plus liabilities.

T F **17.** The major sections of a balance sheet are assets, liabilities, owners' equity, revenues, and expenses.

T F **18.** A business transaction must always involve an exchange of money.

T F **19.** A management information system deals not only with accounting, but with other activities of a business as well.

T F **20.** The income statement is generally considered to be the most important financial statement.

T F **21.** A business should be understood as an entity that is separate and distinct from its owners, customers, and creditors.

T F **22.** Economic planners are accounting information users with a direct financial interest.

T F **23.** The essence of an asset is that it is expected to benefit future operations.

T F **24.** Cash flow is a (performance) measure of profitability.

_____

_____

_____

_____

_____

_____

_____

_____

_____

_____

_____

_____

_____

_____

_____
_____
_____
_____
_____
_____

_____
_____
_____
_____
_____
_____

Multiple Choice

Circle the letter of the best answer.

1. Which of the following accounts would not appear on the balance sheet?
   a. Wages Expense
   b. Common Stock
   c. Notes Receivable
   d. Wages Payable

2. Companies whose stock is publicly traded must file financial statements with the
   a. FASB.
   b. GASB.
   c. SEC.
   d. AICPA.

3. One characteristic of a corporation is
   a. unlimited liability of its owners.
   b. the ease with which ownership is transferred.
   c. ownership by the board of directors.
   d. dissolution upon the death of an owner.

4. Which of the following statements does *not* involve a distinct period of time?
   a. Income statement
   b. Balance sheet
   c. Statement of cash flows
   d. Statement of retained earnings

5. The principal purpose of an audit by a CPA is to
   a. express an opinion on the fairness of a company's financial statements.
   b. detect fraud by a company's employees.
   c. prepare the company's financial statements.
   d. assure investors that the company will be profitable in the future.

6. Collection on an account receivable will
   a. increase total assets and increase total stockholders' equity.
   b. have no effect on total assets, but will increase total stockholders' equity.
   c. decrease both total assets and total liabilities.
   d. have no effect on total assets, liabilities, or stockholders' equity.

7. In a partnership,
   a. profits are always divided equally among partners.
   b. management consists of the board of directors.
   c. no partner is liable for more than a proportion of the company's debts.
   d. dissolution results when any partner leaves the partnership.

8. Which of the following is *not* a major heading on a balance sheet or income statement?
   a. Accounts Receivable
   b. Stockholders' Equity
   c. Liabilities
   d. Revenues

9. Payment of a liability will
   a. decrease total liabilities and decrease total stockholders' equity.
   b. decrease total assets and increase total stockholders' equity.
   c. decrease total assets and decrease total liabilities.
   d. have no effect on total assets, liabilities, or stockholders' equity.

10. The purchase of an asset for cash will
    a. increase total assets and increase total stockholders' equity.
    b. increase total assets and increase total liabilities.
    c. increase total assets and decrease total liabilities.
    d. have no effect on total assets, liabilities, or stockholders' equity.

11. Which of the following is *not* an activity listed on the statement of cash flows?
    a. Investing Activities
    b. Funding Activities
    c. Operating Activities
    d. Financing Activities

APPLYING YOUR KNOWLEDGE

Exercises

1. Moses Steel, Inc., always publishes annual financial statements. This year, however, it has suffered a huge loss and is trying to keep this fact a secret by refusing anyone access to its financial statements. Why might each of the following nevertheless insist on seeing Moses's statements?

   a. Potential investors in Moses

   b. The Securities and Exchange Commission

   c. The bank, which is considering a loan request by Moses

   d. Present stockholders of Moses

   e. Moses's management

2. Einstein Corporation had assets of $100,000 and liabilities of $70,000 at the beginning of the year. During the year assets decreased by $15,000 and stockholders' equity increased by $20,000. What is the amount of liabilities at year end?

   $_____

3. Following are the accounts of Foster's TV Repair Corporation as of December 31, 20xx.

Accounts Payable	$ 1,300
Accounts Receivable	1,500
Building	10,000
Cash	?
Common Stock	14,500
Equipment	850
Land	1,000
Retained Earnings	3,000
Truck	4,500

   Using this information, prepare a balance sheet *in good form*. (You must derive the dollar amount for Cash.)

   Foster's TV Repair Corporation
   Balance Sheet
   December 31, 20xx

   Assets

   Liabilities

   Stockholders' Equity

   ---

4. Following are the transactions for Tellier Paints, Inc., for the first month of operations.

a. Jack and Andrea Tellier invested $20,000 cash in the newly formed business.
b. Purchased paint supplies and equipment for $650 cash.
c. Purchased a company truck on credit for $5,200.
d. Received $525 for painting a house.
e. Paid one-half of the amount due on the truck previously purchased.
f. Billed a customer $150 for painting his garage.
g. Paid $250 for one month's rental of the office.
h. Received full payment from the customer whose garage was painted (transaction f).
i. Performed a service for $20. The customer said he would pay next month.
j. The company declared and paid a $200 cash dividend.

In the form below, show the effect of each transaction on the balance sheet accounts by putting the dollar amount, along with a plus or minus sign, under the proper account. Determine the balance in each account at month's end. As an example, transaction a already has been recorded.

| Transaction | Assets | | | | Liabilities | Stockholders' Equity | |
	Cash	Accounts Receivable	Supplies and Equipment	Trucks	Accounts Payable	Common Stock	Retained Earnings
a	+$20,000					+$20,000	
b							
c							
d							
e							
f							
g							
h							
i							
j							
Balance at end of month							

Crossword Puzzle
for Chapter 1

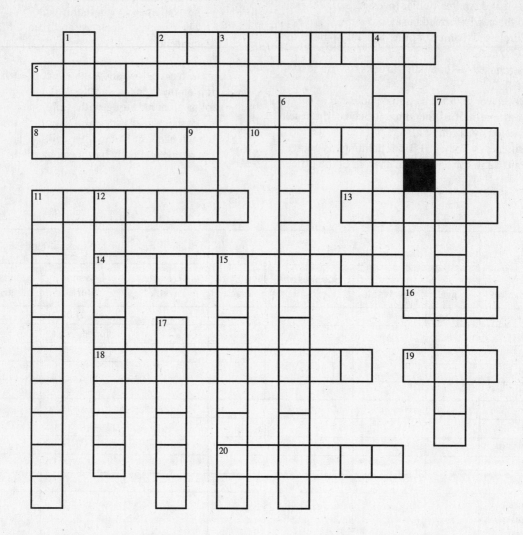

	ACROSS
2.	Accounting mainly for external use
5.	_____ proprietorship
8.	Resources of a company
10.	One to whom another is indebted
11.	_____ sheet
13.	Professional organization of accountants
14.	The language of business
16.	IRS's concern
18.	Measure of debt-paying ability
19.	Data-generating network
20.	Separate _____ concept

	DOWN
1.	See 3-Down
3.	With 1-Down, income statement measure
4.	Independent CPA activity
6.	Measure of business performance
7.	Form of business organization
9.	Regulatory agency of publicly held corporations
11.	Recorder of business transactions
12.	Debt of a company
15.	Impartial
17.	Ownership in a company

HOW TO READ AN ANNUAL REPORT

REVIEWING THE SUPPLEMENT

1. Most of the four million corporations in the United States are *private,* or *closely held, corporations,* so named because ownership is not available to the general public. *Public companies,* though fewer in number, often are owned by thousands of stockholders, creating a far greater economic impact than their closely held counterparts.

2. Public companies are required to register their common stock with the Securities and Exchange Commission (SEC), primarily for the protection of the investing public. In addition, public companies must submit to their stockholders an *annual report,* which contains the requisite financial statements and other vital information about the financial position and performance of the company. Called the *S-1* when filed with the SEC, the annual report is available to the general public through a number of sources (including the Internet and electronic media sources such as *Compact Disclosure).*

3. In addition to the financial statements, the annual report ordinarily contains a letter to the stockholders, a multiyear summary of financial highlights, a description of the business, management's discussion of operating results and financial condition, a report of management's responsibility, the auditors' report, and a list of directors and officers of the corporation.

4. *Consolidated financial statements* are the combined statements of a company and its controlled subsidiaries. A company's financial statements may show data from consecutive periods side by side for comparison. Such statements are called *comparative financial statements.*

5. The consolidated statement of earnings should contain information regarding net income and earnings per share. A measure of a company's profitability, earnings per share equals net income divided by the weighted average number of shares of common stock outstanding.

6. The consolidated balance sheet usually contains classifications such as current assets, current liabilities, and long-term debt, which are useful in assessing a company's liquidity. In addition, stockholders' equity normally contains information on stock issued and bought back by the corporation, on earnings retained by the business, and on certain unusual items, such as foreign currency translation adjustments.

7. Whereas the consolidated statement of earnings reflects a company's profitability, the consolidated statement of cash flows reflects its liquidity. The statement provides information about a company's cash receipts, cash payments, and investing and financing activities during an accounting period.

8. A *consolidated statement of stockholders' equity* is usually presented in a corporate annual report in place of the statement of retained earnings. It explains the changes in each of the components of stockholders' equity.

9. A section called *notes to the financial statements* accompanies, and is considered an integral part of, the financial statements. Its purpose is to help the reader interpret some of the more complex financial statement items.

10. A *summary of significant accounting policies* discloses the generally accepted accounting principles used in preparing the statements. It usually follows the last financial statement, perhaps as the first note to the financial statements.

11. Corporations are often required to issue *interim financial statements*. These statements give financial information covering less than a year (for example, quarterly data). Ordinarily they are reviewed, but not audited, by the independent CPA.

12. An annual report usually also includes a report of management's responsibilities for the financial statements and the internal control structure of the company as well as management's discussion and analysis of operating performance.

13. The *independent auditors' report* conveys to third parties that the financial statements were examined in accordance with generally accepted auditing standards (*scope section*), and expresses the auditors' opinion on how fairly the financial statements reflect the company's financial condition (*opinion section*). In addition, the auditors' report clarifies the nature and purpose of an audit, and emphasizes management's ultimate responsibility for the financial statements.

CHAPTER 2   MEASURING BUSINESS TRANSACTIONS

REVIEWING THE CHAPTER

Objective 1: Explain, in simple terms, the generally accepted ways of solving the measurement issues of recognition, valuation, and classification.

1. Before recording a business transaction, the accountant must determine three things:
   a. When the transaction should be recorded (the **recognition** issue)
   b. What value to place on the transaction (the **valuation** issue)
   c. How the components of the transaction should be categorized (the **classification** issue)

2. A sale is recognized (entered in the accounting records) when the title to merchandise passes from the supplier to the purchaser, regardless of when payment is made or received. This point of sale is referred to as the **recognition point**.

3. The **cost principle** states that the dollar value (**cost**) of any item involved in a business transaction is its original cost (also called *historical cost*). Generally, any change in value after the transaction is not reflected in the accounting records.

Objective 2: Describe the chart of accounts and recognize commonly used accounts.

4. Every business transaction is classified in a filing system consisting of accounts. An account is the basic storage unit for accounting data. Each asset, liability, component of stockholders' equity, revenue, and expense has a separate account.

5. All of a company's accounts are contained in a book or file called the **general ledger** (or simply the *ledger*). In a manual accounting system, each account appears on a separate page. The accounts generally are in the following order: assets, liabilities, stockholders' equity, revenues, and expenses. A list of the accounts with their respective account numbers, called a **chart of accounts,** is presented at the beginning of the ledger for easy reference.

6. Although the accounts used by companies will vary, there are some that are common to most businesses. Some typical assets are Cash, Notes Receivable, Accounts Receivable, Prepaid Expenses, Land, Buildings, and Equipment. Some typical liabilities are Notes Payable, Accounts Payable, and Mortgage Payable.

7. The stockholders' equity section of a corporation's balance sheet contains a common stock account and a retained earnings account. Common stock represents the amount of capital invested by stockholders, whereas retained earnings represent cumulative profits and losses, less cumulative dividends declared. Dividends are distributions of assets (generally cash) to stockholders and may be declared only when sufficient retained earnings (and cash) exist.

8. A separate account is kept for each type of revenue and expense. The exact revenue and expense accounts used will vary, depending on the type of business and the nature of its operations. Revenues cause an increase in retained earnings, whereas expenses cause a decrease.

Objective 3: Define *double-entry system* and state the rules for double entry.

9. The **double-entry system** of accounting requires that for each transaction there must be one or more accounts debited and one or more accounts credited, and that total dollar amounts of debits must equal total dollar amounts of credits.

10. An account in its simplest form, a **T account,** has three parts:
    a. A title that expresses the name of the asset, liability, or stockholders' equity account
    b. A left side, which is called the **debit** side
    c. A right side, which is called the **credit** side

11. At the end of an accounting period, **balances** (also known as *account balances*) are calculated in order to prepare the financial statements. Using T accounts, there are three steps to follow in determining the account balances:
    a. Foot (add) the debit entries. The **footing** (total) should be made in small numbers beneath the last entry.
    b. Foot the credit entries.
    c. Subtract the smaller total from the larger. A debit balance exists when total debits exceed total credits; a credit balance exists when the opposite is the case.

12. To determine which accounts are debited and which are credited in a given transaction, one uses the following rules:
    a. Increases in assets are debited.
    b. Decreases in assets are credited.
    c. Increases in liabilities and stockholders' equity are credited.
    d. Decreases in liabilities and stockholders' equity are debited.
    e. Revenues, common stock, and retained earnings increase stockholders' equity, and are therefore credited.
    f. Dividends and expenses decrease stockholders' equity, and are therefore debited.

13. Transactions may be analyzed and processed by executing the following five steps:
    a. Determine the effect (increase or decrease) of the transaction on assets, liabilities, and stockholders' equity accounts. Each transaction should be supported by a **source document,** such as an invoice or a check.
    b. Apply the rules of double entry.
    c. In **journal form,** enter the transaction (record the entry) into the journal.
    d. Post the journal entry to the general ledger.
    e. Prepare the trial balance.

Objective 4: Apply the steps for transaction analysis and processing to simple transactions.

14. To record a transaction, one must (a) obtain a description of the transaction, (b) determine which accounts are involved and what type each is (for example, asset or revenue), (c) determine which accounts are increased and which are decreased, and (d) apply the rules stated in paragraph 12 a–f.

Objective 5: Prepare a trial balance and describe its value and limitations.

15. Periodically, the accountant must check the equality of the total of debit and credit balances in the ledger. This is done formally by means of a **trial balance.** A normal balance for an account is determined by whether it is increased by entries to the debit side or by entries to the credit side. The side on which increases are recorded dictates what is considered the **normal balance.** For example, asset accounts have a normal debit balance.

16. If the trial balance does not balance, one or more errors have been made in the journal, ledger, or trial balance. The accountant must locate the errors to put the trial balance in balance. It is important to know, however, that it is possible to make errors that would not cause the trial balance to be out of balance (that is, errors that cannot be detected through the trial balance).

17. Ruled lines appear in financial reports before each subtotal, and a double line customarily is placed below the final amount. Although dollar signs are required in financial statements, they are omitted in journals and ledgers. On paper with ruled columns, commas and periods are omitted, and a dash frequently is used to designate zero cents.

Supplemental Objective 6: Record transactions in the general journal.

18. As transactions occur, they are recorded initially and chronologically in a book called the **journal.** The **general journal** is the simplest and most flexible type of journal. Each transaction **journalized** (recorded) in the general journal contains (a) the date, (b) the account names, (c) the dollar amounts debited and credited, (d) an explanation, and (e) the account numbers, if the transaction has been posted. A line should be skipped after each **journal entry,** and more than one debit or credit can be entered for a single transaction (called a **compound entry**).

Supplemental Objective 7: Post transactions from the general journal to the ledger.

19. The general journal records details of each transaction; the results of these details are summarized in the general ledger which updates each account. Each day's journal entries must be posted to the appropriate account in **ledger account form.**

Posting is a transferring process that results in an updated balance for each account. The dates and amounts are transferred from the journal to the ledger, and new account balances are calculated. The Post. Ref. columns are used for cross-referencing between the journal and the ledger.

Summary of Journal Entries Introduced in Chapter 2

A. (LO 4)   Cash   XX (amount invested)
       Common Stock   XX (amount invested)
            Investment of cash into business by owners

B. (LO 4)   Prepaid Rent   XX (amount paid)
       Cash   XX (amount paid)
            Advance payment for rent

C. (LO 4)   Art Equipment   XX (purchase price)
       Cash   XX (amount paid)
            Purchase of art equipment for cash

D. (LO 4)   Office Equipment   XX (purchase price)
       Cash   XX (amount paid)
       Accounts Payable   XX (amount to be paid)
            Purchase of office equipment, partial payment made

E. (LO 4)   Art Supplies   XX (purchase price)
       Office Supplies   XX (purchase price)
       Accounts Payable   XX (amount to be paid)
            Purchase of art and office supplies on credit

F. (LO 4)   Prepaid Insurance   XX (amount paid)
       Cash   XX (amount paid)
            Insurance purchased in advance

G. (LO 4)   Accounts Payable   XX (amount paid)
       Cash   XX (amount paid)
            Payment on a liability

H. (LO 4)   Cash   XX (amount received)
       Advertising Fees Earned   XX (amount earned)
            Received payment for services rendered

I. (LO 4)   Wages Expense   XX (amount incurred)
       Cash   XX (amount paid)
            Recorded and paid wages for the period

J. (LO 4) Cash   XX (amount received)
                Unearned Art Fees   XX (amount received)
                    Received payment for services to be performed

K. (LO 4) Accounts Receivable   XX (amount to be received)
                Advertising Fees Earned   XX (amount earned)
                    Rendered service, payment to be received at later time

L. (LO 4) Utilities Expense   XX (amount incurred)
                Cash   XX (amount paid)
                    Recorded and paid utility bill

M. (LO 4) Telephone Expense   XX (amount incurred)
                Accounts Payable   XX (amount to be paid)
                    Recorded telephone bill, payment to be made at later time

N. (LO 4) Dividends   XX (amount declared)
                Cash   XX (amount paid)
                    Declared and paid a dividend

SELF-TEST

Test your knowledge of the chapter by choosing the best answer for each of the following items.

1. Deciding whether to record a sale when the order for services is received or when the services are performed is an example of a
   a. recognition issue.
   b. valuation issue.
   c. classification issue.
   d. communication issue.

2. Which of the following statements is true?
   a. The chart of accounts usually is presented in alphabetical order.
   b. The general ledger contains all the accounts found in the chart of accounts.
   c. The general journal contains a list of the chart of accounts.
   d. Most companies use the same chart of accounts.

3. Which of the following is a liability account?
   a. Accounts Receivable
   b. Dividends
   c. Rent Expense
   d. Accounts Payable

4. An entry made on the left side of an account is referred to as
   a. the balance.
   b. a debit.
   c. a credit.
   d. a footing.

5. Although debits increase assets, they also
   a. decrease assets.
   b. increase stockholders' equity.
   c. increase expenses.
   d. increase liabilities.

6. Payment for a two-year insurance policy is recorded as a debit to
   a. Prepaid Insurance.
   b. Insurance Expense.
   c. Cash.
   d. Accounts Payable.

7. An agreement to spend $100 a month on advertising beginning next month requires
   a. a debit to Advertising Expense.
   b. a debit to Prepaid Advertising.
   c. no entry.
   d. a credit to Cash.

8. Transactions initially are recorded in the
   a. trial balance.
   b. T account.
   c. journal.
   d. ledger.

9. In posting from the general journal to the general ledger, the page number on which the transaction is recorded appears in the
   a. Post. Ref. column of the general ledger.
   b. Item column of the general ledger.
   c. Post. Ref. column of the general journal.
   d. Description column of the general journal.

10. To test that the total of debits and the total of credits are equal, the accountant periodically prepares a
    a. trial balance.
    b. T account.
    c. general journal.
    d. ledger.

TESTING YOUR KNOWLEDGE

Matching*

Match each term with its definition by writing the appropriate letter in the blank.

_____ 1. Original (historical) cost

_____ 2. Account

_____ 3. Debit

_____ 4. Credit

_____ 5. Account balance

_____ 6. Ledger

_____ 7. Posting

_____ 8. Prepaid expenses

_____ 9. Accounts Payable

_____ 10. Common Stock

_____ 11. Retained Earnings

_____ 12. Double-entry system

_____ 13. Trial balance

_____ 14. Journal

_____ 15. Post. Ref.

_____ 16. Footing

_____ 17. Compound entry

_____ 18. Unearned revenue

_____ 19. Dividends

a. Transferring data from the journal to the ledger

b. The amount in an account at a given point in time

c. An entry with more than one debit or credit

d. A distribution of assets to stockholders, resulting from profitable operations

e. A procedure for checking the equality of debits and credits in the ledger accounts

f. A record that occupies a page of the ledger

g. The book that contains all of a company's accounts

h. Adding a column of numbers

i. A liability arising when payment is received prior to the performance of services

j. Cumulative profits and losses, less dividends declared

k. The proper valuation to place on a business transaction

l. Amounts owed to others for purchases on credit

m. Amounts paid in advance for goods or services

n. The book of original entry

o. The right side of a ledger account

p. The column in the journal and ledger that provides for cross-referencing between the two

q. The left side of a ledger account

r. The method that requires both a debit and a credit for each transaction

s. The account that represents ownership in a corporation

Short Answer

Use the lines provided to answer each item.

1. List the five steps that must be executed to analyze and process transactions.

   _____

   _____

   _____

   _____

   _____

   _____

   *Note to student: The matching quiz might be completed more efficiently by starting with the definition and searching for the corresponding term.

2. Given the following journal entry, indicate which part of the entry applies to each measurement issue listed.

July 14	Cash	150	
	Accounts Receivable		150
	Collection on account		

   a. Recognition issue _____

   b. Valuation issue _____

   c. Classification issue _____

3. Describe a transaction that would require a debit to one asset and a credit to another asset.

_____

_____

4. Describe a transaction that would require a debit to a liability and a credit to an asset.

_____

_____

5. List the three account types that affect the Retained Earnings account.

_____

_____

_____

True-False

Circle T if the statement is true, F if it is false. Please provide explanations for the false answers, using the blank lines at the end of the section.

T F **1.** A sale should be recorded on the date of payment.

T F **2.** *Historical cost* is another term for *original cost.*

T F **3.** There must be a separate account for each asset, liability, component of stockholders' equity, revenue, and expense.

T F **4.** The credit side of an account implies something favorable.

T F **5.** In a given account, total debits must always equal total credits.

T F **6.** Management can determine cash on hand quickly by referring to the journal.

T F **7.** The number and titles of accounts vary among businesses.

T F **8.** Promissory Note is an example of an account title.

T F **9.** Prepaid expenses are classified as assets.

T F **10.** Increases in liabilities are indicated with a credit.

T F **11.** In all journal entries, at least one account must be increased and another decreased.

T F **12.** Journal entries are made after transactions have been entered into the ledger accounts.

T F **13.** In the journal, all liabilities and stockholders' equity accounts must be indented.

T F **14.** A debit is never indented in the journal.

T F **15.** Posting is the process of transferring data from the journal to the ledger.

T F **16.** The Post. Ref. column of a journal or ledger should be empty until posting is done.

T F **17.** In practice, the ledger account form is used, but the T account form is not.

T F **18.** The chart of accounts is a table of contents to the general journal.

T F **19.** Unearned Revenue has a normal debit balance.

T F **20.** Retained Earnings is a cash account placed in the asset section of the balance sheet.

T F **21.** The Common Stock account represents stockholders' investments, but not corporate profits and losses.

_____   _____
_____   _____
_____   _____
_____   _____
_____   _____
_____   _____
_____   _____
_____   _____
_____   _____
_____   _____
_____   _____
_____   _____

Multiple Choice

Circle the letter of the best answer.

1. Which of the following is *not* considered in initially recording a business transaction?
   a. Classification
   b. Recognition
   c. Summarization
   d. Valuation

2. When a liability is paid, which of the following is true?
   a. Total assets and total liabilities remain the same.
   b. Total assets and total stockholders' equity decrease.
   c. Total assets decrease by the same amount that total liabilities increase.
   d. Total assets and total liabilities decrease.

3. Which of the following is *not* true about a proper journal entry?
   a. All credits are indented.
   b. All debits are listed before the first credit.
   c. An explanation is needed for each debit and each credit.
   d. A debit is never indented, even if a liability or stockholders' equity account is involved.

4. When an entry is posted, what is the last step to be taken?
   a. The explanation must be transferred.
   b. The account number is placed in the reference column of the ledger.
   c. The journal page number is placed in the reference column of the journal.
   d. The account number is placed in the reference column of the journal.

5. Which of the following errors will probably be disclosed by the preparation of a trial balance (i.e., would cause it to be out of balance)?
   a. Failure to post an entire journal entry (i.e., nothing is posted).
   b. Failure to record an entry in the journal (i.e., nothing is entered).
   c. Failure to post part of a journal entry.
   d. Posting the debit of a journal entry as a credit, and the credit as a debit.

6. When cash is received in payment of an account receivable, which of the following is true?
   a. Total assets increase.
   b. Total assets remain the same.
   c. Total assets decrease.
   d. Total assets and total stockholders' equity increase.

7. Which of the following is increased by debits?
   a. Dividends
   b. Unearned Revenue
   c. Mortgage Payable
   d. Retained Earnings

8. Which of the following accounts is an asset?
   a. Unearned Revenue
   b. Prepaid Rent
   c. Retained Earnings
   d. Fees Earned

9. Which of the following accounts is a liability?
   a. Interest Payable
   b. Interest Expense
   c. Interest Receivable
   d. Interest Income

10. A company that rents an office (i.e., a lessee or tenant) would never have an entry to which account for that particular lease?
    a. Prepaid Rent
    b. Unearned Rent
    c. Rent Payable
    d. Rent Expense

11. Which of the following accounts has a normal credit balance?
    a. Prepaid Insurance
    b. Dividends
    c. Sales
    d. Advertising Expense

APPLYING YOUR KNOWLEDGE

Exercises

1. Following are all the transactions of Champlain Printing, Inc., for the month of May. For each transaction, provide *in good form* the journal entries required. Use the journal provided on the next page.

May 2 Champlain Printing, Inc., was granted a charter by the state, and investors contributed $28,000 in exchange for 2,800 shares of $10 par value common stock.

3 Rented part of a building for $300 per month. Paid three months' rent in advance.

5 Purchased a small printing press for $10,000 and photographic equipment for $3,000 from Mechan Press, Inc. Paid $2,000 and agreed to pay the remainder as soon as possible.

8 Hired a pressman, agreeing to pay him $200 per week.

9 Received $1,200 from Ebony's Department Store as an advance for brochures to be printed.

11 Purchased paper for $800 from Heritage Paper Company. Issued Heritage a promissory note for the entire amount.

14 Completed a $500 printing job for Franklin Shoes. Franklin paid for half, agreeing to pay the remainder next week.

14 Paid the pressman his weekly salary.

15 Paid Mechan Press, Inc., $1,000 of the amount owed for the May 5 transaction.

18 Received the remainder due from Franklin Shoes for the May 14 transaction.

20 A $700 cash dividend was declared and paid by the corporation.

24 Received an electric bill of $45. Payment will be made in a few days.

30 Paid the electric bill.

2. Following are three balance sheet accounts, selected at random from Chen Company's ledger. For each, determine the account balance.

Accounts Receivable		Accounts Payable	
2,000	1,000	1,200	4,200
750		2,000	

Cash	
15,000	1,000
4,000	1,200
	2,200

a. Accounts Receivable has a (debit or credit) balance of

$_____.

b. Accounts Payable has a (debit or credit) balance of

$_____.

c. Cash has a (debit or credit) balance of

$_____.

General Journal				
Date		Description	Debit	Credit
May	2	Cash	28,000	
		Common Stock		28,000
		To record the stockholders' original investment		

3. Two journal entries are presented below. Post both entries to the ledger accounts provided. Only those accounts needed have been provided, and previous postings have been omitted to simplify the exercise.

		General Journal			Page 7
Date		**Description**	**Post. Ref.**	**Debit**	**Credit**
Apr.	3	Cash		1,000	
		Revenue from Services			1,000
		Received payment from Isham Company for services			
	5	Accounts Payable		300	
		Cash			300
		Paid Evelyn Supply Company for supplies purchased on March 31 on credit			

Cash   **Account No. 11**

					Balance	
Date	**Item**	**Post. Ref.**	**Debit**	**Credit**	**Debit**	**Credit**

Accounts Payable   **Account No. 21**

					Balance	
Date	**Item**	**Post. Ref.**	**Debit**	**Credit**	**Debit**	**Credit**

Revenue from Services   **Account No. 41**

					Balance	
Date	**Item**	**Post. Ref.**	**Debit**	**Credit**	**Debit**	**Credit**

CHAPTER 3 MEASURING BUSINESS INCOME

REVIEWING THE CHAPTER

Objective 1: Define *net income* and its two major components, *revenues* and *expenses*.

1. Profitability, or earning a **profit,** is an important goal of most businesses. A major function of accounting is to measure and report a company's success or failure in achieving this goal. This is done by means of an income statement.

2. **Net income** is the net increase in stockholders' equity resulting from the operations of the company. Net income results when revenues exceed expenses, and a **net loss** results when expenses exceed revenues.

3. **Revenues** are the price of goods sold and services rendered during a specific period of time. Examples of revenues are Sales (the account used when merchandise is sold), Commissions Earned, and Advertising Fees Earned.

4. Also described as the cost of doing business or as expired costs, **expenses** are the costs of goods and services used in the process of earning revenues. Examples of expenses are Telephone Expense, Wages Expense, and Advertising Expense.

Objective 2a: Explain the difficulties of income measurement caused by the accounting period issue.

5. The **periodicity** assumption (the solution to the **accounting period issue**) states that although measurements of net income for short periods of time are approximate, they are nevertheless useful. Income statement comparison is made possible through accounting periods of equal length. A **fiscal year** covers any twelve-month accounting period used by a company. Many companies use a fiscal year that corresponds to a calendar year, which is a twelve-month period that ends on December 31.

Objective 2b: Explain the difficulties of income measurement caused by the continuity issue.

6. Under the **going concern** assumption (the solution to the **continuity issue**), the accountant assumes that the business will continue to operate indefinitely, unless there is evidence to the contrary.

Objective 2c: Explain the difficulties of income measurement caused by the matching issue.

7. When the **cash basis of accounting** is used, revenues are recorded when cash is received, and expenses are recorded when cash is paid. This method, however, can lead to distortion of net income for the period.

8. According to the **matching rule,** revenues should be recorded in the period(s) in which they are actually earned, and expenses should be recorded in the period(s) in which they are used to produce revenue; the timing of cash payments or receipts is irrelevant.

Objective 3: Define *accrual accounting* and explain two broad ways of accomplishing it.

9. **Accrual accounting** consists of all techniques used to apply the matching rule. Specifically, it

involves (1) recognizing revenues when earned (**revenue recognition**) and expenses when incurred, and (2) adjusting the accounts at the end of the period.

10. Because adjusting entries never involve the Cash account, they do not affect cash flow. They are, however, necessary for the accurate measurement of performance. Good judgment must be exercised in the preparation of adjusting entries to avoid the abuse and misrepresentation that can occur.

Objective 4: State four principal situations that require adjusting entries.

11. A problem arises when revenues or expenses apply to more than one accounting period. The problem is solved by making **adjusting entries** at the end of the accounting period. Adjusting entries allocate to the current period the revenues and expenses that apply to that period, deferring the remainder to future periods. A **deferral** is the postponement of the recognition of an expense already paid or of a revenue already received [see 12(a) and (c) below]. An **accrual** is the recognition of an expense or revenue that has arisen but has not yet been recorded [see 12(b) and (d) below].

12. Adjusting entries are required to accomplish several purposes:
    a. To divide recorded costs (such as the cost of machinery or prepaid rent) among two or more accounting periods.
    b. To record unrecorded expenses (such as wages earned by employees after the last pay period in an accounting period).
    c. To divide recorded revenues (such as commissions collected in advance) among two or more accounting periods.
    d. To record unrecorded revenues (such as commissions earned but not yet billed to customers).

Objective 5: Prepare typical adjusting entries.

13. When an expenditure is made that will benefit more than just the current period, the initial debit is usually made to an asset account instead of to an expense account. Then, at the end of the accounting period, the amount that has been used is transferred from the asset account to an expense account.
    a. **Prepaid expenses,** such as Prepaid Rent and Prepaid Insurance, are debited when they are paid for in advance.

b. An account for supplies, such as Office Supplies, is debited when supplies are purchased. At the end of the accounting period, an inventory of supplies is taken. The difference between supplies available for use during the period and ending inventory is the amount used during the period.

c. A long-lived asset such as a building, trucks, or office furniture is debited to an asset account when purchased. At the end of each accounting period, an adjusting entry must be made to transfer a part of the original cost of each long-lived asset to an expense account. The amount transferred or allocated is called **depreciation** or *depreciation expense*.

d. **Accumulated depreciation accounts** are contra-asset accounts used to total the past depreciation expense on specific long-term assets. They are called **contra accounts** because on the balance sheet they are subtracted from their associated asset account. Thus proper balance sheet presentation will show the original cost, the accumulated depreciation as of the balance sheet date, and the undepreciated balance (called **carrying value** or *book value*).

14. In making the adjusting entry to record depreciation, Depreciation Expense is debited and Accumulated Depreciation is credited.

15. Similarly, expenses have often been incurred but not recorded in the accounts because cash has not yet been paid. An adjusting entry must be made to record these **accrued expenses.** For example, interest on a loan may have accrued that does not have to be paid until the next period. A debit to Interest Expense and a credit to Interest Payable will record the current period's interest for the income statement. A similar adjusting entry would be made for estimated income taxes and accrued wages. These entries will also record the liabilities for the balance sheet.

16. Sometimes payment is received for goods before they are delivered or for services before they are rendered. In such cases, a liability account such as **Unearned Revenues** or Unearned Fees would appear on the balance sheet. This account is a liability because it represents revenues that still must be earned by providing the product or service that is owed.

17. Often at the end of an accounting period, revenues have been earned but not recorded because

no payment has been received. An adjusting entry must be made to record these **accrued** (unrecorded) **revenues.** For example, interest that has been earned might not be received until the next period. A debit must be made to Interest Receivable and a credit to Interest Income to record the current period's interest for the income statement. This entry will also record the asset for the balance sheet.

Objective 6: Prepare financial statements from an adjusted trial balance.

18. After all the adjusting entries have been posted to the ledger accounts and new account balances have been computed, an **adjusted trial balance** should be prepared. Once in balance, the adjusted trial balance is then used to prepare the financial statements.

Supplemental Objective 7: Analyze cash flows from accrual-based information.

19. Net income is best determined by applying accrual accounting, whereby revenues are recorded when earned and expenses when incurred. Liquidity, or the ability to pay debts when they fall due, relies upon cash flow (not accrual-based) information. Fortunately, cash receipts and payments can be calculated, given accrual-based net income and related information. The general rule for determining cash flow received from any revenue or paid for any expense (except depreciation) is to determine the potential cash payments or cash receipts and then deduct the amount not paid or received. For example, cash payments for rent would equal rent expense plus an increase (or minus a decrease) in prepaid rent occurring during the period.

Summary of Journal Entries Introduced in Chapter 3

A. (LO 5)   Rent Expense   XX (amount expired)
                  Prepaid Rent   XX (amount expired)
                      Expiration of prepaid rent

B. (LO 5)   Insurance Expense   XX (amount expired)
                  Prepaid Insurance   XX (amount expired)
                      Expiration of prepaid insurance

C. (LO 5)   Art Supplies Expense   XX (amount consumed)
                  Art Supplies   XX (amount consumed)
                      Consumption of art supplies

D. (LO 5)   Office Supplies Expense   XX (amount consumed)
                  Office Supplies   XX (amount consumed)
                      Consumption of office supplies

E. (LO 5)   Depreciation Expense, Art Equipment   XX (amount allocated to period)
                  Accumulated Depreciation, Art Equipment   XX (amount allocated to period)
                      Recording of depreciation expense

F. (LO 5)   Depreciation Expense, Office Equipment   XX (amount allocated to period)
                  Accumulated Depreciation, Office Equipment   XX (amount allocated to period)
                      Recording of depreciation expense

G. (LO 5)   Wages Expense   XX (amount incurred)
                 Wages Payable   XX (amount to be paid)
                     Accrual of unrecorded expense

H. (LO 5)   Income Taxes Expense   XX (amount estimated)
                 Income Taxes Payable   XX (amount estimated to be paid)
                     Accrual of estimated income taxes

I. (LO 5)   Unearned Art Fees   XX (amount earned)
                 Art Fees Earned   XX (amount earned)
                     Performance of services paid for in advance

J. (LO 5)   Fees Receivable   XX (amount to be received)
                 Advertising Fees Earned   XX (amount earned)
                     Accrual of unrecorded revenue

Cash Flow Formulas (SO 7)

Type of Account	Potential Payment or Receipt	Not Paid or Received	Result
Prepaid Expense	Ending Balance + Expense for the Period	– Beginning Balance	= Cash Payments for Expenses
Unearned Revenue	Ending Balance + Revenue for the Period	– Beginning Balance	= Cash Receipts from Revenues
Accrued Payable	Beginning Balance + Expense for the Period	– Ending Balance	= Cash Payments for Expenses
Accrued Receivable	Beginning Balance + Revenue for the Period	– Ending Balance	= Cash Receipts from Revenues

SELF-TEST

Test your knowledge of the chapter by choosing the best answer for each of the following items.

1. The net increase in stockholders' equity that results from business operations is called
   a. net income.
   b. revenue.
   c. an expense.
   d. an asset.

2. Which of the following accounts is an example of a contra account?
   a. Unearned Art Fees
   b. Depreciation Expense, Buildings
   c. Prepaid Insurance
   d. Accumulated Depreciation, Office Equipment

3. A business can choose a fiscal year that corresponds to
   a. the calendar year.
   b. the natural business year.
   c. any twelve-month period.
   d. any of the above.

4. Assigning revenues to the accounting period in which goods are delivered or services performed, and expenses to the accounting period in which they are used to produce revenues is called the
   a. accounting period issue.
   b. continuity assumption.
   c. matching rule.
   d. recognition rule.

5. Accrual accounting involves all of the following except
   a. recording all revenues when cash is received.
   b. applying the matching rule.
   c. recognizing expenses when incurred.
   d. adjusting the accounts.

6. Which of the following is an example of a deferral?
   a. Accruing year-end wages
   b. Recognizing revenues earned but not yet recorded
   c. Recording prepaid rent
   d. Recognizing expenses incurred but not yet recorded

7. Prepaid Insurance shows an ending balance of $2,300. During the period, insurance in the amount of $1,200 expired. The adjusting entry would include a debit to
   a. Prepaid Insurance for $1,200.
   b. Insurance Expense for $1,200.
   c. Unexpired Insurance for $1,100.
   d. Insurance Expense for $1,100.

8. Adjusting entries are used to
   a. make financial statements from one period to the next more comparable.
   b. make net income reflect cash flow.
   c. correct errors in the recording of earlier transactions.
   d. record initial transactions.

9. On July 31 Wages Payable had a balance of $500 and on August 31, the balance was $300. Wages Expense for August was $2,600. How much cash was expended for wages during August?
   a. $2,100
   b. $2,400
   c. $2,600
   d. $2,800

10. Which of the following accounts would probably be contained in an adjusted trial balance, but probably *not* in a trial balance?
    a. Unearned Revenue
    b. Cash
    c. Depreciation Expense
    d. Utilities Expense

TESTING YOUR KNOWLEDGE

Matching*

Match each term with its definition by writing the appropriate letter in the blank.

_____ 1. Net income

_____ 2. Revenues

_____ 3. Expenses

_____ 4. Expired cost

_____ 5. Unexpired cost

_____ 6. Deferral

_____ 7. Accrual

_____ 8. Fiscal year

_____ 9. Going concern assumption

_____ 10. Cash basis of accounting

_____ 11. Accrual accounting

_____ 12. Matching rule

_____ 13. Adjusting entry

_____ 14. Depreciation expense

_____ 15. Accumulated Depreciation

_____ 16. Contra account

_____ 17. Unearned revenue

_____ 18. Adjusted trial balance

a. All the techniques used to apply the matching rule

b. A liability that represents an obligation to deliver goods or render services

c. That portion of an asset that has not yet been charged as an expense

d. A general term for the price of goods sold or services rendered

e. The assumption that a business will continue indefinitely (solution to the continuity problem)

f. Recognition of an expense or revenue that has arisen but has not yet been recorded

g. A method of determining whether accounts are still in balance

h. The requirement to recognize an expense in the same period as the revenue produced by that expense

i. The amount by which revenues exceed expenses (opposite of net loss)

j. An account that is subtracted from an associated account

k. Any twelve-month accounting period used by a company

l. An example of a contra account to assets

m. An end-of-period allocation of revenues and expenses relevant to that period

n. The cost of doing business

o. Recording revenues and expenses when payment is received or made

p. The expired cost of a plant asset for a particular accounting period

q. Postponement of the recognition of an expense already paid or of a revenue already received

r. A descriptive term for expense

---

*Note to student: The matching quiz might be completed more efficiently by starting with the definition and searching for the corresponding term.

Short Answer

Use the lines provided to answer each item.

1. Briefly summarize the four situations that require adjusting entries.

   _____

   _____

   _____

   _____

2. Briefly explain the matching rule.

   _____

   _____

   _____

   _____

3. Define *depreciation* as the term is used in accounting.

   _____

   _____

   _____

4. Distinguish between prepaid expenses and unearned revenues.

   _____

   _____

   _____

   _____

True-False

Circle T if the statement is true, F if it is false. Please provide explanations for the false answers, using the blank lines at the end of the section.

T F 1. Failure to record accrued wages will result in total liabilities that are understated.

T F 2. Expired costs are listed on the income statement.

T F 3. A calendar year refers to any twelve-month period.

T F 4. The cash basis of accounting often violates the matching rule.

T F 5. Under the accrual basis of accounting, the timing of cash receipts and payments is vital for recording revenues and expenses.

T F 6. Adjusting entries must be made immediately after the financial statements are prepared.

T F 7. Prepaid insurance represents an unexpired cost.

T F 8. Office Supplies Expense must be debited for the amount in ending inventory of office supplies.

T F 9. Because Accumulated Depreciation appears in the asset section of the balance sheet, it has a debit balance.

T F 10. As a machine is depreciated, its accumulated depreciation increases and its carrying value decreases.

T F 11. Unearned Revenues is a contra account to Earned Revenues on the income statement.

T F 12. When an expense has accrued but payment has not yet been made, a debit is needed for the expense and a credit for Prepaid Expenses.

T F 13. The adjusted trial balance is the same as the trial balance, except that it has been modified by adjusting entries.

T F 14. If one has made a sale for which the money has not yet been received, one would debit Unearned Revenues and credit Earned Revenues.

T F 15. The original cost of a long-lived asset should appear on the balance sheet even after depreciation has been recorded.

T F 16. Adjusting entries help make financial statements comparable from one period to the next.

_____ _____

_____ _____

_____ _____

_____ _____

_____ _____

_____ _____

_____ _____

_____ _____

_____ _____

_____ _____

_____ _____

_____ _____

Multiple Choice

Circle the letter of the best answer.

1. Which of the following is an unlikely description for an adjusting entry?
   a. Debit to an expense, credit to an asset
   b. Debit to a liability, credit to a revenue
   c. Debit to an expense, credit to a revenue
   d. Debit to an expense, credit to a liability

2. Depreciation does *not* apply to
   a. trucks.
   b. office supplies.
   c. machinery.
   d. office equipment.

3. An account called Unearned Fees is used when
   a. recorded costs must be divided among periods.
   b. recorded revenues must be divided among periods.
   c. unrecorded (accrued) expenses must be recorded.
   d. unrecorded (accrued) revenues must be recorded.

4. Depreciation best applies to
   a. recorded costs that must be divided among periods.
   b. recorded revenues that must be divided among periods.
   c. unrecorded expenses that must be recorded.
   d. unrecorded revenues that must be recorded.

5. Which of the following would *not* appear on the adjusted trial balance?
   a. Prepaid Insurance
   b. Unearned Management Fees
   c. Net Income
   d. Depreciation Expense

6. An adjusting entry made to record accrued interest on a note receivable due next year would consist of a debit to
   a. Cash and a credit to Interest Income.
   b. Cash and a credit to Interest Receivable.
   c. Interest Expense and a credit to Interest Payable.
   d. Interest Receivable and a credit to Interest Income.

7. The periodicity assumption solves the accounting period problem by recognizing that
   a. net income over a short period of time is a useful estimate.
   b. a business is likely to continue indefinitely.
   c. revenues should be recorded in the period earned.
   d. a twelve-month accounting period must be used.

8. Prepaid Rent is a(n)
   a. expense.
   b. contra account.
   c. liability.
   d. asset.

9. An adjusting entry would *never* include
   a. Unearned Revenue.
   b. Cash.
   c. Prepaid Advertising.
   d. Wages Expense.

10. Which of the following accounts would probably contain a lower dollar amount on the adjusted trial balance than on the trial balance?
   a. Accounts Receivable
   b. Dividends
   c. Office Supplies
   d. Rent Expense

APPLYING YOUR KNOWLEDGE

Exercises

1. On January 1, 20xx, Excelsior Transit Company began its business by buying a new bus for $24,000. One-eighth of the cost of the bus is depreciated each year. Complete *in good form* the balance sheet as of December 31, 20x2.

Excelsior Transit Company
Partial Balance Sheet
December 31, 20x2

Assets

Cash	$5,000
Accounts Receivable	3,000
Company Vehicles	
Total Assets	$____

---

2. For each set of facts, provide the dollar amount that would be recorded.

   a. The cost of supplies at the beginning of the period was $510. During the period, supplies that cost $800 were purchased. At the end of the period, supplies that cost $340 remained. Supplies Expense should be recorded for

   $_____.

   b. The company signed a lease and paid $14,000 on July 1, 20xx, to cover the four-year period beginning July 1, 20xx. How much Rent Expense should it record on December 31, 20xx?

   $_____

   c. The company was paid $600 in advance for services to be performed. By the end of the period, only one-fourth of it had been earned. How much of the $600 will appear as Unearned Revenues on the balance sheet?

   $_____

3. In the next column is the trial balance for Grosvenor Company. The facts that follow are based on this trial balance. For each item, make the adjusting entry in the journal provided on the next page. Keep in mind that Grosvenor Company operates on the calendar year.

   a. Cost of supplies on hand, based on a physical count, is $375.
   b. Wages of $2,500 for the five-day workweek ($500 per day) are recorded and paid every Friday. December 31 falls on a Thursday.
   c. Services amounting to $600 were rendered during 20xx for customers who had paid in advance.
   d. Five percent of the cost of buildings is taken as depreciation for 20xx.
   e. One-quarter of the prepaid advertising expired during 20xx.
   f. All of the insurance shown on the trial balance was paid for on July 1, 20xx, and covers the two-year period beginning July 1, 20xx.
   g. Work performed for customers that has not been billed or recorded amounts to $2,200.
   h. Accrued interest on a note payable amounts to $52. This interest will be paid when the note matures.
   i. Accrued income tax expense for the year amounts to $21,700. This amount will be paid early next year.

Grosvenor Company
Trial Balance
December 31, 20xx

	Debit	Credit
Cash	$ 77,300	
Notes Receivable	5,000	
Prepaid Advertising	8,000	
Prepaid Insurance	1,000	
Supplies	500	
Office Equipment	9,000	
Buildings	90,000	
Accumulated Depreciation, Buildings		$ 6,000
Notes Payable		1,500
Unearned Revenues		2,800
Common Stock		100,000
Dividends	13,000	
Revenues from Services		212,000
Wages Expense	118,500	
	$322,300	$322,300

General Journal				
Date		Description	Debit	Credit

4. At year-beginning and year-end, Tsu Industries had the following balance sheet balances:

	Jan. 1	Dec. 31
Wages Payable	$1,200	$3,700
Unearned Revenue	500	900
Prepaid Rent	2,400	1,800

In addition, the following figures were taken from the income statement:

Wages Expense	$ 8,700
Revenue from Services	35,000
Rent Expense	3,600

a. Cash paid for wages during the year =

$_____.

b. Cash received for revenue during the year =

$_____.

c. Cash paid for rent during the year =

$_____.

Crossword Puzzle
for Chapters 2 and 3

ACROSS

1. An account that is subtracted from another
3. See 21-Down
6. Postponement of a revenue or expense
7. Journal column title (same as 2-Down)
9. Where accounts are kept
13. Source of revenues
16. Test of debit and credit equality (2 words)
18. Left side of ledger
19. Monthly or yearly compensation
22. _____ bookkeeping (hyphenated)
23. Realize (revenues)

DOWN

1. Historical _____
2. Post. _____ column
4. Become an expense
5. Hourly or piecework-rate compensation
8. Income statement item
10. _____ estate (land)
11. Record transactions
12. Rule applied through accrual accounting
14. Right side of ledger
15. Assignment of a dollar amount to
17. Recognition of unrecorded revenues or expenses
20. Written promise to pay
21. With 3-Across, the term accountants use to refer to profit

CHAPTER 4 ACCOUNTING SYSTEMS

REVIEWING THE CHAPTER

Objective 1: Identify the principles of accounting systems design.

1. **Accounting systems** summarize a business's financial data, organize the data into useful form, and (through accountants) communicate the results to management. Management then uses the output to make a variety of business decisions. An accounting system is able to accomplish the above objectives through an activity called **data processing.**

2. Most businesses now process their data by means of computerized accounting systems. For such a system to work, however, the individuals involved must possess a solid understanding of the accounting process.

3. In designing an accounting system, the systems designer must adhere to four general principles of systems design:
   a. The **cost-benefit principle** states that the benefits derived from the accounting system must match or exceed its cost.
   b. The **control principle** states that the accounting system must contain the safeguards necessary to protect assets and make sure the data are reliable.
   c. The **compatibility principle** states that the accounting system must be in harmony with the organization and its people.
   d. The **flexibility principle** states that the accounting system should be able to accommodate changes in the volume of transactions and in organizational changes within the business.

Objective 2: State all the steps in the accounting cycle.

4. The steps in the **accounting cycle** are as follows:
   a. The transactions are analyzed from the source documents.
   b. The transactions are recorded in the journal.
   c. The entries are posted to the ledger and a trial balance is prepared.
   d. The accounts are adjusted at the end of the period and the adjusted trial balance is prepared.
   e. The revenue, expense, and dividends accounts are closed to conclude the current accounting period and prepare for the beginning of the new accounting period. Also, a post-closing trial balance is prepared.
   f. Financial statements are prepared from the adjusted trial balance.

Objective 3: Describe how general ledger software and spreadsheet software are used in accounting.

5. Accountants use a variety of software (computer programs), but rely especially upon general ledger software and spreadsheet software.
   a. **General ledger software** consists of programs that perform, in an integrative way, major accounting functions, such as sales, accounts receivable, purchases, accounts payable, and payroll. Most general ledger software uses the Windows® operating system. Windows®, through its **graphical user interface (GUI),** employs symbols, called **icons,** to represent common computer operations. A *mouse* or

trackball may be used with Windows®, or the keyboard may be operated in the usual manner.

b. Unlike general ledger software, which is useful for double-entry transactions, **spreadsheets** assist in data analysis. With such commercial names as Windows® Excel and Lotus, a spreadsheet is a grid of rows and columns, into which are placed data or formulas for accounting tasks such as financial planning and cost estimation.

Objective 4: Identify the basic elements of computer systems, and describe microcomputer accounting systems.

6. A computer data processing system is made up of three basic elements: (a) hardware, (b) software, and (c) personnel.

7. Computer **hardware** consists of the equipment needed to operate a computer system—keyboard, central processing unit (CPU), and printer, for example. Computer **software,** on the other hand, consists of **programs,** or sets of instructions that produce a desired result. The key personnel in a computer system are the **systems analyst** (who designs the data processing system), the **programmer** (who writes the instructions), and the **computer operator** (who runs the computer).

8. Two or more microcomputers can communicate with each other when they are linked through a **network.** A network in one location, as a classroom, is called a **local area network (LAN).** In contrast, a network of computers in different cities or countries is called a **wide area network (WAN).**

9. Most small businesses purchase software that performs, through integrated programs, various accounting functions. Every transaction entered into the accounting records should be supported by **source documents** (invoices, etc.). Posting can be accomplished on a batch posting (end of the day, week, or month) or a real-time posting (immediate) basis.

Objective 5: Explain how accountants use the Internet.

10. The **Internet** is the world's largest computer network, enabling individuals and organizations around the world to communicate with one another. One needs a modem and (usually) an Internet service provide (ISP) to access the Internet.

11. Individuals and organizations can send and receive **electronic mail (e-mail)** through the Internet, and can subscribe to any number of *electronic mailing lists.*

12. The **World Wide Web** (or "the Web") consists of the vast collection of information that can be accessed through the Internet. Browsers, such as Netscape Navigator and Microsoft Internet Explorer, are needed to access the Web.

13. Files can be downloaded (obtained) from the Internet through a process called **information retrieval.** Information can be shared over the Internet by individuals with common interests through **bulletin boards.** Individuals and companies can conduct business through the Internet, in a practice called **electronic commerce.**

Objective 6: Explain the purposes of closing entries and prepare required closing entries.

14. Revenue and expense accounts are sometimes referred to as **temporary** (or *nominal*) **accounts** because they are temporary in nature. Their purpose is to record revenues and expenses during a particular accounting period. At the end of that period, their totals are transferred to Retained Earnings (via the Income Summary account), leaving zero balances to begin the next accounting period.

15. Balance sheet accounts are sometimes referred to as **permanent** (or *real*) **accounts** because their balances can extend past the end of an accounting period. They are *not* set back to zero.

16. **Closing entries** serve two purposes. First, they set the stage for the new accounting period by clearing revenue and expense accounts of their balances. (So that the Retained Earnings account can be updated, the Dividends account also is closed.) Second, they summarize the period's revenues and expenses by transferring the balance of revenue and expense accounts to the **Income Summary** account.

17. There are four closing entries, as follows:
a. Temporary credit balances are closed. This is accomplished with a compound entry that debits each revenue account for the amount required to give it a zero balance and credits Income Summary for the revenue total. The Income Summary account exists only during the closing process and does not appear in the financial statements.
b. Temporary debit balances are closed. This is accomplished with a compound entry that credits each expense for the amount required to give it a zero balance, and debits Income Summary for the expense total.

c. The Income Summary account is closed. After revenue and expense accounts have been closed, the Income Summary account will have either a debit balance or a credit balance. If a credit balance exists, then Income Summary must be debited for the amount required to give it a zero balance, and Retained Earnings is credited for the same amount. The reverse is done when Income Summary has a debit balance.

d. The Dividends account is closed. This is accomplished by crediting Dividends for the amount required to give it a zero balance, and debiting Retained Earnings for the same amount. Note that the Income Summary account is not involved in this closing entry.

Objective 7: Prepare the post-closing trial balance.

18. After the closing entries are posted to the ledger, a **post-closing trial balance** must be prepared to verify again the equality of the debits and credits in the accounts. Only balance sheet accounts appear because all income statement accounts, as well as the Dividends account, have zero balances at this point.

Supplemental Objective 8: Prepare reversing entries as appropriate.

19. At the end of each accounting period, the accountant makes adjusting entries to record accrued revenues and expenses. Many of the adjusting entries are followed in the next period by the receipt or payment of cash. Thus it would become necessary in the next period to make a special entry dividing amounts between the two periods. To avoid this inconvenience, the accountant can make **reversing entries** (dated the beginning of the new period). Reversing entries, though not required, allow the bookkeeper to simply make the routine bookkeeping entry when cash finally changes hands. Not all adjusting entries may be reversed. In the system we will use, only adjustments for accruals may be reversed. Deferrals may not.

Supplemental Objective 9: Prepare a work sheet.

20. Accountants use **working papers** to help organize their work and to provide evidence in support of the financial statements. The **work sheet** is one such working paper. It decreases the chance of overlooking an adjustment, acts as a check on the arithmetical accuracy of the accounts, and helps in preparing financial statements. The work sheet is never published but is a useful tool for the accountant.

21. The five steps in the preparation of the work sheet are as follows:

a. Enter and total the account balances in the Trial Balance columns.

b. Enter and total the adjustments in the Adjustments columns. (A letter identifies the debit and credit for each adjustment and can act as a key to a brief explanation at the bottom of the work sheet.)

c. Enter (by means of **crossfooting**) and total the account balances as adjusted in the Adjusted Trial Balance columns.

d. Extend (transfer) the account balances from the Adjusted Trial Balance columns to the Income Statement columns or the Balance Sheet columns (depending on which type of account is involved).

e. Total the Income Statement columns and the Balance Sheet columns. Enter the net income or net loss in both pairs of columns (one will be a debit, the other a credit) as a balancing figure, and recompute the column totals.

Supplemental Objective 10: Use a work sheet for three different purposes.

22. Once the work sheet is completed, it can be used to (a) record the adjusting entries, (b) record the closing entries, thus preparing the records for the new period, and (c) prepare the financial statements.

a. Formal adjusting entries must be recorded in the journal and posted to the ledger so that the account balances on the books will agree with those on the financial statements. This is easily accomplished by referring to the Adjustments columns (and footnoted explanations) of the work sheet.

b. Formal closing entries are entered into the journal and posted to the ledger, as explained in Objective 6. This is accomplished by referring to the work sheet's Income Statement columns (for the revenue and expense accounts) and its Balance Sheet columns (for the Dividends account).

c. The income statement may be prepared from the information found in the work sheet's Income Statement columns. Calculations of the change in retained earnings for the period are shown on the statement of retained earnings. Information for this calculation may be found in the Balance Sheet columns of the work sheet (beginning retained earnings, net income, and dividends). The balance sheet may be prepared from information found in the work sheet's Balance Sheet columns and on the statement of retained earnings.

Summary of Journal Entries Introduced in Chapter 4

A. (LO 6) Advertising Fees Earned   XX (current credit balance)
         Art Fees Earned   XX (current credit balance)
           Income Summary   XX (sum of revenue amounts)
              To close the revenue accounts

B. (LO 6) Income Summary   XX (sum of expense amounts)
           Wages Expense   XX (current debit balance)
           Utilities Expense   XX (current debit balance)
           Telephone Expense   XX (current debit balance)
           Rent Expense   XX (current debit balance)
           Insurance Expense   XX (current debit balance)
           Art Supplies Expense   XX (current debit balance)
           Office Supplies Expense   XX (current debit balance)
           Depreciation Expense, Art Equipment   XX (current debit balance)
           Depreciation Expense, Office Equipment   XX (current debit balance)
           Income Taxes Expense   XX (current debit balance)
              To close the expense accounts

C. (LO 6) Income Summary   XX (current credit balance)
           Retained Earnings   XX (net income amount)
              To close the Income Summary account
              (profit situation)

D. (LO 6) Retained Earnings   XX (dividends for period)
           Dividends   XX (dividends for period)
              To close the Dividends account

E. (SO 8) Wages Expense   XX (amount accrued)
           Wages Payable   XX (amount to be paid)
              To accrue unrecorded wages

F. (SO 8) Wages Payable   XX (amount previously accrued)
           Wages Expense   XX (amount incurred this period)
           Cash   XX (amount paid)
              Paid wages; entry E above was *not* reversed

G. (SO 8) Wages Payable   XX (amount to be paid)
           Wages Expense   XX (amount accrued)
              Reversing entry for E above (assume Wages
              Expense had been closed at end of period)

H. (SO 8) Wages Expense   XX (amount paid)
           Cash   XX (amount paid)
              Paid wages; entry E above *was* reversed

I. (SO 8) Income Taxes Payable   XX (amount in adjusting entry)
           Income Taxes Expense   XX (amount in adjusting entry)
              To reverse adjusting entry for estimated income taxes

J. (SO 8) Advertising Fees Earned   XX (amount accrued)
           Fees Receivable   XX (amount accrued)
              To reverse adjusting entry for accrued fees receivable

SELF-TEST

Test your knowledge of the chapter by choosing the best answer for each of the following items.

1. Which of the following sequences of actions describes the proper sequence of the accounting cycle?
   a. Post, record, analyze, prepare, close, adjust
   b. Analyze, record, post, adjust, close, prepare
   c. Prepare, record, post, adjust, analyze, close
   d. Enter, record, close, prepare, adjust, analyze

2. One important purpose of closing entries is to
   a. adjust the accounts in the ledger.
   b. set balance sheet accounts to zero to begin the next accounting period.
   c. set income statement accounts to zero to begin the next accounting period.
   d. summarize assets and liabilities.

3. After all the closing entries have been posted, the balance of the Income Summary account should be
   a. a debit if a net income has been earned.
   b. a debit if a net loss has been incurred.
   c. a credit if a net loss has been incurred.
   d. zero.

4. After the closing entries have been posted, all of the following accounts have a zero balance *except*
   a. Service Revenue Earned.
   b. Depreciation Expense.
   c. Unearned Service Revenue.
   d. Wages Expense.

5. The post-closing trial balance
   a. lists income statement accounts only.
   b. lists balance sheet accounts only.
   c. lists both income statement and balance sheet accounts.
   d. is prepared before closing entries are posted to the ledger.

6. For which of the following adjustments would a reversing entry facilitate bookkeeping procedures?
   a. An adjustment for depreciation expense
   b. An adjustment to allocate prepaid insurance to the current period
   c. An adjustment made as a result of an inventory of supplies
   d. An adjustment for wages earned by but not yet paid to employees

7. The work sheet is a type of
   a. ledger.
   b. journal.
   c. working paper.
   d. financial statement.

8. A decision to go ahead with a costly computer system because of potential sales loss and customer discontent under the current system is probably a result of applying the
   a. cost-benefit principle.
   b. control principle.
   c. compatibility principle.
   d. flexibility principle.

9. An example of a hardware output device in a microcomputer system is a
   a. hard disk.
   b. computer program.
   c. central processor.
   d. printer.

10. A person who writes instructions for a computer is called a
    a. systems analyst.
    b. programmer.
    c. graphical user interface.
    d. computer operator.

TESTING YOUR KNOWLEDGE

*Matching**

Match each term with its definition by writing the appropriate letter in the blank.

_____ **1.** Post-closing trial balance

_____ **2.** Working papers

_____ **3.** Work sheet

_____ **4.** Crossfooting

_____ **5.** Reversing entry

_____ **6.** Closing entries

_____ **7.** Income Summary

_____ **8.** Temporary (nominal) accounts

_____ **9.** Permanent (real) accounts

_____ **10.** Spreadsheet

_____ **11.** Information retrieval

_____ **12.** Hardware

_____ **13.** Software

_____ **14.** Systems analyst

_____ **15.** Computer operator

_____ **16.** Icon

_____ **17.** World Wide Web

_____ **18.** Data processing

_____ **19.** Network

a. The vast collection of information accessible through the Internet

b. Accounts whose balances extend beyond the end of an accounting period

c. Gathering, organizing, and communicating information

d. A symbol representing a common computer operation

e. The means of transferring net income or loss to the Retained Earnings account

f. The linkage of two or more microcomputers

g. A working paper that facilitates the preparation of financial statements

h. A final proof that the accounts are in balance

i. The equipment used in a computer data processing system

j. A person who runs a computer

k. The opposite of an adjusting entry, journalized to facilitate routine bookkeeping

l. Computer programs, instructions, and routines

m. An account used only during the closing process

n. Software employing a grid of rows and columns

o. Adding from left to right

p. Documents that help accountants organize their work

q. Accounts that begin each period with zero balances

r. The downloading of files from the Internet

s. A person who designs computer systems

Note to student: The matching quiz might be completed more efficiently by starting with the definition and searching for the corresponding term.

Short Answer

Use the lines provided to answer each item.

1. What four accounts or kinds of accounts are closed out each accounting period?

_____

_____

_____

_____

2. List the five columnar headings of a work sheet in their proper order.

_____

_____

_____

_____

_____

3. In general, what accounts appear in the post-closing trial balance? What accounts do *not* appear?

_____

_____

_____

4. Briefly, explain the purpose of reversing entries.

_____

_____

_____

5. The six steps in the accounting cycle are presented here in the wrong order. Place the numbers 1 through 6 in the spaces provided to indicate the correct order.

_____ The entries are posted to the ledger.

_____ The temporary accounts are closed.

_____ The transactions are analyzed from the source documents.

_____ The accounts are adjusted.

_____ The transactions are recorded in the journal.

_____ Financial statements are prepared from the adjusted trial balance.

6. List the four general principles of systems design, and briefly describe the significance of each.

a. _____

_____

b. _____

_____

c. _____

_____

d. _____

_____

_____

7. List the three basic elements of a computer system.

_____

_____

_____

Circle T if the statement is true, F if it is false. Please provide explanations for the false answers, using the blank lines at the end of the section.

T F **1.** The work sheet is prepared before the formal adjusting entries have been made in the journal.

T F **2.** Preparation of a work sheet helps reduce the possibility of overlooking an adjustment.

T F **3.** Total debits will differ from total credits in the Balance Sheet columns of a work sheet by the amount of the net income or loss.

T F **4.** The statement of retained earnings is prepared after the formal income statement, but before the formal balance sheet.

T F **5.** The Income Summary account can be found on the statement of retained earnings.

T F **6.** Closing entries convert real and nominal accounts to zero balances.

T F **7.** When revenue accounts are closed, the Income Summary account will be credited.

T F **8.** The Dividends account is closed to the Income Summary account.

T F **9.** When the Income Summary account is closed, it always requires a debit.

T F **10.** Reversing entries are never required.

T F **11.** The work sheet is published with the balance sheet and income statement, as a supplementary statement.

T F **12.** A key letter is needed in the Adjusted Trial Balance columns of a work sheet to show whether the entry is extended to the Balance Sheet columns or the Income Statement columns.

T F **13.** If total debits exceed total credits (before balancing) in the Income Statement columns of a work sheet, a net loss has occurred.

T F **14.** The post-closing trial balance will contain the Dividends account.

T F **15.** Reversing entries update the accounts at the end of the accounting period.

T F **16.** Retained Earnings is an example of a permanent (real) account.

T F **17.** The CPU is an important part of a computer's software.

T F **18.** A computer network within a college campus is an example of a local area network (LAN).

T F **19.** A graphical user interface (GUI) uses icons to make software easier to use.

T F **20.** The software used to navigate the World Wide Web is called a spreadsheet.

_____

_____

_____

_____

_____

_____

_____

_____

Multiple Choice

Circle the letter of the best answer.

1. Which account will appear on the post-closing trial balance?
   a. Interest Income
   b. Income Summary
   c. Retained Earnings
   d. Dividends

2. Which of the following statements is true?
   a. Closing entries are prepared before formal adjusting entries.
   b. The work sheet is prepared after the post-closing trial balance.
   c. Formal adjusting entries are prepared before the work sheet.
   d. Closing entries are prepared after the adjusted trial balance.

3. Reversing entries
   a. are dated as of the end of the period.
   b. are the opposite of adjusting entries.
   c. may be made for depreciation previously recorded.
   d. are the opposite of closing entries.

4. If total debits exceed total credits (before balancing) in the Balance Sheet columns of a work sheet,
   a. a net income has occurred.
   b. a net loss has occurred.
   c. a mistake has definitely been made.
   d. no conclusions can be drawn until the closing entries have been made.

5. Which of the following accounts would *not* be involved in closing entries?
   a. Unearned Commissions
   b. Retained Earnings
   c. Telephone Expense
   d. Dividends

6. When a net loss has occurred,
   a. all expense accounts are closed with debits.
   b. the Income Summary account is closed with a credit.
   c. the Dividends account is closed with a debit.
   d. all revenue accounts are closed with credits.

7. Which of the following is *not* an objective of closing entries?
   a. To transfer net income or loss to Retained Earnings
   b. To produce zero balances in all nominal accounts
   c. To update the revenue and expense accounts
   d. To be able to measure net income for the following period

8. A corporation began the accounting period with $50,000 in retained earnings, ended with $75,000 in retained earnings, and had declared $30,000 in dividends. What was the corporation's net income or loss for the period?
   a. $55,000 net income
   b. $30,000 net loss
   c. $5,000 net loss
   d. $5,000 net income

9. Which of the following is an example of a temporary account?
   a. Prepaid Rent
   b. Unearned Revenues
   c. Wages Expense
   d. Accumulated Depreciation, Building

10. Being able to accommodate changes in a business is a description of the
    a. control principle.
    b. compatibility principle.
    c. flexibility principle.
    d. cost-benefit principle.

11. Information is shared over the Internet by individuals with common interests through
    a. bulletin boards.
    b. Internet service providers.
    c. electronic commerce.
    d. general ledger software.

APPLYING YOUR KNOWLEDGE

Exercises

1. Following are the accounts of an Adjusted Trial Balance for the month of July. In the journal provided, make the necessary closing entries. All accounts have normal balances.

Accounts Payable	$ 1,000
Accounts Receivable	2,000
Cash	13,500
Common Stock	10,000
Dividends	2,500
Rent Expense	500
Retained Earnings	3,000
Revenue from Services	4,700
Telephone Expense	50
Utilities Expense	150

General Journal				
Date		Description	Debit	Credit

2. Using the information from Exercise 1, complete the following statement of retained earnings.

Karen's Fix-It Services, Inc.
Statement of Retained Earnings
For the Month Ended July 31, 20xx

_____

3. The following items **a** through **g** provide the information needed to make adjustments for Dillon's Maintenance, Inc., as of December 31, 20xx. Complete the entire work sheet on the next page using this information. Remember to use key letters for each adjustment.

a. On December 31, there is $200 of unexpired rent on the storage garage.

b. Depreciation taken on the lawn equipment during the period amounts to $1,500.

c. An inventory of lawn supplies shows $100 rmaining on December 31.

d. Accrued wages on December 31 amount to $280.

e. Grass-cutting fees earned but as yet uncollected amount to $50.

f. Of the $300 landscaping fees paid for in advance, $120 had been earned by December 31.

g. Accrued income tax expense for the year amounts to $1,570. This amount will be paid early next year.

Dillon's Maintenance, Inc.
Work Sheet
For the Year Ended December 31, 20xx

Account Name	Trial Balance		Adjustments		Adjusted Trial Balance		Income Statement		Balance Sheet	
	Debit	Credit	Debit	Credit	Debit	Credit	Debit	Credit	Debit	Credit
Cash	2,560									
Accounts Receivable	880									
Prepaid Rent	750									
Lawn Supplies	250									
Lawn Equipment	10,000									
Accum. Deprec., Lawn Equipment		2,000								
Accounts Payable		630								
Unearned Landscaping Fees		300								
Common Stock		5,000								
Retained Earnings		1,000								
Dividends	6,050									
Grass-Cutting Fees		15,000								
Wages Expense	3,300									
Gasoline Expense	140									
	23,930	23,930								
Rent Expense										
Depreciation Expense, Lawn Equipment										
Lawn Supplies Expense										
Landscaping Fees Earned										
Wages Payable										
Income Taxes Expense										
Income Taxes Payable										
Net Income										

4. On December 1, Barasch Company borrowed $20,000 from a bank on a note for 90 days at 12 percent (annual) interest. Assuming that interest is not included in the face amount, prepare the following journal entries:

a. December 1 entry to record the note
b. December 31 entry to record accrued interest
c. December 31 entry to close interest account
d. January 1 reversing entry
e. March 1 entry to record payment of the note plus interest

General Journal				
Date		**Description**	**Debit**	**Credit**

CHAPTER 5 FINANCIAL REPORTING AND ANALYSIS

REVIEWING THE CHAPTER

Objective 1: State the objectives of financial reporting.

1. Financial reporting should fulfill three objectives. It should (a) provide information that is useful in making investment and credit decisions; (b) provide information that is useful in assessing cash flow prospects; and (c) provide information about business resources, claims to those resources, and changes in them. General-purpose external financial statements are the main way of presenting financial information to interested parties. They consist of the balance sheet, income statement, statement of retained earnings, and statement of cash flows.

Objective 2: State the qualitative characteristics of accounting information and describe their interrelationships.

2. Accounting attempts to provide decision makers with information that displays certain **qualitative characteristics,** or standards:
   a. **Understandability,** carrying the intended meaning, is a key qualitative characteristic.
   b. Another very important standard is **usefulness.** For it to be useful, information must be relevant and reliable. **Relevance** means that the information is capable of influencing the decision. Relevant information provides feedback, helps in making predictions, and is timely. **Reliability** means that accounting information accurately reflects what it is meant to reflect, that it is credible, verifiable, and neutral.

Objective 3: Define and describe the use of the conventions of *comparability* and *consistency, materiality, conservatism, full disclosure,* and *cost-benefit.*

3. To help users interpret financial information, accountants depend on five **conventions,** or rules of thumb: comparability and consistency, materiality, conservatism, full disclosure, and cost-benefit.
   a. **Comparability** means that the information allows the decision maker to compare the same company over two or more accounting periods, or different companies over the same accounting period. **Consistency** means that a particular accounting procedure, once adopted, should not be changed unless the company can justify the change and discloses the dollar effect on the statements.
   b. The **materiality** convention states that strict accounting practice need not be applied to items of insignificant dollar value. Whether a dollar amount is material or not is a matter of professional judgment, which should be exercised in a fair and accurate manner.
   c. The **conservatism** convention states that an accountant who has a choice of acceptable accounting procedures should choose the one that is least likely to overstate assets and income. Applying the lower-of-cost-or-market rule to inventory valuation is an example of conservatism.
   d. The **full disclosure** convention states that financial statements and their notes should contain all information relevant to the user's understanding of the statements.

e. The **cost-benefit** convention states that the cost of providing additional accounting information should not exceed the benefits to be gained from the information.

Objective 4: Explain management's responsibility for ethical financial reporting and define *fraudulent financial reporting*.

4. Users depend on management and its accountants to act ethically and with good judgment in the preparation of financial statements. This responsibility is often expressed in the report of management that accompanies financial statements.

5. The intentional preparation of misleading financial statements is called **fraudulent financial reporting.** It can result from the distortion of records, falsified transactions, or the misapplication of accounting principles. Individuals who perpetrate fraudulent financial reporting are subject to criminal and financial penalties.

Objective 5: Identify and describe the basic components of a classified balance sheet.

6. **Classified financial statements** divide assets, liabilities, owners' equity, revenues, and expenses into subcategories to offer the reader more useful information.

7. On a classified balance sheet, assets are usually divided into four categories: (a) current assets; (b) investments; (c) property, plant, and equipment; and (d) intangible assets. (Sometimes another category called "other assets" is added for miscellaneous items.)

8. These categories are usually listed in order of liquidity (the ease with which an asset can be turned into cash).

9. **Current assets** are cash and assets that are expected to be turned into cash or used up within the normal operating cycle of the company or one year, whichever is longer. (From here on we will call this time period the current period.)
   a. A company's normal operating cycle is the average time between the purchase of inventory and the collection of cash from the sale of that inventory.
   b. Cash, short-term investments, accounts receivable, notes receivable, prepaid expenses, supplies, and inventory are current assets.

10. Examples of **investments** are stock and bonds held for long-term investment, land held for future use, plant or equipment not used in the busi-

ness, special funds, and a controlling interest in another company.

11. **Property, plant, and equipment** (also called *operating assets, fixed assets, tangible assets, long-lived assets,* or *plant assets*) include things like land, buildings, delivery equipment, machinery, office equipment, and natural resources. Most of the assets in this category are subject to depreciation.

12. **Intangible assets** have no physical substance. More importantly, they represent certain long-lived rights or privileges. Examples are patents, copyrights, goodwill, franchises, and trademarks.

13. **Other assets** is used as a category by some companies to group all assets other than current assets and property, plant, and equipment. In this case, other assets can include investments and intangible assets.

14. The liabilities of a classified balance sheet are usually divided into current and long-term liabilities.
   a. **Current liabilities** are obligations for which payment (or performance) is due in the current period. They are paid from current assets or by incurring new short-term liabilities. Examples are notes payable, accounts payable, taxes payable, and unearned revenues.
   b. **Long-term liabilities** are debts that are due after the current period or that will be paid from noncurrent assets. Examples are mortgages payable, long-term notes payable, bonds payable, employee pension obligations, and long-term leases.

15. The owner's equity section of a classified balance sheet is usually called owner's equity, partners' equity, or stockholders' equity. The exact name depends on whether the business is a sole proprietorship, a partnership, or a corporation. Other descriptive terms for owner's equity are *proprietorship, capital,* and the somewhat misleading term *net worth.*

16. In a corporation, the stockholders' equity section consists of contributed capital (also called *paid-in capital*) and retained earnings.

17. In a sole proprietorship or partnership, the owner's or partners' equity section shows the name of the owner or owners. Each is followed by the word *capital* and the dollar amount of investment as of the balance sheet date.

18. One difficult aspect of reading a balance sheet is understanding the numerical relationships and

patterns among the various accounts listed. That is, the dollar amount assigned to an account has little meaning by itself, but becomes significantly more pertinent when put into proper perspective. Fortunately, software has been developed to present balance sheet figures in graphical form. This visual presentation enables the reader to easily grasp the relative magnitude of the numbers, and to plainly see their relationship to the whole.

Objective 6: Prepare multistep and single-step classified income statements.

19. An income statement may be presented in either multistep or single-step form.
    a. The **multistep income statement** is the more detailed of the two, containing several subtractions and subtotals. It has separate sections for cost of goods sold, operating expenses, and other (nonoperating) revenues and expenses. One important subtotal is **income from operations** (or *operating income*), which equals gross margin minus operating expenses. See paragraph 20 for an illustration of the multistep form.
    b. In the **single-step income statement,** the revenues section lists all revenues, including other revenues, and the operating costs section lists all expenses, including other expenses. The difference is labeled net income or net loss.

20. Service companies calculate net income by simply deducting expenses from revenues. However, the income of **merchandising companies** (which buy and sell finished products) and **manufacturing companies** (which make and sell products) is computed as follows:

    Net Sales
    − Cost of Goods Sold
    = Gross Margin
    − Operating Expenses
    = Income from Operations
    ± Other Revenues and Expenses
    = Income before Income Taxes
    − Income Taxes
    = **Net Income**

    Merchandising companies include both wholesalers and retailers.

21. **Net sales** (or simply *sales*) consist of gross proceeds from the sale of merchandise (**gross sales**) less sales returns and allowances and sales discounts.

22. **Cost of goods sold** (also called *cost of sales*) is the amount that the merchandising company originally paid for the goods that it sold during a given period. If, for example, a merchandising firm sells for $100 a radio that cost the company $70, then revenues from sales are $100, cost of goods sold is $70, and **gross margin** (also called *gross profit*) is $30. This $30 gross margin helps pay for **operating expenses** (all expenses other than cost of goods sold and income taxes). What is left after subtracting operating expenses represents income from operations (also called *operating income*).

23. Then, **other revenues and expenses** (nonoperating items such as interest expense and interest income) are deducted or added to arrive at **income before income taxes.** Finally, a corporation's income statement should disclose provision for income taxes, or simply **income taxes,** separately from the other expenses. (The income statement of a sole proprietorship or a partnership would *not* contain a provision for income taxes because these forms of business are not taxable units.)

24. Operating expenses consist of selling expenses and general and administrative expenses. Selling expenses are advertising expenses, salespeople's salaries, sales office expenses, **freight out expense** (also called *delivery expense*), and all other expenses directly related to the sales effort. General and administrative expenses are all expenses not directly related to the manufacturing or sales effort. Examples are general office expenses and executive salaries.

25. **Earnings per share,** also called *net income per share,* equals net income divided by the average number of shares of common stock outstanding. It usually appears below net income in the income statement and is a measure of the company's profitability.

26. Presently an income statement in the manner described above provides useful information to management, which is continually trying to improve its profitability. A *graphical* presentation can make analysis of the income statement even more manageable.

Objective 7: Evaluate liquidity and profitability using classified financial statements.

27. Classified financial statements help the reader evaluate liquidity and profitability.

28. **Liquidity** refers to a company's ability to pay its bills when they are due and to meet unexpected

needs for cash. Two measures of liquidity are working capital and the current ratio.

    a. **Working capital** equals current assets minus current liabilities. It is the amount of current assets that would remain if all the current debts were paid.

    b. The **current ratio** equals current assets divided by current liabilities. A current ratio of 1:1, for example, shows that current assets are just enough to pay current liabilities. A 2:1 current ratio would be considered more satisfactory.

29. **Profitability** means more than just a company's net income. And to draw conclusions, one must compare profitability measures with industry averages and past performance. Five common measures of profitability are profit margin, asset turnover, return on assets, debt to equity ratio, and return on equity.

    a. The **profit margin** equals net income divided by net sales. A 12.5 percent profit margin, for example, means that 12½¢ has been earned on each dollar of sales.

    b. **Asset turnover** equals net sales divided by average total assets. This measures how efficiently assets are used to produce sales.

    c. **Return on assets** equals net income divided by average total assets. This measure shows how efficiently the company is using its assets.

    d. The **debt to equity** ratio measures the proportion of a business financed by creditors relative to the proportion financed by owners. It equals total liabilities divided by stockholders' equity. A debt to equity ratio of 1.0, for instance, indicates equal financing by creditors and owners.

    e. **Return on equity** shows what percentage was earned on the owners' investment. It equals net income divided by average stockholders' equity.

SELF-TEST

Test your knowledge of the chapter by choosing the best answer for each of the following items.

1. Goodwill is categorized as
   a. a current asset.
   b. revenue.
   c. an intangible asset.
   d. property, plant, and equipment.

2. Accounting information is said to be useful if it is
   a. timely and biased.
   b. relevant and reliable.
   c. relevant and certain.
   d. accurate and faithful.

3. To ignore an amount because it is small in relation to the financial statements taken as a whole is an application of
   a. materiality.
   b. conservatism.
   c. full disclosure.
   d. comparability.

4. Accounting is concerned with providing information to decision makers. The overall framework of rules within which accountants work to provide this information is best described as
   a. business transactions.
   b. data processing.
   c. generally accepted accounting principles.
   d. income tax laws.

5. A note receivable due in two years normally would be classified as
   a. a current asset.
   b. an investment.
   c. property, plant, and equipment.
   d. an intangible asset.

6. The current portion of long-term debt is normally classified as
   a. current assets.
   b. current liabilities.
   c. long-term liabilities.
   d. stockholders' equity.

7. A disadvantage of the single-step income statement is that
   a. gross margin is not disclosed separately.
   b. other revenues and expenses are separated from operating items.
   c. interest expense is not disclosed.
   d. the cost of goods sold cannot be determined.

8. Net income is a component in determining each of the following ratios *except*
   a. profit margin.
   b. return on assets.
   c. debt to equity.
   d. return on equity.

9. Asset turnover is expressed in (as)
   a. dollars.
   b. a percentage.
   c. times.
   d. days.

10. Which of the following terms does not mean the same as the others listed?
    a. Net worth
    b. Owner's equity
    c. Proprietorship
    d. Working capital

TESTING YOUR KNOWLEDGE

Matching*

Match each term with its definition by writing the appropriate letter in the blank.

_____ 1. Qualitative characteristics

_____ 2. Relevance

_____ 3. Reliability

_____ 4. Fraudulent financial reporting

_____ 5. Classified financial statements

_____ 6. Liquidity

_____ 7. Current assets

_____ 8. Property, plant, and equipment

_____ 9. Intangible assets

_____ 10. Current liabilities

_____ 11. Long-term liabilities

_____ 12. Other revenues and expenses

_____ 13. Earnings per share (*net income per share*)

_____ 14. Merchandising company

_____ 15. Cost of goods sold

_____ 16. Gross margin (*gross profit*)

_____ 17. Operating expenses

a. A buyer and seller of goods that are in finished form

b. Long-lived tangible assets

c. The intentional preparation of misleading financial statements

d. All expenses except for cost of goods sold and income taxes

e. Guidelines for evaluating the quality of accounting reports

f. Short-term obligations

g. Financial reports broken down into subcategories

h. What a merchandising company paid for the goods it sold during the period

i. Net income divided by average number of outstanding shares of common stock

j. The income statement section that contains nonoperating items

k. The subcategory of assets that are expected to be turned into cash or used up within one year or the normal operating cycle, whichever is longer

l. The standard that accounting information should be related to the user's needs

m. Long-term assets that lack physical substance and that grant rights or privileges to their owner

n. Net sales minus cost of goods sold

o. Obligations due after the current period

p. The standard that accounting information should accurately reflect what it is meant to represent

q. The ability to pay bills when due and to meet unexpected needs for cash

---

Note to student: The matching quiz might be completed more efficiently by starting with the definition and searching for the corresponding term.

Short Answer

Use the lines provided to answer each item.

1. List the three forms of business organization, with each one's name for the owners' equity section of the balance sheet.

Business Organization

a. _____

b. _____

c. _____

Name for Owners' Equity Section

a. _____

b. _____

c. _____

2. What does each of the following ratios have to do with a company's profitability?

Profit margin

_____

_____

_____

Asset turnover

_____

_____

_____

Return on assets

_____

_____

_____

Return on equity

_____

_____

_____

Debt to equity

_____

_____

_____

3. Define each of the following liquidity ratios.

Working capital

_____

_____

Current ratio

_____

_____

4. Explain the basic point of each of the following conventions:

Consistency and comparability

_____

_____

Materiality

_____

_____

Cost-benefit

_____

_____

Conservatism

_____

_____

Full disclosure

_____

_____

Circle T if the statement is true, F if it is false. Please provide explanations for the false answers, using the blank lines at the end of the section.

T F **1.** Receivables are not current assets if collection requires more than one year.

T F **2.** Freight out expense is a type of operating expense.

T F **3.** Gross margin minus operating expenses equals income from operations.

T F **4.** Operating expenses are made up of selling expenses and cost of goods sold.

T F **5.** Accounting information is relevant if it could make a difference to the outcome of a decision.

T F **6.** The net income figure is needed to compute the profit margin, the return on assets, and the return on equity.

T F **7.** The investments section of a balance sheet would include both short- and long-term investments in stock.

T F **8.** One meaning of the term *profitability* is the ease with which an asset can be converted into cash.

T F **9.** A company's normal operating cycle cannot be less than one year.

T F **10.** Net worth refers to the current value of a company's assets.

T F **11.** Other revenues and expenses is a separate classification in a multistep income statement.

T F **12.** The net income figures for a multistep and a single-step income statement will differ, given the same accounting period for the same company.

T F **13.** Both wholesalers and retailers are types of merchandising companies.

T F **14.** Working capital equals current assets divided by current liabilities.

T F **15.** The proportion of a company financed by the owners is revealed by the debt to equity ratio.

T F **16.** The qualitative characteristic of relevance means that accounting information can be confirmed or duplicated by independent parties.

T F **17.** Earnings per share is an important measure of liquidity.

_____

_____

_____

_____

_____

_____

_____

_____

_____

_____

_____

_____

_____

_____

Circle the letter of the best answer.

1. The basis for classifying assets as current or non-current is the period of time normally required by the business to turn cash invested in
   a. noncurrent assets back into current assets.
   b. receivables back into cash, or 12 months, whichever is shorter.
   c. inventories back into cash, or 12 months, whichever is longer.
   d. inventories back into cash, or 12 months, whichever is shorter.

2. Which of the following will not be found anywhere in a single-step income statement?
   a. Cost of goods sold
   b. Other expenses
   c. Gross margin
   d. Operating expenses

3. The current ratio would probably be of *most* interest to
   a. stockholders.
   b. creditors.
   c. management.
   d. customers.

4. Which item below will *not* appear in the stockholders' equity section of a corporation's balance sheet?
   a. Retained earnings
   b. Common stock
   c. Paid-in capital in excess of par value
   d. Benjamin El Hallel, Capital

5. Net income divided by net sales equals
   a. profit margin.
   b. return on assets.
   c. working capital.
   d. income from operations.

6. Operating expenses consist of
   a. other expenses and cost of goods sold.
   b. selling expenses and cost of goods sold.
   c. selling expenses and general and administrative expenses.
   d. selling expenses, general and administrative expenses, and other expenses.

7. Applying the lower-of-cost-or-market rule to inventory valuation follows the convention of
   a. consistency.
   b. materiality.
   c. conservatism.
   d. full disclosure.

8. Which of the following is *not* an objective of financial reporting, according to FASB *Statement of Financial Accounting Concepts No. 1?*
   a. To provide information about the timing of cash flows
   b. To provide information to investors and creditors
   c. To provide information about business resources
   d. To provide information to management

9. If a company has a profit margin of 4.0 percent and an asset turnover of 3.0 times, its return on assets is approximately
   a. 1.3 percent.
   b. 3.0 percent.
   c. 4.0 percent.
   d. 12.0 percent.

APPLYING YOUR KNOWLEDGE

Exercises

1. Assume that Kobe Company uses the following group headings on its classified balance sheet:

   a. Current Assets
   b. Investments
   c. Property, Plant, and Equipment
   d. Intangible Assets
   e. Current Liabilities
   f. Long-Term Liabilities
   g. Stockholders' Equity

   Indicate by letter where each of the following should be placed. Write an "X" next to items that do not belong on the balance sheet.

   _____ 1. Franchises
   _____ 2. Short-term advances from customers
   _____ 3. Accumulated depreciation
   _____ 4. Common stock
   _____ 5. Prepaid rent
   _____ 6. Delivery truck
   _____ 7. Office supplies
   _____ 8. Fund for the purchase of land
   _____ 9. Notes payable due in ten years
   _____ 10. Bonds payable currently due (payable out of current assets)
   _____ 11. Goodwill
   _____ 12. Short-term investments
   _____ 13. Provision for income taxes
   _____ 14. Inventory
   _____ 15. Accounts payable

2. The following information relates to Direct Appliances, Inc., for 20xx:

Current Assets	$ 60,000
Average Total Assets	200,000
Current Liabilities	20,000
Long-Term Liabilities	30,000
Average Stockholders' Equity	150,000
Net Sales	250,000
Net Income	25,000

   In the spaces provided, indicate each measure of liquidity and profitability.

   a. Working capital = $ _____
   b. Current ratio = _____
   c. Profit margin = _____%
   d. Return on assets = _____%
   e. Return on equity = _____%
   f. Asset turnover = _____ times

3. The following data relate to Corvus Corporation for 20xx:

Cost of Goods Sold	$150,000
Interest Income	2,000
Income Taxes	5,000
Net Sales	200,000
Common Stock Outstanding	3,500 shares
Operating Expenses	30,000

   a. In the space provided below, complete the condensed multistep income statement in good form. Include earnings per share information in the proper place.

Corvus Corporation Income Statement (Multistep) For the Year Ended December 31, 20xx		

b. In the space provided, complete the condensed single-step income statement in good form. Include earnings per share information in the proper place.

Corvus Corporation Income Statement (Single-step) For the Year Ended December 31, 20xx		

Crossword Puzzle
for Chapters 4 and 5

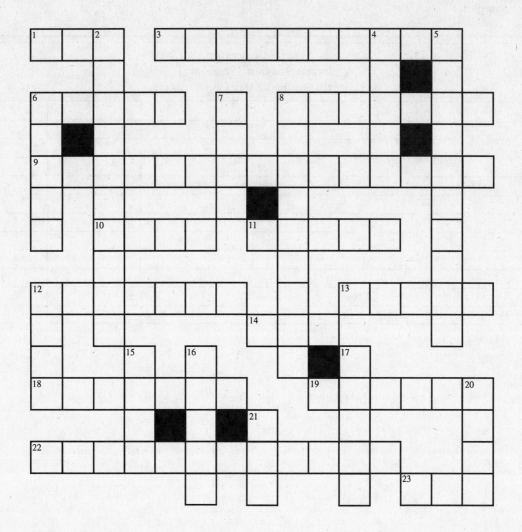

ACROSS

1. Strong proponent of 10-Across
3. Relevance and reliability
6. Ownership stake
8. Short-term
9. Inventory-related expense (4 words)
10. _____ disclosure
11. _____ turnover
12. _____ out expense
13. _____ revenues and expenses
14. Provision _____ income taxes
18. Cost-_____ convention
19. Cleared, as temporary accounts
22. Another term for 13-Across
23. _____ worth

DOWN

2. Financial statement form
4. Profits (verb)
5. Income statement form (hyphenated)
6. Normal operating _____
7. Hourly pay
8. Add horizontally
12. Issuer of financial-reporting objectives
15. Balance of a cleared account
16. Asset category
17. Property, _____, and equipment
20. _____ to equity ratio
21. A natural resource

CHAPTER 6 MERCHANDISING OPERATIONS AND INTERNAL CONTROL

REVIEWING THE CHAPTER

Objective 1: Identify the management issues related to merchandising businesses.

1. Accounting for service businesses, such as movers and dry cleaners, is relatively easy because this type of business does not have inventory (goods for resale) to manage.

2. A **merchandising business,** on the other hand, is a wholesaler or retailer that buys and sells goods in finished form. This kind of firm uses the same basic accounting methods as a service company. However, the merchandiser must also account for its inventory, requiring a more complicated process and producing a more sophisticated income statement.

3. The merchandiser engages in a series of transactions known as the **operating cycle,** consisting of (a) the purchase of **merchandise inventory,** (b) the payment for purchases made on credit, (c) the sale of the inventory for cash or on credit, and (d) the collection of cash from credit sales.

4. Merchandisers must carefully manage cash flow, or liquidity. Such **cash flow management** is essential for the business to pay its bills when they fall due. **Profitability management** is also important for the merchandiser. It involves purchasing goods at favorable prices, selling those goods at a price that will cover costs and help earn a profit, and controlling operating expenses.

5. One effective way to control expenses is to use operating budgets. An **operating budget** consists of a detailed listing of selling and general and administrative expenses, along with their projected amounts. Periodically, management should compare these budgeted amounts with actual amounts expensed, analyze the items that are significantly over or under budget, and adjust operations accordingly.

6. The merchandising company must choose a system to account for its inventory. The two basic systems are the periodic inventory system and the perpetual inventory system.

7. The **perpetual inventory system** is used when management wishes to keep a record of the quantity (and usually the cost) of inventory as it is both purchased and sold. As a result, management can quickly determine product availability, avoid running out of stock, and control the costs of carrying its inventory. Under the perpetual inventory system, the Merchandise Inventory account and Cost of Goods Sold are updated whenever goods are sold.

8. The **periodic inventory system** is used when it is unnecessary or impractical to keep track of the quantity of inventory or the cost of each item. Under this method, the company waits until the end of the accounting period to take a physical inventory. This physical count figure is then multiplied by a derived cost-per-unit figure (explained in Chapter 8) to arrive at the cost of ending inventory.

9. The periodic inventory system is simpler and less costly to maintain than the perpetual inventory

system. However, its lack of detailed records may lead to inefficiencies, lost sales, and higher operating costs.

10. A merchandising business typically handles a great deal of cash and inventory. Unfortunately, these assets are very susceptible to theft and embezzlement. Accordingly, a good system of internal control must be established to help protect the company's assets.

11. Merchandise inventory appears as an asset on the balance sheet and includes all salable goods owned by the company, no matter where the goods are located. Goods in transit to which a company has acquired title are included in ending inventory. However, goods that the company has formally sold are not included, even if the company has not yet delivered them. To simplify the taking of a **physical inventory,** which usually takes place on the last day of the fiscal year, many companies end their fiscal year during the slow season, when inventories are relatively low.

Objective 2: Define and distinguish the terms of sale for merchandising transactions.

12. As a matter of convenience, manufacturers and wholesalers frequently quote prices of merchandise based on a discount from the list or catalogue price (called a **trade discount**). Neither the list price nor the trade discount is entered into the accounting records.

13. When goods are sold on credit, terms will vary as to when payment must be made. For instance, n/30 means that full payment is due within 30 days after the invoice date, and n/10 eom means that full payment is due 10 days after the end of the month.

14. Often a customer is given a discount for early payment, and the merchandiser records a **sales discount.** Terms of 2/10, n/30, for example, mean that a 2 percent discount will be given if payment is made within 10 days of the invoice date. Otherwise, the full amount is due within 30 days.

15. Freight charges are borne by the buyer or seller of the goods, depending upon the terms specified. A merchandiser in Chicago, for instance, must pay the freight in from Boston if the terms specify FOB Boston or **FOB shipping point.** However, the supplier in Boston pays if the terms are FOB Chicago or **FOB destination.** FOB terms are also related to when the title of the merchandise passes from the seller to the buyer.

Objective 3: Prepare an income statement and record merchandising transactions under the perpetual inventory system.

16. The net income of a merchandising firm is computed as follows:

Net Sales
- Cost of Goods Sold
= Gross Margin
- Operating Expenses
= Income Before Income Taxes
- Income Taxes
= Net Income

17. When a merchandising firm incurs transportation costs on goods purchased, it debits Freight In (or Transportation In) and credits Accounts Payable. Under the perpetual inventory system, cost of goods sold and merchandise inventory are updated whenever a purchase, sale, or other inventory transaction takes place. In addition, **freight in** (also called *transportation in*) is usually included in cost of goods sold.

18. Transactions are recorded under the perpetual inventory system as explained below:
   a. For the purchase of merchandise on credit, Merchandise Inventory is debited and Accounts Payable is credited.
   b. Transportation costs for goods received are recorded with a debit to Freight In and a credit to Accounts Payable or Cash.
   c. The return of goods to the supplier (for credit) is recorded with a debit to Accounts Payable and a credit to Merchandise Inventory.
   d. Payment on account is recorded with a simple debit to Accounts Payable and credit to Cash.
   e. When goods are sold on credit, Accounts Receivable is debited and Sales is credited. However, an additional entry must be made, debiting Cost of Goods Sold and crediting Merchandise Inventory.
   f. Delivery costs for goods sold are recorded with a debit to **Freight Out Expense** (also called *delivery expense*) and a credit to Accounts Payable or Cash.
   g. When a credit customer returns goods for a refund, **Sales Returns and Allowances** is debited and Accounts Receivable is credited. The Sales Returns and Allowances account is debited instead of the Sales account to provide management with data about dissatisfied

customers. Under the perpetual inventory system, a second entry is needed to reinstate Merchandise Inventory (a debit) and to reduce Cost of Goods Sold (a credit).

  h. The receipt of payment on account is recorded with a simple debit to Cash and credit to Accounts Receivable.

Objective 4: Prepare an income statement and record merchandising transactions under the periodic inventory system.

19. Under the periodic inventory system, cost of goods sold and merchandise inventory are *not* updated for purchases, sales, and other inventory transactions. In addition, its income statement contains a specific calculation of cost of goods sold, as illustrated below:

  Beginning Inventory

  + Net Cost of Purchases (see paragraph 20)

  = **Goods Available for Sale**

  – Ending Inventory

  = Cost of Goods Sold

20. **Net cost of purchases** is calculated as follows:

  (Gross) Purchases

  – Purchases Returns and Allowances

  – Purchases Discounts

  = **Net Purchases**

  + Freight In

  = Net Cost of Purchases

21. Transactions are recorded under the periodic inventory system as explained below:

  a. All purchases of merchandise are debited to the **Purchases** account and credited to Accounts Payable. The purpose of the Purchases account is to accumulate the cost of merchandise purchased for resale during the period.

  b. Transportation costs for goods purchased are recorded with a debit to Freight In and a credit to Accounts Payable or Cash.

  c. The return of goods to the supplier (for credit) is recorded with a debt to Accounts Payable and a credit to **Purchases Returns and Allowances.** The latter appears as a contra account to Purchases on the income statement.

  d. Payment on account is recorded with a simple debit to Accounts Payable and credit to Cash.

  e. When a cash sale is made, Cash is debited and Sales is credited for the amount of the sale.

When a credit sale is made, Accounts Receivable is debited and Sales is credited. Generally, a sale is recorded when the goods are delivered and title passes to the customer, regardless of when payment is made.

  f. Delivery costs for goods sold are recorded with a debit to Freight Out Expense and a credit to Accounts Payable or Cash.

  g. When a credit customer returns goods for a refund, Sales Returns and Allowances is debited and Accounts Receivable is credited.

  h. The receipt of payment on account is recorded with a simple debit to Cash and credit to Accounts Receivable.

22. Companies that allow customers to use national credit cards (such as MasterCard) must follow special accounting procedures. The credit card company reimburses the merchant for the sale, less a service charge. The credit card company levies this service charge because it is responsible for establishing credit and collecting money from the customer. Assuming that the merchant deposits its credit card sales invoices into a special bank account for immediate credit, it would debit Cash and Credit Card Discount Expense and credit Sales.

23. Inventory losses result from theft and spoilage, and are included in cost of goods sold. As one might imagine, these losses are easier to track under the perpetual system than under the periodic system.

Objective 5: Define *internal control*, identify the five components of internal control, and explain seven examples of control activities.

24. **Internal control** encompasses all the policies and procedures management uses to assure (a) the reliability of financial reporting, (b) compliance with laws and regulations, and (c) the effectiveness and efficiency of operations. To achieve these objectives, management must establish the following five components of internal control: the control environment, risk assessment, information and communication, control activities, and monitoring.

  a. The **control environment** reflects management's philosophy and operating style, the company's organizational structure, methods of assigning authority and responsibility, and personnel policies and practices.

  b. **Risk assessment** entails identification of areas where risk of asset loss or inaccuracy of records is especially high.

c. **Information and communication** involves the establishment of the accounting systems by management, as well as the communication of each individual's responsibility within those systems.

d. **Control activities** are the specific procedures and policies established by management to ensure that the objectives of internal control are met. These activities are discussed in more detail in the following paragraph.

e. **Monitoring** consists of management's regular assessment of the quality of internal control.

25. Examples of control activities are (a) requiring authorization for all transactions, (b) recording all transactions, (c) the design and use of adequate documents, (d) physical controls, as over the accounting records, (e) periodic checks of records and assets, (f) separation of duties, and (g) sound personnel procedures. **Bonding** an employee (an example of a good control activity) means reducing or eliminating the risk of theft by that individual against the company.

Objective 6: Describe the inherent limitations of internal control.

26. A system of internal control relies on the people who carry out the control procedures. Human error, mistakes in judgment, collusion, and changing conditions all can limit the effectiveness of a system of internal control.

Objective 7: Apply internal control activities to common merchandising transactions.

27. Accounting controls over merchandising transactions help prevent losses from theft or fraud, and help ensure accurate accounting records. Administrative controls over merchandising transactions should help keep inventory levels balanced, keep enough cash on hand to make timely payments for purchases discounts, and avoid credit losses.

28. Procedures should be followed to achieve effective internal control over sales and the exchange of cash.

29. Cash received by mail should be handled by two or more employees. Cash received from sales over the counter should be controlled through the use of cash registers and prenumbered sales tickets. At the end of each day, total cash receipts should be reconciled and recorded in the cash receipts journal following the principle of separation of duties.

30. All cash payments for purchases should be made by check and only with authorization. The system of authorization and the documents used differ among companies, but these are the most common documents:

a. A **purchase requisition** is completed by a department requesting that the company purchase something for the department.

b. A **purchase order** is completed by the department responsible for the company's purchasing activities; it is sent to the vendor.

c. An **invoice** is the bill sent from the vendor to the buyer's accounting department.

d. A **receiving report** is completed by the receiving department and forwarded to the accounting department; it contains information about the quantity and condition of the goods received.

e. A **check authorization**, issued by the accounting department, is a document showing that the purchase order, invoice, and receiving report are in agreement, and that payment is approved.

f. When payment is approved, a **check** is issued to the vendor for the amount of the invoice, less the appropriate discount. A remittance advice, which shows what the check is paying, should be attached to the check.

Supplemental Objective 8: Apply sales and purchases discounts to merchandising transactions.

31. Often a merchandising company offers (and is offered) a discount if payment is received (or made) within a given number of days.

a. Sales discounts are recorded when payment is received within the discount period. Cash and Sales Discounts are debited; Accounts Receivable is credited. Sales Discounts is a contra account to Gross Sales on the income statement.

b. A purchase is initially recorded at the gross purchase price. If the company makes payment within the discount period, it debits Accounts Payable, credits Purchases Discounts, and credits Cash. **Purchases Discounts** is a contra account to Purchases on the Income Statement.

Perpetual Inventory System

A. (LO 3) Merchandise Inventory   XX (purchase price)
    Accounts Payable   XX (amount due)
      Purchased merchandise on credit

B. (LO 3) Freight In   XX (price charged)
    Accounts Payable   XX (amount due)
      Incurred transportation charges

C. (LO 3) Accounts Payable   XX (amount returned)
    Merchandise Inventory   XX (amount returned)
      Returned merchandise to supplier for credit

D. (LO 3) Accounts Payable   XX (amount paid)
    Cash   XX (amount paid)
      Made payment on account

E. (LO 3) Accounts Receivable   XX (amount to be received)
    Sales   XX (sales price)
      Sold merchandise on credit

    Cost of Goods Sold   XX (inventory cost)
    Merchandise Inventory   XX (inventory cost)
      Recorded cost of goods sold and updated the
      inventory account for goods sold above

F. (LO 3) Freight Out Expense   XX (amount incurred)
    Cash   XX (amount paid)
      Paid delivery costs for goods shipped
      to customer

G. (LO 3) Sales Returns and Allowances   XX (price of goods returned)
    Accounts Receivable   XX (amount credited to account)
      Customer returned goods for credit

    Merchandise Inventory   XX (inventory cost)
    Cost of Goods Sold   XX (inventory cost)
      Reinstated inventory and reduced cost of
      goods sold for goods returned above

H. (LO 3) Cash   XX (amount received)
    Accounts Receivable   XX (amount settled)
      Received payment on account

Periodic Inventory System

I. (LO 4) Purchases   XX (purchase price)
     Accounts Payable   XX (amount due)
       Purchased merchandise on credit

J. (LO 4) Freight In   XX (price charged)
     Accounts Payable   XX (amount due)
       Incurred transportation charges

K. (LO 4) Accounts Payable   XX (amount returned)
     Purchases Returns and Allowances   XX (amount returned)
       Returned merchandise to supplier for credit

L. (LO 4) Accounts Payable   XX (amount paid)
     Cash   XX (amount paid)
       Made payment on account

M. (LO 4) Accounts Receivable   XX (amount to be received)
     Sales   XX (sales price)
       Sold merchandise on credit

N. (LO 4) Freight Out Expense   XX (amount incurred)
     Cash   XX (amount paid)
       Paid delivery costs for goods shipped
       to customer

O. (LO 4) Sales Returns and Allowances   XX (price of goods returned)
     Accounts Receivable   XX (amount credited to account)
       Customer returned goods, account credited

P. (LO 4) Cash   XX (amount received)
     Accounts Receivable   XX (amount settled)
       Received payment on account

Q. (LO 4) Cash   XX (amount net of fee)
     Credit Card Discount Expense   XX (fee charged)
     Sales   XX (gross amount sold)
       Sales on credit card (invoices deposited
       in special credit card bank account)

R. (SO 8) Cash   XX (net amount received)
     Sales Discounts   XX (discount given)
     Accounts Receivable   XX (gross amount settled)
       Received payment from customer within
       discount period

S. (SO 8) Accounts Payable   XX (gross amount settled)
     Purchases Discounts   XX (discount taken)
     Cash   XX (net amount paid)
       Paid supplier within discount period

Chapter 6

SELF-TEST

Test your knowledge of the chapter by choosing the best answer for each of the following items.

1. Management determines that, on average, customers are taking five more days to pay for sales made on credit. To which of the following management concerns does this payment pattern directly relate?
   a. Cash flow management
   b. Profitability management
   c. Choice of inventory system
   d. Control of merchandise operations

2. A pretax income always results when
   a. the cost of goods sold exceeds operating expenses.
   b. revenues exceed the cost of goods sold.
   c. revenues exceed operating expenses.
   d. the gross margin exceeds operating expenses.

3. Which of the following appears as an operating expense on the income statement of a merchandising concern?
   a. Freight In
   b. Freight Out Expense
   c. Sales Returns and Allowances
   d. Purchases Returns and Allowances

4. If beginning and ending merchandise inventories are $400 and $700, respectively, and the cost of goods sold is $3,400, net cost of purchases
   a. is $3,700.
   b. is $3,400.
   c. is $3,100.
   d. cannot be determined.

5. A sale is made on June 1 for $200, terms 2/10, n/30, on which a sales return of $50 is granted on June 7. The dollar amount received for payment in full on June 9 is
   a. $200.
   b. $150.
   c. $147.
   d. $196.

6. Under a periodic inventory system, a purchase of merchandise for $750 including freight of $50 under terms of n/30, FOB shipping point would include a
   a. debit to Freight In of $50.
   b. debit to Purchases of $750.
   c. credit to Accounts Payable of $700.
   d. credit to Freight Payable of $50.

7. A firm, which maintains perpetual inventory records, sells on account, for $2,000, goods which had cost $1,400. The entries to record this transaction should include a
   a. debit to Merchandise Inventory for $1,400.
   b. debit to Sales for $2,000.
   c. credit to Accounts Receivable for $2,000.
   d. debit to Cost of Goods Sold for $1,400.

8. Which of the following does *not* constitute a component of internal control?
   a. Monitoring
   b. Risk assessment
   c. Reporting
   d. Control activities

9. The separation of duties in terms of cash transactions means that separate individuals should be responsible for authorization, custody, and
   a. approval.
   b. recordkeeping.
   c. control.
   d. protection.

10. Which of the following documents should be presented and agreed on before a check authorization is prepared?
    a. Purchase requisition and purchase order
    b. Purchase order and receiving report
    c. Purchase requisition, purchase order, and invoice
    d. Purchase order, invoice, and receiving report

TESTING YOUR KNOWLEDGE

Matching*

Match each term with its definition by writing the appropriate letter in the blank.

_____ 1. Trade discount

_____ 2. Invoice

_____ 3. Receiving report

_____ 4. Check authorization

_____ 5. Sales returns and allowances

_____ 6. Sales discounts

_____ 7. Freight out expense

_____ 8. Purchases

_____ 9. Goods available for sale

_____ 10. Perpetual inventory system

_____ 11. Periodic inventory system

_____ 12. Freight in

_____ 13. FOB (free on board)

_____ 14. Purchases returns and allowances

_____ 15. Purchases discounts

_____ 16. Internal control

_____ 17. Purchase requisition

_____ 18. Purchase order

a. Transportation cost for goods purchased

b. A document that authorizes payment

c. Delivery charge for goods sold

d. A system whereby continuous cost records are maintained for merchandise

e. A bill sent by the vendor to the purchaser

f. The point after which the buyer must bear the transportation cost

g. Under the periodic inventory system, the account used to accumulate the cost of goods bought during the period

h. A deduction off a list or catalogue price

i. Beginning inventory plus net cost of purchases

j. A document requesting the purchasing department to order certain items

k. The account used by the seller to record the discount when the buyer pays for goods within the discount period

l. The account used by the seller when the buyer returns goods

m. A system whereby continuous cost records are *not* maintained for merchandise

n. The account used by the buyer to record the discount when it pays for goods within the discount period

o. An order for goods that is sent to the vendor

p. Under the periodic inventory system, the account used by the buyer when it returns goods

q. A description of goods received by a company

r. A system designed to safeguard assets, promote operational efficiency, encourage adherence to managerial policies, and help achieve accounting accuracy

---

*Note to student: The matching quiz might be completed more efficiently by starting with the definition and searching for the corresponding term.

Short Answer

Use the lines provided to answer each item.

1. List seven control activities that help make a system of internal control effective.

   _____

   _____

   _____

   _____

   _____

   _____

   _____

2. List any six procedures that may be employed to control and safeguard cash.

   _____

   _____

   _____

   _____

   _____

   _____

3. What three documents should be in agreement before an invoice is paid?

   _____

   _____

   _____

4. Assuming a periodic inventory system, list the items in the condensed cost of goods sold section of an income statement. Use mathematical signs to indicate their relationship.

   _____

   _____

   _____

   _____

   _____

5. Using mathematical signs, list the sequence of items involved in computing net cost of purchases in a periodic inventory system.

   _____

   _____

   _____

   _____

   _____

   _____

True-False

Circle T if the statement is true, F if it is false. Please provide explanations for the false answers, using the blank lines at the end of the section.

T F   1. Ending merchandise inventory is needed to calculate goods available for sale.

T F   2. Terms of n/10 eom mean that payment must be made 10 days before the end of the month.

T F   3. An operating budget will disclose the differences between budgeted and actual operating expenses.

T F   4. Inventory losses are normally included in the cost of goods sold.

T F 5. FOB destination means that the seller is bearing the transportation cost.

T F 6. Sales Discounts is a contra account to Net Sales.

T F 7. Using a periodic inventory system, ending inventory is needed for both the balance sheet and the income statement.

T F 8. Cost of goods available for sale minus cost of goods sold equals ending inventory.

T F 9. The perpetual inventory system requires more detailed recordkeeping than does the periodic system.

T F 10. The beginning inventory of a period is the same as the ending inventory of the previous period.

T F 11. Sales Returns and Allowances normally has a credit balance.

T F 12. Under the periodic inventory system, a cash purchase of office supplies that are meant to be used in the day-to-day operation of a business requires a debit to Purchases and a credit to Cash.

T F 13. A Purchases Returns and Allowances account would not be used under the perpetual inventory system.

T F 14. Credit Card Discount Expense is treated by the merchant as a contra account to Sales.

T F 15. Under a periodic inventory system, as soon as a sale is made, cost of the goods sold must be recorded and the inventory account must be decreased.

T F 16. One example of a trade discount is 2/10, n/30.

T F 17. When goods are shipped FOB shipping point, title passes when the goods are received by the buyer.

T F 18. A good system of internal control will guarantee that the accounting records are accurate.

T F 19. Collusion refers to a secret agreement between two or more persons to defraud a company.

T F 20. The mail should be opened in the accounting department so that transactions may be recorded immediately.

T F 21. A company orders goods by sending the supplier a purchase requisition.

T F 22. Rotating employees in job assignments is poor internal control because employees would continually be forced to learn a new job skill.

T F 23. One of the five components of internal control is "information and communication."

_____
_____
_____
_____
_____
_____
_____
_____
_____
_____
_____
_____
_____
_____

_____
_____
_____
_____
_____
_____
_____
_____
_____
_____
_____
_____
_____
_____

_____   _____
_____   _____
_____   _____
_____   _____
_____   _____

Multiple Choice

Circle the letter of the best answer.

1. Dew buys $600 of merchandise from Allen, with terms of 2/10, n/30. Dew immediately returns $100 of goods and pays for the remainder eight days after the purchase. Dew's entry on the date of payment would include a
   a. debit to Accounts Payable for $600.
   b. debit to Sales Discounts for $12.
   c. credit to Purchases Returns and Allowances for $100.
   d. credit to Purchases Discounts for $10.

2. Which of the following accounts normally has a credit balance?
   a. Sales Discounts
   b. Merchandise Inventory
   c. Purchases Returns and Allowances
   d. Freight In

3. Which of the following accounts is irrelevant in computing cost of goods sold in a periodic inventory system?
   a. Freight In
   b. Freight Out Expense
   c. Merchandise Inventory, beginning
   d. Merchandise Inventory, ending

4. Which of the following documents is prepared (by a buyer of goods) before all of the others listed?
   a. Purchase order
   b. Receiving report
   c. Check authorization (or voucher)
   d. Purchase requisition

5. Which of the following is an example of poor internal control?
   a. Having the receiving department compare goods received with the related purchase order
   b. Forcing employees to take earned vacations
   c. Requiring someone other than the petty cash custodian to enter petty cash transactions into the accounting records
   d. Bonding employees

6. Which of the following accounts is *not* used in conjunction with a perpetual inventory system?
   a. Cost of Goods Sold
   b. Freight In
   c. Purchases
   d. Merchandise Inventory

7. The operating cycle does *not* include which of the following transactions?
   a. Sale of inventory
   b. Cash payment for operating expenses
   c. Purchase of inventory
   d. Cash collection from inventory sales

8. A company has credit card sales for the day of $1,000. If the credit card company charges 5 percent, the company's journal entry to record sales and the receipt of cash upon depositing the credit card invoices at the bank would include a
   a. credit to Sales for $950.
   b. credit to Credit Card Discount Expense for $50.
   c. debit to Sales for $1,000.
   d. debit to Cash for $950.

APPLYING YOUR KNOWLEDGE

Exercises

1. Following are the May transactions of Chill Merchandising Corporation. For each transaction, prepare the journal entry in the journal provided on the next page. Assume that the periodic inventory system is used.

May 1 Purchased merchandise for $500 on credit, terms 2/10, n/60.

3 Sold merchandise for $500 on credit, terms 2/10, 1/20, n/30.

4 Received invoice and paid $42 for freight charges relating to a merchandise purchase of April.

5 Purchased office supplies for $100, on credit.

6 Returned $20 of the May 5 office supplies, for credit.

7 Returned $50 of merchandise purchased on May 1, for credit.

9 Sold merchandise for $225, on credit, terms 2/10, 1/15, n/30.

10 Paid for the merchandise purchased on May 1, less the return and any discount.

14 The customer of May 9 returned $25 of merchandise, for credit.

22 The customer of May 9 paid for the merchandise, less the return and any discount.

26 The customer of May 3 paid for the merchandise.

2. Using the information below, prepare a partial income statement showing just the computation of gross margin.

Advertising Expense	$ 5,000
Dividends	12,000
Freight In	2,000
Freight Out Expense	4,000
Income Taxes Expense	4,780
Income Taxes Payable	4,780
Interest Income	150
Merchandise Inventory (Jan. 1)	10,000
Merchandise Inventory (Dec. 31)	8,000
Purchases	50,000
Purchases Discounts	500
Purchases Returns and Allowances	500
Rent Expense	3,000
Retained Earnings	15,000
Sales	100,000
Sales Discounts	300
Sales Returns and Allowances	200
Wages Expense	7,000

Jordan Merchandising Company
Partial Income Statement
For the Year 20xx

		General Journal		
Date		Description	Debit	Credit

CHAPTER 7   SHORT-TERM LIQUID ASSETS

REVIEWING THE CHAPTER

Objective 1: Identify and explain the management issues related to short-term liquid assets.

1. It is management's responsibility to use company assets to maximize income while maintaining liquidity. **Short-term liquid assets** are financial assets that arise from cash transactions, the investment of cash, and the extension of credit. Examples are cash and cash equivalents, short-term investments, accounts receivable, and notes receivable.

2. A common measure of the adequacy of short-term liquid assets is the **quick ratio,** which equals short-term liquid assets divided by current liabilities. A quick ratio of 1.0 is generally considered a benchmark, but industry characteristics and company trends should also be carefully examined.

3. To maintain adequate liquidity, management must (a) manage cash needs during seasonal cycles, (b) set credit policies, and (c) consider the financing of receivables.
   a. During the course of a year, most businesses experience periods of both strong and weak sales, as well as variations in cash flow. For a business to remain liquid, management must carefully plan for cash inflows, cash outflows, borrowing, and investing.
   b. Companies sell on credit to be competitive and to increase sales. However, a business must carefully review the financial backgrounds of its potential credit customers before selling to them on credit. The effect of a company's credit policies is commonly measured by the **receivable turnover** (net sales divided by average net accounts receivable) and the **average days' sales uncollected** (365 divided by the receivable turnover).
   c. Occasionally, companies cannot afford to wait until their receivables are collected. They can use the receivables to obtain cash by borrowing funds and pledging the accounts receivable as collateral. Also, a business can sell its receivables to a **factor** (e.g., a bank or finance company) through a process called **factoring.** Receivables can be factored without recourse (as with major credit cards) or with recourse. The factoring fee is much greater when receivables are factored without recourse because of the greater risk involved. When receivables are sold with recourse, the seller of the receivable has a **contingent liability** in the event of nonpayment. Finally, a business can obtain financing through the **discounting** (selling) of its notes receivable.

Objective 2: Explain *cash, cash equivalents,* and the importance of electronic funds transfer.

4. **Cash** consists of coin and currency on hand, checks and money orders from customers, and deposits in checking accounts. A company's Cash account also can include a **compensating balance,** the minimum amount a bank requires a company to keep in its bank account.

5. **Cash equivalents** consist of investments, such as certificates of deposit and U.S. Treasury notes, that have a term of less than 90 days. Cash and

cash equivalents often are combined on the balance sheet.

6. Most companies need to keep some currency and coins on hand, for cash registers and for paying expenses that are impractical to pay by check. One way to control a cash fund or cash advances is through the use of an **imprest system.** A common form of this is the petty cash fund, which is established at a fixed amount. Each payment from the fund is documented by a receipt. The petty cash fund is replenished periodically to restore it to its original amount.

7. Making payment by check reduces the need for currency and provides a permanent record of the payment itself. However, the use of checks can be partially avoided through an **electronic funds transfer (EFT).**

8. Banks provide a variety of services to their customers, as well as convenient means for conducting their banking transactions. In recent years, the use of automated teller machines (ATMs), banking by phone, and *debit cards* have become commonplace. When a purchase is made with a debit card, the purchase amount is deducted directly from the customer's bank account.

Objective 3: Account for short-term investments.

9. Companies frequently have excess cash on hand for short periods of time. To put this idle cash to good use, most companies purchase **short-term investments,** or **marketable securities.** Short-term investments are categorized as held-to-maturity securities, trading securities, or available-for-sale securities.

10. **Held-to-maturity securities** are debt securities, such as U.S. Treasury bills, that are expected to be held until the maturity date and whose cash value is not needed until then. Upon purchase of these securities, Short-Term Investments is debited and Cash credited. At year end, accrued interest is recognized with a debit to Short-Term Investments and a credit to Interest Income; the investment would be valued on the balance sheet at its amortized cost. At maturity, Cash is debited for the maturity amount, and Short-Term Investments and Interest Income are credited.

11. **Trading securities** consist of both debt and equity securities that will be held for just a short period of time. These securities are valued on the balance sheet at their fair or market value, if available. Also, dollar increases or decreases in the total trading portfolio during the period are reflected on that period's income statement.

a. Upon the purchase of trading securities, Short-Term Investments is debited and Cash is credited.

b. At year end, the cost and market (fair) value of the securities are compared, and an adjustment is made. When a decline in value has been suffered, Unrealized Loss on Investments (an income statement account) is debited and Allowance to Adjust Short-Term Investments to Market (a contra-asset account) is credited. When, on the other hand, an increase in value is experienced, Allowance to Adjust Short-Term Investments to Market is debited and Unrealized Gain on Investments is credited. In either case, the investments are reported on the balance sheet at market value.

c. When an investment is sold, Cash is debited for the proceeds, Short-Term Investments is credited for the original cost, and Realized Gain (or Realized Loss) on Investments is credited (or debited) for the difference.

12. **Available-for-sale securities** are equity and debt securities that do not qualify as either held-to-maturity or trading securities. These securities are recorded in the same way as trading securities, except that unrealized gains and losses are reported in the stockholders' equity section of the balance sheet (as Accumulated Other Comprehensive Income) rather than on the income statement.

13. Dividend and interest income for all three categories of investments is recorded in the Other Income and Expenses section of the income statement.

Objective 4: Define *accounts receivable* and apply the allowance method of accounting for uncollectible accounts, using both the percentage of net sales method and the accounts receivable aging method.

14. **Accounts receivable** are short-term liquid assets that represent payment due from credit customers. This type of credit is called **trade credit.**

15. **Installment accounts receivable** are receivables that will be collected in a series of payments; they usually are classified on the balance sheet as current assets.

16. When loans and sales are made to the company's employees, officers, or owners, they should be shown separately on the balance sheet with a title such as Receivables from Employees and Officers.

17. When a customer overpays, his or her account shows a credit balance. When a balance sheet is

prepared, Accounts Receivable should be the sum of all accounts with debit balances. The sum of all accounts with credit balances should be shown as current liabilities.

18. Regardless of how thorough and efficient its control system is, a company will always have some customers who cannot or will not pay. **Uncollectible accounts** (also called *bad debts*), the accounting term for credit accounts that are not paid, are an expense of selling on credit. The company can afford such an expense because extending credit allows it to sell more, thereby increasing company earnings.

19. Some companies recognize the loss from an uncollectible account at the time it is determined to be uncollectible. This **direct charge-off method** is used by small companies and by all companies for tax purposes, but companies that follow GAAP do not use it on their financial statements because it does not match revenues and expenses.

20. The matching rule requires that uncollectible accounts expense is recognized in the same accounting period as the corresponding sale, even if the customer defaults in a future period. Of course, at the time of a credit sale, the company does not know which customers are not going to pay. Therefore, an estimate of uncollectible accounts must be made at the end of the accounting period. Then an adjusting entry is made, debiting Uncollectible Accounts Expense and crediting Allowance for Uncollectible Accounts for the estimated amount. This method of accounting for uncollectible accounts is called the **allowance method.** Uncollectible Accounts Expense appears on the income statement and is closed out as are other expenses. **Allowance for Uncollectible Accounts** (also called *Allowance for Bad Debts*) is a contra account to Accounts Receivable, reducing Accounts Receivable to the amount estimated to be collectible.

21. The two most common methods for estimating uncollectible accounts are the percentage of net sales method and the accounts receivable aging method.

22. Under the **percentage of net sales method,** the estimated percentage for uncollectible accounts is multiplied by net sales for the period. The answer determines the amount of the adjusting entry for uncollectible accounts. Any previous balance in Allowance for Uncollectible Accounts represents estimates from previous years that have not yet been written off. Under this method, that balance has no bearing on the adjusting entry for this period.

23. Under the **accounts receivable aging method,** customers' accounts are placed in a "not yet due" category or in one of several "past due" categories (called the **aging of accounts receivable**). The amounts in each category are totaled. Each total then is multiplied by a different percentage for estimated bad debts. The sum of these answers represents estimated bad debts in ending Accounts Receivable. Again, the debit is to Uncollectible Accounts Expense, and the credit is to Allowance for Uncollectible Accounts. However, the entry is for the amount that will bring Allowance for Uncollectible Accounts to the figure arrived at in the aging calculation.

24. When it becomes clear that a specific account will not be collected, it should be written off by a debit to Allowance for Uncollectible Accounts and a credit to Accounts Receivable. The debit is not made to Uncollectible Accounts Expense. After a specific account is written off, Accounts Receivable and Allowance for Uncollectible Accounts decrease by the same amount, but the net figure for expected receivables stays the same.

25. When a customer whose account has been written off pays in part or in full, two entries must be made. First, the customer's receivable is reinstated by a debit to Accounts Receivable and a credit to Allowance for Uncollectible Accounts for the amount now thought to be collectible. Second, Cash is debited and Accounts Receivable is credited for each collection.

Objective 5: Define and describe a *promissory note,* and make calculations and journal entries involving promissory notes.

26. A **promissory note** is a written promise to pay a definite sum of money on demand or at a future date. The person who signs the note and thereby promises to pay is called the *maker* of the note. The person to whom money is owed is called the *payee.* The payee records short- or long-term **notes receivable,** and the maker records short- or long-term **notes payable.**

27. The **maturity date** and the **duration of note** must be stated on the promissory note, or it must be possible to figure them out from the information on the note.

28. To the borrower, **interest** is the cost of borrowing money. To the lender, it is the reward for lending money. Principal is the amount of money borrowed or loaned. The interest rate is the annual charge for borrowing money and is expressed as a percentage. A note can be either interest-bearing or non-interest-bearing.

29. Interest (not the interest rate) is a dollar figure, which is computed as follows:

Interest = Principal
          × Interest Rate
          × Time (length of loan)

For example, interest on $800 at 5 percent for 90 days is $10: $800 × 5/100 × 90/360. A 360-day year is used to simplify the computation. If the length of the note was expressed in months, then the third fraction would be the number of months divided by 12.

30. The **maturity value** of an interest-bearing note is the face value of the note (principal) plus interest. For a non-interest-bearing note, maturity value is equal to the face amount (which, however, includes implied interest).

31. There are four situations that result in journal entries for notes receivable: (a) receipt of a note, (b) collection on a note, (c) recording a dishonored note, and (d) recording adjusting entries.

32. When a promissory note is received—for example, in settlement of an existing account receivable—Notes Receivable is debited and Accounts Receivable is credited. Other situations could require the credit to be made to a revenue account instead.

33. When collection is made on a note, Cash is debited for the maturity value, Notes Receivable is credited for the face value, and Interest Income is credited for the difference.

34. A **dishonored note** is one that is not paid at the maturity date. The payee debits Accounts Receivable for the maturity value, and credits Notes Receivable and Interest Income.

35. End-of-period adjustments must be made for notes that apply to both the current and future periods. In this way, interest can be divided correctly among the periods.

Supplemental Objective 6: Prepare a bank reconciliation.

36. The end-of-month balance in a bank statement rarely agrees with the balance on the company's books for that date. Thus, the accountant must prepare a **bank reconciliation** to account for the difference and to locate any errors made by the bank or the company. The bank reconciliation begins with the balance per books and balance per bank figures as of the bank statement date. Each figure is adjusted by additions and deductions, resulting in two adjusted cash balance figures, which must agree. The balance per books figure is adjusted by information that the bank knew on the bank statement date but the company did not. The balance per bank figure is adjusted by information that the company knew on the bank statement date but the bank did not. For example:

a. Outstanding checks are a deduction from the balance per bank.

b. Deposits in transit are an addition to the balance per bank.

c. Service charges by the bank appear on the bank statement and are a deduction from the balance per books.

d. A customer's non-sufficient funds (NSF) check is deducted from the balance per books.

e. Interest earned on a checking account is added to the balance per books.

f. Miscellaneous charges are deducted from the balance per books. Miscellaneous credits are added to the balance per books.

g. Errors must be identified and corrected.

37. After the bank reconciliation has been prepared, adjusting entries must be made so that the accounting records reflect the new information supplied by the bank statement. Each adjustment includes either a debit or a credit to Cash.

A. (LO 3) Short-Term Investments   XX (purchase price)
           Cash   XX (amount paid)
              Purchase of U.S. Treasury bills

B. (LO 3) Short-Term Investments   XX (accrued interest)
           Interest Income   XX (accrued amount)
              Accrual of interest on U.S. Treasury bills

C. (LO 3) Cash   XX (maturity amount)
           Short-Term Investments   XX (debit balance)
           Interest Income   XX (interest this period)
              Receipt of cash at maturity of U.S. Treasury bills
              and recognition of related income

D. (LO 3) Short-Term Investments   XX (purchase price)
           Cash   XX (amount paid)
              Investment in stocks for trading

E. (LO 3) Unrealized Loss on Investments   XX (market decline)
           Allowance to Adjust Short-Term Investments to Market   XX (market decline)
              Recognition of unrealized loss on trading portfolio

F. (LO 3) Cash   XX (proceeds on sale)
           Short-Term Investments   XX (purchase price)
           Realized Gain on Investments   XX (the difference)
              Sale of stock at a gain

G. (LO 3) Allowance to Adjust Short-Term Investments to Market   XX (market increase)
           Unrealized Gain on Investments   XX (market increase)
              Recognition of unrealized gain on trading portfolio

H. (LO 4) Uncollectible Accounts Expense   XX (amount estimated)
           Allowance for Uncollectible Accounts   XX (amount estimated)
              To record the estimated uncollectible accounts
              expense for the year

I. (LO 4) Allowance for Uncollectible Accounts   XX (defaulted amount)
           Accounts Receivable   XX (defaulted amount)
              To write off receivable of specific customer as
              uncollectible

J. (LO 4) Accounts Receivable   XX (amount reinstated)
           Allowance for Uncollectible Accounts   XX (amount reinstated)
              To reinstate the portion of a specific customer's
              account now considered collectible

K. (LO 4) Cash   XX (amount received)
           Accounts Receivable   XX (amount received)
              Collection from customer in J

L. (LO 5) Notes Receivable   XX (establishing amount)

           Accounts Receivable   XX (eliminating amount)

             Received note in payment of account

M. (LO 5) Cash   XX (maturity amount)

           Notes Receivable   XX (face amount)

           Interest Income   XX (amount earned)

             Collected note

N. (LO 5) Accounts Receivable   XX (maturity amount)

           Notes Receivable   XX (face amount)

           Interest Income   XX (amount earned)

             To record dishonored note

O. (LO 5) Interest Receivable   XX (amount accrued)

           Interest Income   XX (amount earned)

             To accrue interest earned on a note receivable

P. (LO 5) Cash   XX (maturity amount)

           Notes Receivable   XX (face amount)

           Interest Receivable   XX (interest previously accrued)

           Interest Income   XX (interest this period)

             Receipt of note receivable plus interest (see O above)

Q. (SO 6) After a bank reconciliation is prepared, journal entries must be made to record the items on the bank statement that the company has not yet recorded (service charges, NSF checks, etc.). The sample entries presented in the textbook are not duplicated here, but please notice that all entries contain either a debit or a credit to Cash.

SELF-TEST

Test your knowledge of the chapter by choosing the best answer for each of the following items.

1. Because Tamara Company's sales are concentrated in the summer, management must carefully plan its borrowing needs and short-term investments. This is an example of management's responsibility to
   a. finance receivables.
   b. manage cash needs during seasonal cycles.
   c. set reasonable credit policies.
   d. finance purchases of long-term assets.

2. At year end, RJN Company has coin and currency on hand of $3,400, deposits in checking accounts of $32,000, U.S. Treasury bills due in 60 days of $58,000, and U.S. Treasury bonds due in 180 days of $88,000. On its balance sheet, cash and cash equivalents will be shown as
   a. $3,400.
   b. $35,400.
   c. $93,400.
   d. $181,400.

3. A $100,000 U.S. Treasury bill due in 180 days is purchased for $97,000. When cash in the amount of $100,000 is received, the journal entry would contain
   a. a credit to Interest Income for $3,000.
   b. a debit to Gain on Investment for $3,000.
   c. a credit to Investment Loss for $3,000.
   d. a credit to Gain on Investment for $3,000.

4. The matching rule
   a. necessitates the recording of an estimated amount for bad debts.
   b. is violated when the allowance method is employed.
   c. results in the recording of an exact amount for bad debt losses.
   d. requires that bad debt losses be recorded when an individual customer defaults.

5. Which of the following methods of recording uncollectible accounts expense would best be described as an income statement method?
   a. Accounts receivable aging method
   b. Direct charge-off method
   c. Percentage of net sales method
   d. Both **a** and **b**

6. Using the percentage of net sales method, uncollectible accounts expense for the year is estimated to be $54,000. If the balance of Allowance for Uncollectible Accounts is a $16,000 credit before adjustment, what is the balance after adjustment?
   a. $16,000
   b. $38,000
   c. $54,000
   d. $70,000

7. Using the accounts receivable aging method, estimated uncollectible accounts are $74,000. If the balance of Allowance for Uncollectible Accounts is an $18,000 credit before adjustment, what is the balance after adjustment?
   a. $18,000
   b. $56,000
   c. $74,000
   d. $92,000

8. Each of the following is a characteristic of a promissory note, with the exception of
   a. a payee who has an unconditional right to receive a definite amount on a definite date.
   b. an amount to be paid that can be determined on the date the note is signed.
   c. a due date that can be determined on the date the note is signed.
   d. a maker who agrees to pay a definite sum subject to conditions to be determined at a later date.

9. The maturity value of a $6,000, 90-day note at 10 percent is
   a. $600.
   b. $5,850.
   c. $6,600.
   d. $6,150.

10. Unrealized Loss on Investments (for trading securities) appears
    a. on the balance sheet within the stockholders' equity section.
    b. on the income statement.
    c. on the balance sheet within the liabilities section.
    d. on the balance sheet within the assets section.

TESTING YOUR KNOWLEDGE

*Matching**

Match each term with its definition by writing the appropriate letter in the blank.

_____ 1. Trade credit

_____ 2. Factoring

_____ 3. Uncollectible accounts expense

_____ 4. Allowance for uncollectible accounts

_____ 5. Installment accounts receivable

_____ 6. Promissory note

_____ 7. Maker

_____ 8. Payee

_____ 9. Maturity date

_____ 10. Maturity value

_____ 11. Interest rate

_____ 12. Interest

_____ 13. Principal

_____ 14. Contingent liability

_____ 15. Dishonored note

_____ 16. Discounting

_____ 17. Compensating balance

_____ 18. Cash equivalents

_____ 19. Cash

_____ 20. Bank reconciliation

a. Short-term investments of less than 90 days

b. Coins, currency, checks, money orders, and bank deposits

c. The charge for borrowing money, expressed as a percentage

d. A note that is not paid at the maturity date

e. A written promise to pay

f. Estimated bad debts as shown on the income statement

g. Selling or transferring accounts receivable

h. A potential obligation

i. The time when payment is due on a note

j. Allowing customers to pay for merchandise over a period of time

k. An accounting for the difference between book balance and bank balance at a particular date

l. The creditor named in a promissory note

m. Estimated bad debts as represented on the balance sheet

n. Selling a note prior to maturity

o. The charge for borrowing money, expressed in dollars

p. Receivables that will be collected in a series of payments

q. A minimum amount that a bank requires a company to keep in its account

r. The debtor named in a promissory note

s. The amount of money borrowed or loaned

t. A note's principal plus interest

Note to student: The matching quiz might be completed more efficiently by starting with the definition and searching for the corresponding term.

Short Answer

Use the lines provided to answer each item.

1. List three methods used in computing uncollectible accounts expense.

   _____

   _____

   _____

2. Explain the concept of contingent liability as it relates to discounted notes receivable.

   _____

   _____

   _____

3. Under what circumstance would there be a debit balance in Allowance for Uncollectible Accounts?

   _____

   _____

4. List the three categories of short-term investments.

   _____

   _____

   _____

5. List four examples of short-term liquid assets.

   _____

   _____

   _____

   _____

6. List three items that would be deducted from the balance per books in a bank reconciliation.

   _____

   _____

   _____

True-False

Circle T if the statement is true, F if it is false. Please provide explanations for the false answers, using the blank lines at the end of the section.

T F   1. Under the direct charge-off method, Allowance for Uncollectible Accounts does not exist.

T F   2. The percentage of net sales method violates the matching rule.

T F   3. Under the accounts receivable aging method, the balance in Allowance for Uncollectible Accounts is ignored in making the adjusting entry.

T F   4. Allowance for Uncollectible Accounts is a contra account to Accounts Receivable.

T F   5. Loans to officers of the company should not be included in Accounts Receivable on the balance sheet.

T F   6. When a customer overpays, his or her account on the company's books has a credit balance.

T F   7. Interest of 5 percent on $700 for 90 days would be computed as follows:
      $700 \times .05 \times 90$.

T F   8. *Trade credit* refers to credit sales made to customers by wholesalers or retailers.

T F   9. When a note is discounted at the bank, the maker must make good on the note if the payee defaults.

T F 10. A note dated December 14 and due February 14 has a duration of 60 days.

T F 11. The number for receivable turnover is built into the average days' sales uncollected calculation.

T F 12. Under the allowance method, the entry to write off a specific account as uncollectible decreases total assets.

T F   **13.** The maturity value of an interest-bearing note equals principal plus interest.

T F   **14.** Under the allowance method, a specific account is written off with a debit to Uncollectible Accounts Expense and a credit to Accounts Receivable.

T F   **15.** When a note is dishonored, the payee nevertheless should record interest earned.

T F   **16.** Uncollectible accounts are an expense of selling on credit.

T F   **17.** Accounts receivable are an example of a cash equivalent.

T F   **18.** The use of a major credit card (e.g., MasterCard) is an example of factoring with recourse.

T F   **19.** The quick ratio equals current assets divided by current liabilities.

T F   **20.** A check that is outstanding for two consecutive months should be included in both months' bank reconciliations.

T F   **21.** A credit memorandum on a bank statement indicates an addition to the bank balance.

T F   **22.** After a bank reconciliation has been completed, the company must make journal entries to adjust for all outstanding checks.

T F   **23.** A bank reconciliation for the month of September should begin with the balance per books and the balance per bank on September 1.

T F   **24.** *Imprest system* refers to the mechanics of a petty cash fund.

T F   **25.** Held-to-maturity securities consist of debt securities, but not equity securities.

T F   **26.** Trading securities appear on the balance sheet at original cost.

Circle the letter of the best answer.

1. A company's bank statement erroneously shows a $1,000 deposit as $100, and the bank is notified. The $900 error appears on the bank reconciliation as a(n)
   a. addition to the balance per bank.
   b. deduction from the balance per bank.
   c. addition to the balance per books.
   d. deduction from the balance per books.

2. Which of the following does *not* equal the others?
   a. $600 for 60 days at 6 percent
   b. $1,200 for 120 days at 3 percent
   c. $300 for 120 days at 6 percent
   d. $600 for 30 days at 12 percent

3. A company estimates at the balance sheet date that $1,500 of net sales for the year will not be collected. A debit balance of $600 exists in Allowance for Uncollectible Accounts. Under the percentage of net sales method, Uncollectible Accounts Expense and Allowance for Uncollectible Accounts would be debited and credited for
   a. $600.
   b. $1,100.
   c. $1,500.
   d. $2,100.

4. A contingent liability exists when
   a. a note is discounted.
   b. a note is dishonored.
   c. interest accrues on a note.
   d. a note reaches maturity.

5. Based on the accounts receivable aging method, a company estimates that $850 of end-of-period accounts receivable will not be collected. A credit balance of $300 exists in Allowance for Uncollectible Accounts. Uncollectible Accounts Expense should be recorded for
   a. $300.
   b. $550.
   c. $850.
   d. $1,150.

6. Under the accounts receivable aging method, a specific customer's account is written off by debiting
   a. Uncollectible Accounts Expense and crediting Allowance for Uncollectible Accounts.
   b. Accounts Receivable and crediting Allowance for Uncollectible Accounts.
   c. Allowance for Uncollectible Accounts and crediting Accounts Receivable.
   d. Uncollectible Accounts Expense and crediting Accounts Receivable.

7. Which of the following *cannot* be determined from the information on a note?
   a. Discount rate
   b. Interest rate
   c. Interest
   d. Maturity date

8. Which method for handling bad debts often violates the matching rule?
   a. Percentage of net sales method
   b. Direct charge-off method
   c. Accounts receivable aging method
   d. Both a and c

9. Which of the following is *not* considered a short-term liquid asset?
   a. Notes receivable
   b. Short-term investments
   c. Inventory
   d. Cash

10. After the bank reconciliation has been completed, a company must make journal entries to adjust for all of the following *except*
    a. bank service charges.
    b. deposits in transit.
    c. a note collected by the bank.
    d. interest earned.

11. Interest earned on a checking account should be included on a bank reconciliation as a(n)
    a. addition to the balance per bank.
    b. deduction from the balance per bank.
    c. addition to the balance per books.
    d. deduction from the balance per books.

APPLYING YOUR KNOWLEDGE

Exercises

1. For the following set of facts, make the necessary entries for Green's Department Store in the journal provided on the next page.

Dec. 31 Interest of $75 has accrued on notes receivable.

31 Net sales for the year were $600,000. It is estimated that 4 percent will not be collected. Make the entry for uncollectible accounts.

Jan. 3 Anna Kohn purchased $10,000 worth of goods on credit in November. She now issues Green's her $10,000, 30-day, 6 percent note, thus extending her credit period.

8 Tom O'Brien goes bankrupt and notifies Green's that he cannot pay for the $1,000 worth of goods he had purchased last year on account.

25 Tom O'Brien notifies Green's that he will be able to pay $600 of the $1,000 that he owes.

28 A check for $200 is received from Tom O'Brien.

2. Calculate interest on the following amounts:

   a. $7,200 at 4% for 20 days = _____

   b. $52,000 at 7% for 3 months = _____

   c. $4,317 at 6% for 60 days = _____

   d. $18,000 at 8% for 1 day = _____

3. On November 17, 20x1, Ameci Corporation purchased 2,000 shares of Simpson Corporation stock for $30 per share. The purchase was made for trading purposes. At December 31, 20x1, the stock had a market value of $28 per share. On January 12, 20x2, Ameci sold all 2,000 shares for $66,000. In the journal provided below, prepare the entries for November 17, December 31, and January 12.

General Journal				
Date		**Description**	**Debit**	**Credit**

General Journal				
Date		Description	Debit	Credit

4. The facts that follow are needed to prepare a bank reconciliation for the Nelson Company as of March 32, 20xx. For each, write the correct letter (a, b, c, or d) indicate where it should appear.

a = Addition to the balance per bank

b = Deduction from the balance per bank

c = Addition to the balance per books

d = Deduction from the balance per books

_____ 1. The service charge by the bank was $8.

_____ 2. A $1,700 note receivable was collected for the company by the bank. No collection fee was charged.

_____ 3. There were two outstanding checks, totaling, $3,200.

_____ 4. A $355 NSF check drawn by a customer was deducted from the company's bank account and returned to the company.

_____ 5. A deposit of $725 was made after banking hours on March 31.

_____ 6. Check no. 185 was drawn for $342 but was recorded erroneously in the company's books as $324.

Crossword Puzzle
for Chapters 6 and 7

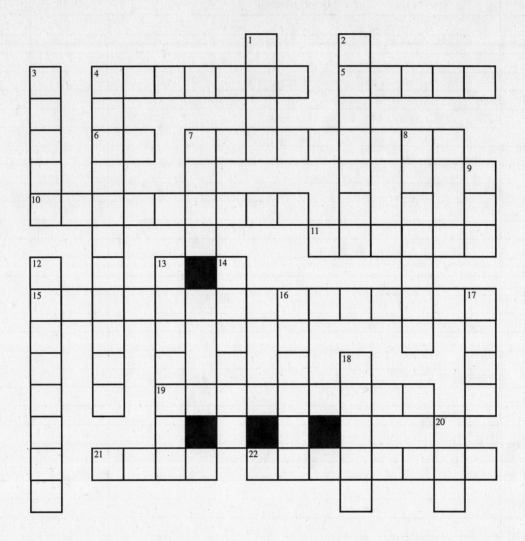

ACROSS

4. Banking statement item
5. Purchase _____
6. Bank fee (abbr.)
7. Conspiracy for fraudulent purposes
10. Cost of _____ (2 words)
11. Receiving _____
15. System of regulatory procedures (2 words)
19. Temporary, as investments (hyphenated)
21. Written promise to pay
22. Uncollectible accounts (2 words)

DOWN

1. Invoice
2. Available-_____ securities (2 words hyphenated)
3. Method to account for 22-Across
4. Method of selling notes receivable
7. _____ flow management
8. The "OB" of FOB (2 words)
9. Electronic funds transfer, for short
12. Default upon
13. Deposits in _____
14. Buyer of accounts receivable
16. Account such as Allowance of Uncollectible Accounts
17. Unrealized _____ on Investments
18. Engages in interest-earning activities
20. Banking convenience, for short

CHAPTER 8   INVENTORIES

REVIEWING THE CHAPTER

Objective 1: Identify and explain the management issues associated with accounting for inventories.

1. The **merchandise inventory** of a merchandising business consists of all goods owned and held for sale in the regular course of business. The inventory of a manufacturer, on the other hand, consists of raw materials, work in process, and finished goods. Inventory appears in the current asset section of the balance sheet.

2. To measure income properly and observe the matching rule, the following two questions must be answered for each nonfinancial asset:
   a. How much of the asset has been used up (expired) during the current period and should be transferred to expense?
   b. How much of the asset is unused (unexpired) and should remain on the balance sheet as an asset?

3. It is important for a merchandiser to maintain a sufficient level of inventory to satisfy customer demand. However, the higher the level maintained, the more costly it is for the business. Management can evaluate the level of inventory by calculating and analyzing the inventory turnover and average days' inventory on hand.
   a. **Inventory turnover** indicates the number of times a company's average inventory is sold during the period. It equals cost of goods sold divided by average inventory.
   b. **Average days' inventory on hand** indicates the average number of days required to sell the average inventory. It equals 365 divided by the inventory turnover.

4. Many companies, in an attempt to reduce their inventory, are changing to a **just-in-time operating environment.** They work closely with suppliers to coordinate and schedule shipments so that the goods arrive just in time to be used or sold.

Objective 2: Define *inventory cost* and relate it to goods flow and cost flow.

5. **Inventory cost** is the purchase price of the inventory less purchase discounts, plus freight or transportation in, including insurance in transit, and applicable taxes and tariffs.

6. Goods in transit should be included in inventory only if the company has title to the goods. When goods are sent FOB shipping point, title passes to the buyer when the goods reach the common carrier. When goods are sent FOB destination, title passes when the goods reach the buyer. Goods that have been sold but are still on hand should not be included in the seller's inventory count.

7. When goods are held on **consignment,** the consignee (who earns a commission on making the sale) has possession of the goods, but the consignor retains title and, thus, includes the goods on its balance sheet.

8. When identical items of merchandise are purchased at different prices during the year, it is usually impractical to monitor the actual **goods flow**

and record the corresponding costs. Instead, the accountant makes an assumption of the **cost flow** and uses one of the following methods: (a) specific identification, (b) average-cost, (c) first-in, first-out (FIFO), or (d) last-in, first-out (LIFO). Ending inventory is computed by (a) counting the items on hand, (b) finding the cost of each item, and (c) multiplying the unit cost by the quantity to determine the total cost.

Objective 3a: Calculate the pricing of inventory, using the cost basis under the periodic inventory system, according to the specific identification method.

9. Under the **specific identification method,** the units of ending inventory can be identified as having come from specific purchases. The flow of costs reflects the actual flow of goods in this case. However, the specific identification method is not practical in most cases.

Objective 3b: Calculate the pricing of inventory, using the cost basis under the periodic inventory system, according to the average-cost method.

10. Under the **average-cost method,** the average cost per unit is figured for the goods available for sale during the period. That is, the cost of goods available for sale is divided by the units available for sale. Then, the average cost per unit is multiplied by the number of units in ending inventory to get the cost of ending inventory.

Objective 3c: Calculate the pricing of inventory, using the cost basis under the periodic inventory system, according to the first-in, first-out (FIFO) method.

11. Under the **first-in, first-out (FIFO) method,** the cost of the first items purchased is assigned to the first items sold. Therefore, ending inventory cost is determined from the prices of the most recent purchases. During periods of rising prices, FIFO yields the highest income before income taxes of the four methods.

Objective 3d: Calculate the pricing of inventory, using the cost basis under the periodic inventory system, according to the last-in, first-out (LIFO) method.

12. Under the **last-in, first-out (LIFO) method,** the cost of last items purchased are assigned to the first items sold. Therefore, the ending inventory cost is determined from the prices of the earliest

purchases. During periods of rising prices, LIFO yields the lowest income before income taxes of the four methods. However, it best matches current merchandise costs with current sales prices.

Objective 4: Apply the perpetual inventory system to the pricing of inventories at cost.

13. When the periodic inventory system is used, a physical inventory is taken at the end of the period, and the cost of goods sold is calculated by subtracting ending inventory from the cost of goods available for sale.

14. The perpetual inventory system is used by companies that want more control over their inventories. A continuous record is kept of the balance of each inventory item. As goods are sold, costs are transferred from the Inventory account to Cost of Goods Sold.

15. The perpetual inventory system lends itself to specific identification, average-cost, FIFO, and LIFO calculations. Under specific identification and FIFO, figures for inventory and cost of goods sold should match those under the periodic inventory system. The perpetual LIFO method, though time-consuming to apply manually, is facilitated by the use of computers.

Objective 5: State the effects of inventory methods and misstatements of inventory on income determination, income taxes, and cash flows.

16. During periods of rising prices, FIFO produces a higher net income than LIFO. During periods of falling prices, the reverse is true. The average-cost method produces income before income taxes figures that are somewhere between those of FIFO and LIFO. Because the specific identification method depends on the particular items sold, no generalization can be made about the effect of changing prices. Even though LIFO best follows the matching rule, FIFO provides a more up-to-date ending inventory figure for balance sheet purposes.

17. There are several rules for the valuation of inventory for federal income tax purposes. For example, even though a business has a wide choice of methods, once a method has been chosen, it must be applied consistently. In addition, several regulations apply to LIFO, such as the requirement that LIFO also be used for the accounting records when it is being used for tax purposes.

18. A **LIFO liquidation** occurs when sales have reduced inventories below the levels established in earlier years. When prices have been rising steadily, a LIFO liquidation produces unusually high profits.

19. Beginning inventory plus purchases equals the cost of goods available for sale. The cost of goods sold is determined indirectly by deducting ending inventory from the cost of goods available for sale.

20. Because the cost of ending inventory is needed to compute the cost of goods sold, it affects income before income taxes dollar for dollar. It is important to match the cost of goods sold with sales so that income before income taxes is reasonably accurate.

21. This year's ending inventory automatically becomes next year's beginning inventory. Because beginning inventory also affects income before income taxes dollar for dollar, an error in this year's ending inventory results in misstated income before income taxes for both this year and next year.
    a. When ending inventory is understated, income before income taxes for the period is understated.
    b. When ending inventory is overstated, income before income taxes for the period is overstated.
    c. When beginning inventory is understated, income before income taxes for the period is overstated.
    d. When beginning inventory is overstated, income before income taxes for the period is understated.

22. A company's choice of inventory method will affect not only its profitability, but also its liquidity and cash flows. The use of LIFO, for example, will usually produce a lower income before income taxes than will FIFO. However, the reduced tax liability under LIFO will have a positive effect on cash flow. Liquidity-related measures such as the current ratio, inventory turnover, and average days' inventory on hand will be affected by the inventory method chosen.

Objective 6: Apply the lower-of-cost-or-market (LCM) rule to inventory valuation.

23. The **market** value of inventory (current replacement cost) can fall below its cost as a result of physical deterioration, obsolescence, or decline in price level. Accordingly, it should be valued based on the **lower of cost or market (LCM) rule.** The two basic methods of valuing inventory at the lower of cost or market are the **item-by-item method** and the **major category method.** Both methods are acceptable by GAAP and for federal income tax purposes.

Supplemental Objective 7a: Estimate the cost of ending inventory using the retail inventory method.

24. The **retail method** of inventory estimation can be used when the difference between the cost and sale prices of goods is a constant percentage over a period of time. It can be used whether or not the business makes a physical count of goods. To apply the retail method, goods available for sale are figured both at cost and at retail. Next, a cost-to-retail ratio is computed. Sales for the period then are subtracted from goods available for sale at retail, to produce ending inventory at retail. Finally, ending inventory at retail is multiplied by the cost-to-retail ratio to produce an estimate of ending inventory at cost.

Supplemental Objective 7b: Estimate the cost of ending inventory using the gross profit method.

24. The **gross profit method** of inventory estimation assumes that the gross margin for a business remains relatively stable from year to year. This method is used when inventory records are lost or destroyed, and when records of beginning inventory and purchases are not kept at retail. To apply the gross profit method, the cost of goods available for sale is determined by adding purchases to beginning inventory. Then, the cost of goods sold is estimated as follows:

Sales × (1 – Gross Margin %)

Finally, the estimated cost of goods sold is subtracted from the cost of goods available for sale to arrive at the estimated ending inventory.

SELF-TEST

Test your knowledge of the chapter by choosing the best answer for each of the following items.

1. An overstatement of ending inventory in one period results in
   a. an overstatement of the ending inventory of the next period.
   b. an understatement of income before income taxes of the next period.
   c. an overstatement of income before income taxes of the next period.
   d. no effect on income before income taxes of the next period.

2. Which of the following costs would *not* be included in the cost of inventory?
   a. Goods held on consignment
   b. Purchased goods in transit, FOB shipping point
   c. Freight In
   d. Invoice price

3. Sept. 1 Inventory 10 @ $4.00
   8 Purchased 40 @ $4.40
   17 Purchased 20 @ $4.20
   25 Purchased 30 @ $4.80 Sold 70

   Using this information, cost of goods sold under the average-cost method is
   a. $133.20.
   b. $444.00.
   c. $310.80.
   d. $304.50.

4. Assuming the same facts as in **3,** cost of goods sold under the first-in, first-out (FIFO) method is
   a. $144.00.
   b. $300.00.
   c. $388.50.
   d. $444.00.

5. Assuming the same facts as in **3,** ending inventory under the last-in, first-out (LIFO) method is
   a. $316.
   b. $444.
   c. $300.
   d. $128.

6. Inventory turnover equals average inventory divided into
   a. number of days in a year.
   b. cost of goods available for sale.
   c. number of months in a year.
   d. cost of goods sold.

7. In a period of rising prices, which of the following inventory methods generally results in the lowest income before income taxes figure?
   a. Average-cost method
   b. FIFO method
   c. LIFO method
   d. Cannot tell without more information

8. When applying the lower-of-cost-or-market rule to inventory, *market* generally means
   a. original cost, less physical deterioration.
   b. resale value.
   c. original cost.
   d. replacement cost.

9. Which of the following companies would be most likely to use the retail inventory method?
   a. A farm supply company
   b. A TV repair company
   c. A dealer in heavy machinery
   d. A men's clothing shop

10. A retail company has goods available for sale of $1,000,000 at retail and $600,000 at cost and ending inventory of $100,000 at retail. What is the estimated cost of goods sold?
    a. $60,000
    b. $100,000
    c. $900,000
    d. $540,000

TESTING YOUR KNOWLEDGE

Matching*

Match each term with its definition by writing the appropriate letter in the blank.

_____ 1. LIFO liquidation

_____ 2. Merchandise inventory

_____ 3. Specific identification method

_____ 4. FIFO method

_____ 5. LIFO method

_____ 6. Average-cost method

_____ 7. Lower of cost or market

_____ 8. Retail method

_____ 9. Gross profit method

_____ 10. Periodic inventory system

_____ 11. Perpetual inventory system

_____ 12. Market

_____ 13. Consignment

a. The inventory method that utilizes an average-cost-per-unit figure

b. The current replacement cost of inventory

c. The inventory estimation method used when inventory is lost or destroyed

d. The inventory method in which the assumed flow of costs matches the actual flow of goods

e. The inventory system that maintains continuous records

f. The rule that governs how inventory should be valued on the financial statements

g. The inventory method that yields the highest ending inventory during periods of rising prices

h. Goods held for sale in the regular course of business

i. The inventory estimation method that uses a cost-to-retail ratio

j. The inventory method that best follows the matching principle

k. An arrangement whereby one company sells goods for another company, for a commission

l. The inventory system that does not maintain continuous records

m. An occurrence that produces unusually high profits under steadily rising prices

---

Note to student: The matching quiz might be completed more efficiently by starting with the definition and searching for the corresponding term.

Short Answer

Use the lines provided to answer each item.

1. List the four basic cost-flow assumptions used to determine the cost of merchandise inventory.

_____

_____

_____

_____

2. List the two basic methods of valuing inventory at the lower of cost or market.

_____

_____

3. List two methods of estimating ending inventory.

_____

_____

4. Briefly distinguish between the periodic and perpetual inventory systems in terms of recordkeeping and inventory taking.

_____

_____

_____

_____

_____

True-False

Circle T if the statement is true, F if it is false. Please provide explanations for the false answers, using the blank lines at the end of the section.

T F 1. The figure for inventory turnover is needed to calculate average days' inventory on hand.

T F 2. When beginning inventory is understated, the cost of goods sold for the period also is understated.

T F 3. When ending inventory is overstated, income before income taxes for the period also is overstated.

T F 4. An error in 20x1's ending inventory will cause income before income taxes to be misstated in both 20x1 and 20x2.

T F 5. Goods in transit belong in the buyer's ending inventory only if the buyer has paid for them.

T F 6. If prices were never to change, all four methods of inventory valuation would result in identical income before income taxes figures.

T F 7. Under FIFO, goods are sold in exactly the same order as they are purchased.

T F 8. Of the four inventory methods, LIFO results in the lowest income during periods of falling prices.

T F 9. Under the retail method, each item sold must be recorded at both cost and retail.

T F 10. Under the gross profit method, the cost of goods sold is estimated by multiplying the gross profit percentage by sales.

T F 11. Under rising prices, the average-cost method results in a lower income before income taxes than LIFO does.

T F 12. If FIFO is being used for tax purposes, it must be used for reporting purposes as well.

T F 13. When goods are held on consignment, the consignee has both possession and title until the goods are sold.

T F 14. The inventory method that produces the highest profitability won't necessarily generate the highest cash flow.

_____

_____

_____

_____

_____

_____

_____

_____

_____

_____

_____

_____

_____

_____

_____

_____

_____

_____

_____

_____

_____

_____

_____

_____

_____

_____

_____

_____

_____

_____

_____

_____

Multiple Choice

Circle the letter of the best answer.

1. Which of the following is least likely to be included in the cost of inventory?
   a. Freight in
   b. Cost to store goods
   c. Purchase cost of goods
   d. Excise tax on goods purchased

2. Under rising prices, which of the following inventory methods probably results in the highest income before income taxes?
   a. FIFO
   b. LIFO
   c. Specific identification
   d. Average-cost

3. Forgetting to include in inventory an item of merchandise in a warehouse results in
   a. overstated income before income taxes.
   b. overstated total assets.
   c. understated stockholders' equity.
   d. understated cost of goods sold.

4. Which inventory method is best suited for low-volume, high-priced goods?
   a. FIFO
   b. LIFO
   c. Specific identification
   d. Average-cost

5. Which of the following is *not* used or computed in applying the retail inventory method?
   a. Ending inventory at retail
   b. Freight at retail
   c. Beginning inventory at cost
   d. Sales during the period

6. The cost of inventory becomes an expense in the period in which the
   a. inventory is sold.
   b. merchandiser obtains title to the inventory.
   c. merchandiser pays for the inventory.
   d. merchandiser is paid for inventory that it has sold.

7. Goods in transit should be included in the inventory of
   a. neither the buyer nor the seller.
   b. the buyer when the goods have been shipped FOB destination.
   c. the seller when the goods have been shipped FOB shipping point.
   d. the company that has title to the goods.

8. Insurance companies often verify the extent of inventory lost or destroyed by applying the
   a. specific identification method.
   b. retail method.
   c. item-by-item method.
   d. gross profit method.

Exercises

1. Chang Company had a beginning inventory of 100 units at $20. The firm made successive purchases as follows:

Feb. 20 Purchased 200 units at $22
May   8   Purchased 150 units at $20
Oct. 17 Purchased 250 units at $24

Calculate the cost that would be assigned to the ending inventory of 310 units and the cost of goods sold under the following methods (assume a periodic inventory system):

		Cost of Ending Inventory	Cost of Goods Sold
a.	LIFO	$ _____	$ _____
b.	FIFO	$ _____	$ _____
c.	Average-cost	$ _____	$ _____

2. The records of Arbo Company show the following data for the month of May:

Sales	$156,000
Beginning inventory, at cost	70,000
Beginning inventory, at retail	125,000
Net purchases, at cost	48,000
Net purchases, at retail	75,000
Freight in	2,000

Compute the estimated cost of ending inventory using the retail inventory method.

3. At the beginning of the accounting period, the cost of merchandise inventory was $150,000. Net sales during the period were $300,000; net purchases totaled $120,000; and the historical gross margin has been 20 percent. Compute the estimated cost of ending inventory using the gross profit method.

4. Wilds Enterprises uses the perpetual LIFO method for valuing its inventory. On May 1, its inventory consisted of 100 units that cost $10 each. Successive purchases and sales for May were as follows:

May 4   Purchased 60 units at $12 each
     8   Sold 50 units
     17 Purchased 70 units at $11 each
     25 Sold 100 units

In the space provided, calculate ending inventory and cost of goods sold.

CHAPTER 9 CURRENT LIABILITIES AND THE TIME VALUE OF MONEY

REVIEWING THE CHAPTER

Objective 1: Identify the management issues related to recognition, valuation, classification, and disclosure of current liabilities.

1. **Liabilities** are one of the three major parts of the balance sheet. They are present obligations for either the future payment of assets or the future performance of services. The primary reason for incurring current liabilities is to meet needs for cash during the operating cycle. Management must carefully manage the cash flows related to current liabilities; the appropriate level of liabilities is critical to business success.

2. Two common measures of the length of time creditors allow for payment are the payables turnover and the average days' payable. **Payables turnover** (measured in "times") shows the relative size of a company's accounts payable, and is calculated as follows:

$$\frac{\text{Cost of Goods Sold} \pm \text{Change in Merchandise Inventory}}{\text{Average Accounts Payable}}$$

Average days' payable, on the other hand, shows the average length of time a company takes to pay its accounts payable. It is computed as follows:

$$\frac{365 \text{ days}}{\text{Payables Turnover}}$$

3. A liability generally should be recorded when an obligation arises, but it is also necessary to make end-of-period adjustments for accrued and estimated liabilities. On the other hand, contracts representing future obligations are not recorded as liabilities until they become current obligations.

4. Liabilities are valued at the actual or estimated amount due, or at the fair market value of goods or services that must be delivered.

5. **Current liabilities** are present obligations that are expected to be satisfied within one year or the normal operating cycle, whichever is longer. Payment is expected to be out of current assets or by taking on another current liability. **Long-term liabilities** are obligations that are not expected to be satisfied in the current period.

6. Supplemental disclosure of liabilities may be required in the notes to the financial statements. An explanation of special credit arrangements, for example, can be very helpful to the financial statement user.

Objective 2: Identify, compute, and record definitely determinable and estimated current liabilities.

7. Current liabilities consist of definitely determinable liabilities and estimated liabilities.

8. **Definitely determinable liabilities** are obligations that can be measured exactly. They include accounts payable, short-term notes payable, dividends payable, sales and excise taxes payable, current portions of long-term debt, accrued liabilities, payroll liabilities, and unearned or deferred revenues.

a. Accounts payable, sometimes called trade accounts payable, are current obligations due to suppliers of goods and services.

b. Companies often obtain a **line of credit** from a bank in order to finance operations. In addition, a company may borrow short-term funds by issuing **commercial paper** (unsecured loans sold to the public).

c. Short-term notes payable are current obligations evidenced by promissory notes. Interest may be either stated separately or included in the face amount. In the latter case, the actual amount borrowed is less than the face amount.

d. Accrued liabilities are actual or estimated liabilities that exist at the balance sheet date but are unrecorded. An end-of-period adjustment is needed to record both the expenses and the accrued liabilities.

e. Dividends payable is an obligation to distribute the earnings of a corporation to its stockholders. It arises only when the board of directors declares a dividend.

f. Most states and many cities levy a sales tax on retail transactions. The federal government also charges an excise tax on some products. The merchant must collect the taxes at the time of the sale and would record both the receipt of cash and the proper tax liabilities.

g. If a portion of long-term debt is due within the next year and is to be paid from current assets, then this amount should be classified as a current liability; the remaining debt should be classified as a long-term liability.

h. Payroll liabilities consist of the employee-related obligations incurred by a business. Not only is the business responsible for paying **wages,** paid at an hourly rate, and **salaries,** paid at a monthly or yearly rate, earned by its employees, it is obligated for such items as social security taxes, Medicare, and unemployment taxes. It is also liable for amounts withheld from its employees' gross earnings that must be remitted to government and other agencies.

i. The three general types of liabilities associated with payroll accounting are (a) liabilities for employee compensation, (b) liabilities for employee payroll withholdings, and (c) liabilities for employer payroll taxes. An employee is under the direct supervision and control of the company. An independent contractor (such as a lawyer or a CPA) is not and, therefore, is not accounted for under the payroll system.

j. **Unearned revenues** represent obligations to deliver goods or services in return for advance payment. When delivery takes place, Unearned Revenue is debited and a revenue account is credited.

9. **Estimated liabilities** are definite obligations. However, the amount of the obligation must be estimated at the balance sheet date because the exact figure will not be known until a future date. Examples of estimated liabilities are income taxes, property taxes, product warranties, and vacation pay.

   a. A corporation's income tax depends on its net income, a figure that often is not determined until well after the balance sheet date.

   b. Property taxes are taxes levied on real and personal property. Very often a company's accounting period ends before property taxes have been assessed. Therefore, the company must make an estimate. The debit is to Property Tax Expense, and the credit is to Estimated Property Tax Payable.

   c. When a company sells its products, many of the warranties will still be in effect during subsequent accounting periods. However, the warranty expense and liability must be recorded in the period of the sale no matter when the company makes good on the warranty. Therefore, at the end of each accounting period, the company should make an estimate of future warranty expense that will apply to the present period's sales.

   d. In most companies, employees earn vacation pay for working a certain length of time. Therefore, the company must estimate the vacation pay that applies to each payroll period. The debit is to Vacation Pay Expense, and the credit is to Estimated Liability for Vacation Pay. The liability decreases (is debited) when an employee receives vacation pay.

Objective 3: Define *contingent liability*.

10. A **contingent liability** is a potential liability that may or may not become an actual liability. The uncertainty about its outcome is settled when a future event does or does not occur. Two conditions must be met when a contingency is entered in the accounting records. The liability must be probable and it must be reasonably estimated. Contingent liabilities arise from things like pending lawsuits, tax disputes, and failure to follow government regulations. A contingent liability should be accrued

when its realization is probable and the amount of the loss can be reasonably estimated.

Objective 4: Define *interest* and distinguish between simple and compound interest.

11. The timing of the receipt and payment of cash (measured in interest) should be a consideration in making business decisions. **Interest** is the cost of using money for a specific period of time; it may be calculated on a simple or compound basis.

    a. When **simple interest** is computed for one or more periods, the amount on which interest is computed does not increase each period (that is, interest is not computed on principal plus accrued interest).

    b. However, when **compound interest** is computed for two or more periods, the amount on which interest is computed *does* increase each period (that is, interest is computed on principal plus accrued interest).

Objective 5: Use compound interest tables to compute the future value of a single invested sum at compound interest and of an ordinary annuity.

12. **Future value** is the amount an investment will be worth at a future date if invested at compound interest.

    a. Future value may be computed on a single sum invested at compound interest. Table 1 in your text facilitates this computation.

    b. Future value may also be computed on an **ordinary annuity** (i.e., a series of equal payments made at the end of equal intervals of time) at compound interest. Table 2 in your text facilitates this computation.

Objective 6: Use compound interest tables to compute the present value of a single sum due in the future and of an ordinary annuity.

13. **Present value** is the amount that must be invested now at a given rate of interest to produce a given future value or values.

    a. Present value may be computed on a single sum due in the future. Table 3 in your text facilitates this computation.

    b. Present value may also be computed on an ordinary annuity. Table 4 in your text facilitates this computation.

14. All four tables facilitate both annual compounding and compounding for less than a year. For example, when computing 12 percent annual interest that is compounded quarterly, one would refer to the 3 percent column for four periods per year.

Objective 7: Apply the concept of present value to simple accounting situations.

15. Present value may be used in accounting to (a) impute interest on non-interest-bearing notes, (b) determine the value of an asset (or business) being considered for purchase, (c) calculate deferred payments for the purchase of an asset, (d) account for the investment of idle cash, (e) accumulate funds needed to pay off a loan, and (f) determine numerous other accounting quantities, such as the value of a bond, pension and lease obligations, and depreciation.

Summary of Journal Entries Introduced in Chapter 9

Interest Stated Separately

A. (LO 2) Cash   XX (amount received)
      Notes Payable   XX (face amount)
         Issued promissory note with interest
         stated separately

B. (LO 2) Notes Payable   XX (face amount)
      Interest Expense   XX (amount incurred)
         Cash   XX (maturity amount)
         Payment of note with interest
         stated separately

C. (LO 2) Interest Expense   XX (amount accrued)
      Interest Payable   XX (amount accrued)
         To record interest expense on note
         with interest stated separately

Interest in Face Amount

D. (LO 2) Cash   XX (face amount minus interest)
      Discount on Notes Payable   XX (interest in face amount)
         Notes Payable   XX (face amount)
         Issued promissory note with interest
         included in face amount

E. (LO 2) Notes Payable   XX (face amount)
         Cash   XX (face amount)
         Payment of note with interest included
         in face amount (see also F below)

F. (LO 2) Interest Expense   XX (amount accrued)
      Discount on Notes Payable   XX (amount accrued)
         To record interest expense on note
         with interest included in face amount

G. (LO 2) Cash   XX (amount collected)
      Sales   XX (price charged)
      Sales Tax Payable   XX (amount to remit)
      Excise Tax Payable   XX (amount to remit)
         Sale of merchandise and collection
         of sales and excise taxes

H.	(LO 2)	Wages Expense	XX	(gross amount)
		Employees' Federal Income Taxes Payable	XX	(amount withheld)
		Employees' State Income Taxes Payable	XX	(amount withheld)
		Social Security Tax Payable	XX	(employees' share)
		Medicare Tax Payable	XX	(employees' share)
		Medical Insurance Payable	XX	(employees' share)
		Pension Contributions Payable	XX	(employees' share)
		Wages Payable	XX	(take-home pay)
		To record payroll		
I.	(LO 2)	Payroll Taxes and Benefits Expense	XX	(total employer payroll taxes)
		Social Security Tax Payable	XX	(employer's share)
		Medicare Tax Payable	XX	(employer's share)
		Medical Insurance Payable	XX	(employer's share)
		Pension Contributions Payable	XX	(employer's share)
		Federal Unemployment Tax Payable	XX	(amount incurred)
		State Unemployment Tax Payable	XX	(amount incurred)
		To record payroll taxes and other costs		
J.	(LO 2)	Cash	XX	(amount prepaid)
		Unearned Subscriptions	XX	(amount to earn)
		Receipt of annual subscriptions in advance		
K.	(LO 2)	Unearned Subscriptions	XX	(amount earned)
		Subscription Revenues	XX	(amount earned)
		Delivery of monthly magazine issues		
L.	(LO 2)	Income Taxes Expense	XX	(amount estimated)
		Estimated Income Taxes Payable	XX	(amount estimated)
		To record estimated federal income taxes		
M.	(LO 2)	Property Tax Expense	XX	(amount estimated)
		Estimated Property Tax Payable	XX	(amount estimated)
		To record estimated property tax expense		
N.	(LO 2)	Estimated Property Tax Payable	XX	(amount incurred)
		Prepaid Property Tax	XX	(amount to be incurred)
		Cash	XX	(amount paid)
		Payment of property tax		
O.	(LO 2)	Product Warranty Expense	XX	(estimated amount)
		Estimated Product Warranty Liability	XX	(estimated amount)
		To record estimated product warranty expense		
P.	(LO 2)	Cash	XX	(fee charged)
		Estimated Product Warranty Liability	XX	(cost of part)
		Service Revenue	XX	(fee charged)
		Merchandise Inventory	XX	(cost of part)
		Replacement of part under warranty		

Q.   (LO 2)   Vacation Pay Expense   XX (amount incurred)
                  Estimated Liability for Vacation Pay   XX (amount owed or accrued)
                     Estimated vacation pay expense

R.   (LO 2)   Estimated Liability for Vacation Pay   XX (amount taken)
                  Cash (or Wages Payable)   XX (amount paid or payable)
                     Wages of employees on vacation

S.   (LO 7)   Purchases   XX (present value of note)
                  Discount on Notes Payable   XX (imputed interest)
                     Notes Payable   XX (face amount)
                        Purchase of merchandise, non-
                        interest-bearing note issued

T.   (LO 7)   Interest Expense   XX (amount accrued)
                  Discount on Notes Payable   XX (amount accrued)
                     Interest expense for period
                     (see S above)

U.   (LO 7)   Interest Expense   XX (interest for period)
              Notes Payable   XX (face amount)
                  Discount on Notes Payable   XX (interest for period)
                  Cash   XX (face amount)
                     Payment of note (see S above)

V.   (LO 7)   Notes Receivable   XX (face amount)
                  Discount on Notes Receivable   XX (imputed interest)
                  Sales   XX (present value of note)
                     Sale of merchandise, non-interest-
                     bearing note received

W.   (LO 7)   Discount on Notes Receivable   XX (amount accrued)
                  Interest Income   XX (amount accrued)
                     Interest income for period
                     (see V above)

X.   (LO 7)   Discount on Notes Receivable   XX (interest for period)
              Cash   XX (face amount)
                  Interest Income   XX (interest for period)
                  Notes Receivable   XX (face amount)
                     Receipt of note (see V above)

Y.   (LO 7)   Tractor   XX (present value of payment)
                  Accounts Payable   XX (present value of payment)
                     Purchase of tractor, payment deferred

Z.   (LO 7)   Accounts Payable   XX (present value of payment)
              Interest Expense   XX (imputed amount)
                  Cash   XX (amount paid)
                     Payment on account including
                     imputed interest expense
                     (see Y above)

AA.	(LO 7)	Accounts Receivable	XX (present value of payment)
		Sales	XX (present value of payment)
		Sale of tractor, payment deferred	

BB.	(LO 7)	Cash	XX (amount received)
		Accounts Receivable	XX (present value of payment)
		Interest Income	XX (imputed amount)
		Receipt on account including imputed interest earned (see AA above)	

CC.	(LO 7)	Short-Term Investments	XX (amount invested)
		Cash	XX (amount invested)
		Investment of cash	

DD.	(LO 7)	Short-Term Investments	XX (interest for period)
		Interest Income	XX (interest for period)
		Interest income for period	

EE.	(LO 7)	Loan Repayment Fund	XX (amount contributed)
		Cash	XX (amount contributed)
		Annual contribution to loan repayment fund	

SELF-TEST

Test your knowledge of the chapter by choosing the best answer for each of the following items.

1. Failure to record a liability will probably
   a. have no effect on net income.
   b. result in overstated net income.
   c. result in overstated total assets.
   d. result in overstated total liabilities and owner's equity.

2. The amount received by a borrower on a $3,000, one-year, 10 percent note with interest included in the face value is
   a. $3,000.
   b. $2,700.
   c. $3,300.
   d. $2,990.

3. If product J cost $100 and had a 2 percent failure rate, the estimated warranty expense in a month in which 1,000 units were sold would be
   a. $2,000.
   b. $100.
   c. $20.
   d. $20,000.

4. Of a company's employees, 70 percent typically qualify to receive two weeks' paid vacation per year. The amount of estimated vacation pay liability for a week in which the total payroll is $3,000 is
   a. $2,100.
   b. $42.
   c. $84.
   d. $120.

5. A contingent liability would be recorded in the accounting records if it is
   a. not probable but can be reasonably estimated.
   b. not probable but cannot be estimated.
   c. probable and can be reasonably estimated.
   d. probable but cannot be reasonably estimated.

6. Payroll Taxes and Benefits Expense includes all the following except
   a. federal unemployment tax payable.
   b. social security tax payable.
   c. federal income tax payable.
   d. state unemployment tax payable.

7. A business accepts a $10,000 12 percent note due in three years. Assuming simple interests, how much will the business receive when the note falls due?
   a. $10,360
   b. $14,049
   c. $10,000
   d. $13,600

8. The present value of a single sum table would *not* include the factor
   a. 1.000.
   b. 0.926.
   c. 0.744.
   d. 0.837.

9. Marina wishes to deposit an amount into her savings account that will enable her to withdraw $1,000 per year for the next four years. She should deposit $1,000 multiplied by
   a. the future value of a single sum factor.
   b. the present value of a single sum factor.
   c. the future value of an ordinary annuity factor.
   d. the present value of an ordinary annuity factor.

10. A company sells merchandise on a deferred payment plan, ultimately receiving $7,000 on the account receivable. On the payment date, the company would
    a. credit Accounts Receivable for less than $7,000.
    b. debit the asset account for $7,000.
    c. debit Interest Income for the imputed amount.
    d. credit Sales for less than $7,000.

TESTING YOUR KNOWLEDGE

*Matching**

Match each term with its definition by writing the appropriate letter in the blank.

_____ 1. Current liabilities

_____ 2. Long-term liabilities

_____ 3. Definitely determinable liabilities

_____ 4. Estimated liabilities

_____ 5. Contingent liabilities

_____ 6. Unearned revenues

_____ 7. Vacation pay

_____ 8. Interest

_____ 9. Simple interest

_____ 10. Compound interest

_____ 11. Future value

_____ 12. Present value

_____ 13. Ordinary annuity

_____ 14. Line of credit

_____ 15. Commercial paper

a. The amount that must be invested now to produce a given future value

b. Unsecured loans sold to the public

c. The computation whereby interest is computed without considering accrued interest

d. Obligations that exist but cannot be precisely measured at the balance sheet date

e. A series of equal payments made at the end of each period

f. Obligations that can be precisely measured

g. The cost of using money for a specific period of time

h. The amount an investment will be worth at a future date

i. An arrangement with the bank that allows a company to borrow funds when needed

j. The computation whereby interest is computed on the original amount plus accrued interest

k. Obligations that are not expected to be satisfied in the current period

l. Potential liabilities that may or may not become actual liabilities

m. Obligations to deliver goods or services in return for advance payment

n. Obligations that are expected to be satisfied within one year or the normal operating cycle, whichever is longer

o. Compensation received during an employee's earned time off

---

*Note to student: The matching quiz might be completed more efficiently by starting with the definition and searching for the corresponding term.

Short Answer

Use the lines provided to answer each item.

1. Current liabilities fall into two principal categories. What are they?

_____

_____

2. Give three examples of contingent liabilities.

_____

_____

_____

3. Give three examples of estimated liabilities.

_____

_____

_____

4. Give three examples of definitely determinable liabilities.

_____

_____

_____

5. List four withholdings from an employee's salary that are always or almost always required.

_____

_____

_____

_____

6. List the four components of payroll taxes and benefits expense.

_____

_____

_____

_____

True-False

Circle T if the statement is true, F if it is false. Please provide explanations for the false answers, using the blank lines at the end of the section.

T F **1.** Unearned revenues can be found on the income statement.

T F **2.** A contract to purchase goods in the future does not require the recording of a current liability.

T F **3.** Failure to record an accrued liability will result in an overstatement of net income.

T F **4.** The current portion of a long-term debt is a current liability (assume that it is to be satisfied with cash).

T F **5.** Sales Tax Payable is an example of an estimated liability.

T F **6.** Warranties fall into the category of definitely determinable liabilities.

T F **7.** The multipliers incorporated into the "present value of a single sum to be received in the future" table are all less than 1.000.

T F **8.** An ordinary annuity is a series of equal payments made at the beginning of equal intervals of time.

T F **9.** The higher the interest rate applied, the higher the present value of an amount or annuity to be received in the future.

T F **10.** Every contingent liability must eventually become an actual liability or no liability at all.

T F **11.** The account Discount on Notes Payable is associated with notes whose interest is stated separately on the face of the note.

T F **12.** If a refrigerator is sold in year 1 and repairs are made in year 2, Product Warranty Expense should be recorded in year 2.

T F **13.** When the payroll is recorded, Wages Payable is credited for gross earnings.

T F **14.** Social security taxes are borne by both the employer and employee.

T F **15.** Typically, unemployment taxes are a component of Payroll Taxes and Benefits Expense.

T F **16.** A decrease in the payables turnover will produce an increase in the average days' payable.

_____

_____

_____

_____

_____

_____

_____

_____

_____

_____

_____

_____

_____

_____

_____

_____

_____

_____

_____

_____

_____

_____

_____

_____

_____

_____

_____

_____

Multiple Choice

Circle the letter of the best answer.

1. Which of the following is not a definitely determinable liability?
   a. Dividends payable
   b. Unearned revenues
   c. Estimated property tax payable
   d. Excise tax payable

2. Estimated liabilities would not apply to
   a. warranties.
   b. vacation pay.
   c. a corporation's income tax.
   d. pending lawsuits.

3. When an employee receives vacation pay, the company should
   a. debit Vacation Pay Expense and credit Cash.
   b. debit Vacation Pay Receivable and credit Cash.
   c. debit Estimated Liability for Vacation Pay and credit Cash.
   d. debit Vacation Pay Expense and credit Estimated Liability for Vacation Pay.

4. A company that uses the calendar year receives a property tax bill each March (for that particular calendar year), to be paid by April 10. If entries are made at the end of each month to record property tax expense, the April 10 entry to record payment would include a

a. debit to Cash.

b. credit to Estimated Property Tax Payable.

c. debit to Property Tax Expense.

d. debit to Prepaid Property Tax.

5. Compound interest is computed semiannually on $100 in the bank for five years at 10 percent annual interest. The future value table is used by multiplying the $100 by which multiplier?

a. 5 periods at 10 percent

b. 10 periods at 5 percent

c. 10 periods at 10 percent

d. 5 periods at 5 percent

Use the following present and future value information to answer Questions 6 and 7.

Period	Present Value of $1 Discounted at 12% Per Period	Future Value of $1 at 12% Per Period
1	0.893	1.120
2	0.797	1.254

6. What amount should be deposited in a bank today at 12 percent interest (compounded annually) to grow to $100 two years from today?

a. $100/0.797

b. $100 × 0.893 × 2

c. ($100 × 0.893) + ($100 × 0.797)

d. $100 × 0.797

7. If $200 were placed in the bank today at 12 percent interest (compounded annually), what amount would be available two years from today?

a. $200 × 1.120 × 2

b. $200/1.254

c. $200 × 1.254

d. $200/1.120

8. Blue Water, Inc., purchased some equipment by executing a $10,000 non-interest-bearing note due in three years. The equipment should be recorded by Blue Water at

a. $10,000 minus the discounted interest on the note.

b. $10,000 plus the discounted interest on the note.

c. the amount of the discounted interest on the note.

d. $10,000.

9. When accounting for a note whose interest is included in its face amount, the account Discount on Notes Payable is eventually converted into

a. Interest Receivable.

b. Interest Expense.

c. Interest Payable.

d. Interest Income.

APPLYING YOUR KNOWLEDGE

Exercises

1. During 20x1, Kwang's Appliance Store sold 300 washing machines, each with a one-year guarantee. It was estimated that 5 percent of the washing machines eventually will require some type of repair, with an average cost of $35. Prepare the adjusting entry that Kwang's would make concerning the warranty. Also, prepare the entry that the store would make on April 9, 20x2, for one such repair that cost $48.

General Journal				
Date		**Description**	**Debit**	**Credit**

2. Sue Diamond, an office worker who is paid $6.50 per hour, worked 40 hours during the week ended May 11. Social security taxes are 6.20 percent; Medicare taxes are 1.45 percent; union dues are $5; state taxes withheld are $8; and federal income taxes withheld are $52. In addition, Diamond's employer must pay (on the basis of gross earnings) social security taxes of 6.20 percent, Medicare taxes of 1.45 percent, federal unemployment taxes of 0.8 percent, and state unemployment taxes of 5.4 percent. Prepare journal entries in the form on the next page that summarize Diamond's earnings for the week and that record the employer's payroll taxes. Round off amounts to the nearest cent.

General Journal				
Date		Description	Debit	Credit

3. Use the time value of money tables in your text to answer the following questions.

   a. What amount received today is equivalent to $1,000 receivable at the end of five years, assuming a 6 percent annual interest rate compounded annually?

      $_____

   b. If payments of $1,000 are invested at 8 percent annual interest at the end of each quarter for one year, compute the amount that will accumulate by the time the last payment is made.

      $_____

   c. If $1,000 is invested on June 30, 20x1, at 6 percent annual interest compounded semiannually, how much will be in the account on June 30, 20x3?

      $_____

   d. Compute the equal annual deposits required to accumulate a fund of $100,000 at the end of twenty years, assuming a 10 percent interest rate compounded annually.

      $_____

4. The manager of City Center Lanes is considering replacing the existing automatic pinsetters with improved ones that cost $10,000 each. It is estimated that each new pinsetter will save $2,000 annually and will last for ten years. Using an interest rate of 18 percent and the time value of money tables in your text, what is the present value of the savings of each new pinsetter to City Center Lanes?

   $_____

   Should the purchase be made?

   _____

5. On January 1, 20x1, Douglas Corporation purchased equipment from Courtright Sales by signing a two-year, non-interest-bearing note for $10,000. Douglas currently pays 10 percent interest on money borrowed. In the journal provided below, prepare Douglas's journal entries (a) to record the purchase and the note, (b) to adjust the accounts after one year, and (c) to record payment of the note after two years. Use the time value of money tables in your text for time value of money information. Omit explanations.

6. Morgan Corporation has current assets of $100,000 and current liabilities of $40,000, of which accounts payable are $30,000. Morgan's cost of goods sold is $290,000, its merchandise decreased by $15,000, and accounts payable were $20,000 the prior year. In the spaces below, provide the following short-term liquidity measures:

a. Working capital: _____

b. Payables turnover: _____

c. Average days' payable: _____

	General Journal			
Date		**Description**	**Debit**	**Credit**

Crossword Puzzle
for Chapters 8 and 9

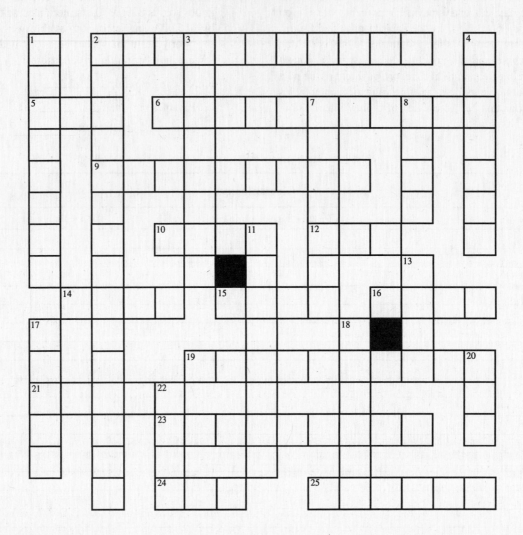

ACROSS

2. Goods-sold-by-one-for-another arrangement
5. Inventory valuation rule (abbr.)
6. Goods
9. Type of liability
10. Method that produces most up-to-date ending inventory (abbr.)
12. Accounting Principles Board, for short
14. Hourly compensation
15. Like unproductive assets
16. _____ liquidation (abbr.)
19. Potential, as a liability
21. Bank activity (pl.)
23. Normal _____ cycle
24. Payable
25. Inventory estimation technique

DOWN

1. Monthly or yearly compensation (pl.)
2. Unsecured loans sold to the public (2 words)
3. _____ identification method
4. With 17-Down, time value of money concept
7. _____ days' inventory on hand
8. _____-by-item method
11. Type of annuity
13. _____ of credit
17. See 4-Down
18. Just-_____ operating environment (hyph.)
20. Government-related liability
22. Cost of Goods _____

CHAPTER 10 LONG-TERM ASSETS

REVIEWING THE CHAPTER

Objective 1: Identify the types of long-term assets and explain the management issues related to accounting for them.

1. **Long-term assets** (also called *fixed assets*) are assets that (a) have a useful life of more than one year, (b) are acquired for use in the operation of the business, and (c) are not intended for resale to customers. Assets such as land and buildings that are not being used in the normal course of business should be classified as long-term investments. Property, plant, and equipment is the balance sheet classification for **tangible assets,** which have physical substance, such as land, buildings, equipment, and **natural resources. Intangible assets** is the balance sheet classification for assets that do not have physical substance, such as patents, trademarks, goodwill, copyrights, leaseholds, and franchises.

2. The allocation of costs to different accounting periods is called **depreciation** in the case of plant and equipment (plant assets), **depletion** in the case of natural resources, and **amortization** in the case of intangible assets. Because land has an unlimited useful life, its cost never is converted into an expense. The unexpired portion of a plant asset's cost is called **carrying value,** or *book value.* It is calculated by deducting accumulated depreciation from original cost.

3. Long-term assets are generally reported at carrying value. However, if **asset impairment** occurs, the long-term asset's carrying value is reduced to reflect its current fair value (measured by the present value of future cash flows). A loss for the amount of the writedown would also be recorded.

4. The decision to acquire long-term assets is called capital budgeting. One common capital budgeting technique compares the amount and timing of cash inflows and outflows over the life of the proposed asset. If the net present value of those cash flows is positive, then the asset should probably be purchased. Information concerning long-term asset acquisitions may be found in the investing activities section of the statement of cash flows.

5. Long-term assets that cannot be purchased for cash must be financed. Common financing techniques include issuing stock, bonds, and long-term notes.

6. In dealing with long-term assets, the major accounting problem is to figure out how much of the asset has benefited the current period, and how much should be carried forward as an asset to benefit future periods. To resolve these issues, one must determine (a) the cost of the asset; (b) the method of matching the cost with revenues; (c) the treatment of subsequent expenditures such as repairs, maintenance, and additions; and (d) the treatment of the asset at time of disposal.

Objective 2: Distinguish between capital and revenue expenditures, and account for the cost of property, plant, and equipment.

7. Before recording an expenditure in connection with a long-term asset, one must determine whether it was a capital expenditure or a revenue

expenditure. A **capital expenditure** is an **expenditure** (a payment or an incurrence of liability) for the purchase or expansion of long-term assets. A capital expenditure is recorded as an asset because it will benefit several accounting periods. A **revenue expenditure** is an expenditure for repairs, maintenance, fuel, and anything else necessary to maintain and operate the plant and equipment. A revenue expenditure is charged as an expense in the period in which it is incurred, under the theory that it benefits only the current accounting period.

8. Treating a capital expenditure as a revenue expenditure, or vice versa, can result in a mismatching of revenues and expenses. Accordingly, great care must be taken to draw the appropriate distinction.

9. The cost of a long-term asset includes the purchase cost, freight charges, insurance while in transit, installation, and other costs involved in acquiring the asset and getting it ready for use. Interest incurred during the construction of a plant asset is included in the cost of the asset. However, interest incurred for the purchase of a plant asset is expensed when incurred.

10. When land is purchased, the Land account should be debited for the price paid for the land, real estate commissions, lawyers' fees, and such expenses as back taxes assumed; draining, clearing, and grading costs; assessments for local improvements; and the cost (less salvage value) of tearing down buildings on the property.

11. Land improvements, such as driveways, parking lots, and fences, are subject to depreciation and require a separate Land Improvements account.

12. When long-term assets are purchased for a lump sum, the cost should be divided among the assets acquired in proportion to their appraisal values.

Objective 3: Define *depreciation*, state the factors that affect its computation, and show how to record it.

13. *Depreciation,* as used in accounting, refers to the allocation of the cost (less the residual value) of a tangible asset to the periods benefited by the asset. It does not refer to the physical deterioration or the decrease in market value of the asset. That is, it is a process of allocation, not valuation.

14. A tangible asset should be depreciated over its estimated useful life in a systematic and rational manner. Tangible assets have limited useful lives because of **physical deterioration** (limitations resulting from use and exposure to the elements) and **obsolescence** (the process of becoming out of date).

15. Depreciation is computed after the asset's cost, residual value, depreciable cost, and estimated useful life are determined. **Residual value** is the estimated value at the disposal date and often is referred to as *salvage value* or *disposal value.* **Depreciable cost** equals the asset's cost less its residual value. **Estimated useful life** can be meas-ured in time or in units, and requires careful consideration by the accountant.

Objective 4a: Compute periodic depreciation under the straight-line method.

16. The most common depreciation methods are (a) straight-line, (b) production, and (c) declining-balance. The last is described as an accelerated method.

17. Under the **straight-line method,** the depreciable cost is spread evenly over the life of the asset. Depreciation for each year is computed as follows:

$$\frac{\text{Cost} - \text{Residual Value}}{\text{Estimated Useful Life (Years)}}$$

Objective 4b: Compute periodic depreciation under the production method.

18. Under the **production method,** depreciation is based not on time but on use of the asset in units. Under this method, depreciation for each year is computed as follows:

$$\frac{\text{Cost} - \text{Residual Value}}{\begin{array}{c}\text{Estimated Units of}\\\text{Useful Life}\end{array}} \times \begin{array}{c}\text{Actual Units}\\\text{of Output}\end{array}$$

Objective 4c: Compute periodic depreciation under the declining-balance method.

19. The declining-balance method is called an **accelerated method** because depreciation is greatest in the first year and decreases each year thereafter. This method is justified by the matching rule (high depreciation charges in the most productive years) and by the smoothing effect that results when annual depreciation and repair expense are combined (that is, over the years, depreciation charges decrease and repair costs increase).

20. Under the **declining-balance method,** depreciation is computed by multiplying the remaining carrying value (the unexpired part of the cost) of the asset by a fixed percentage. The **double-declining-balance method** is a form of the

declining-balance method that uses a fixed percentage that is twice the straight-line percentage. Under the double-declining-balance method, depreciation for each year is computed as shown below.

$$2 \times \frac{100\%}{\text{Useful Life in Years}} \times \frac{\text{Remaining}}{\text{Carrying Value}}$$

Under the declining-balance or double-declining-balance method, as with other methods, an asset should not be depreciated below its residual value.

Objective 5: Account for the disposal of depreciable assets not involving exchanges.

21. When an asset is still in use after it has been fully depreciated, no more depreciation should be recorded. The asset should not be written off until its disposal. Disposal occurs when the asset is discarded, sold, or traded in.

22. When a business disposes of an asset, depreciation should be recorded for the current period preceding disposal. This brings the asset's Accumulated Depreciation account up to the date of disposal.

23. When a machine, for example, is discarded (thrown out), Accumulated Depreciation, Machinery is debited and Machinery is credited for the present balance in the Accumulated Depreciation account. If the machine has not been fully depreciated, then Loss on Disposal of Machinery must be debited for the carrying value to balance the entry.

24. When a machine is sold for cash, Cash is debited, Accumulated Depreciation, Machinery is debited, and Machinery is credited. If the cash received is less than the carrying value of the machine, then Loss on Sale of Machinery also would be debited. On the other hand, if the cash received is greater than the carrying value, Gain on Sale of Machinery would be credited to balance the entry.

Objective 6: Account for the disposal of depreciable assets involving exchanges.

25. When an asset is traded in (exchanged) for a similar one, the gain or loss is computed first, as follows:

> Trade-In Allowance
> − Carrying Value of Asset Traded In
> = Gain (Loss) on Trade-In

a. For financial reporting purposes, both gains and losses should be recognized (recorded) on the exchange of dissimilar assets, and losses should be recognized on the exchange of similar assets. However, gains are not recognized on the exchange of similar assets.

b. For income tax purposes, neither gains nor losses should be recognized on the exchange of similar assets, but both should be recognized on the exchange of dissimilar assets.

c. When a gain or loss is recognized, the asset acquired should be debited for its list price—cash paid plus trade-in allowance—using a realistic trade-in value. The old asset is removed from the books, as explained in paragraph 24.

d. When a gain or loss is not recognized, the asset acquired should be debited for the carrying value of the asset traded in plus cash paid (this results in the nonrecognition of the gain or loss).

Objective 7: Identify the issues related to accounting for natural resources and compute depletion.

26. Natural resources are tangible assets in the form of valuable substances that can be cut, pumped, or mined and sold. They include standing timber, oil and gas fields, and mineral deposits.

27. *Depletion* refers both to the exhaustion of the resource and to the allocation of a natural resource's cost to accounting periods based on the amount extracted in each period. Depletion for each year is computed as follows:

$$\frac{\text{Cost} - \text{Residual Value}}{\substack{\text{Estimated Units} \\ \text{Available}}} \times \substack{\text{Units Extracted} \\ \text{and Sold} \\ \text{During Period}}$$

Units extracted but not sold in one year are recorded as inventory, to be charged as an expense in the year they are sold.

28. Assets that are acquired in conjunction with the natural resource, and that cannot be used after the natural resource is depleted, should be depreciated on the same basis as depletion is computed.

29. In accounting for the exploration and development of oil and gas resources, two methods have been used. Under **successful efforts accounting,** the cost of a dry well is written off immediately as a loss. The **full-costing** method, on the other hand, capitalizes and depletes the costs of both successful and dry wells. Both methods are in accordance with GAAP.

Objective 8: Apply the matching rule to intangible assets, including research and development costs and goodwill.

30. Intangible assets are long-term assets that have no physical substance. They represent certain rights and advantages to their owner. Examples of intangible assets are patents, copyrights, trademarks, goodwill, leaseholds, leasehold improvements, franchises, licenses, brand names, formulas, and processes. An intangible asset should be written off over its useful life (not to exceed 40 years) through amortization. This is to be accomplished by a direct reduction of the asset account and an increase in amortization expense.

   a. A **patent** is an exclusive right granted by the federal government for a period of 17 years to make a particular product or use a specific process.

   b. A **copyright** is an exclusive right granted by the federal government to the possessor to publish and sell literary, musical, and other artistic materials (including computer programs) for a period of the author's life plus 50 years.

   c. A **leasehold** is a right to occupy land or buildings under a long-term rental contract.

   d. **Leasehold improvements** are improvements to leased property that become the property of the lessor at the end of the lease.

   e. A **trademark** is a registered symbol that gives the holder the right to use it to identify a product or service.

   f. A **brand name** is a registered name that gives the holder the right to use it to identify a product or service.

   g. A **franchise** is the right to an exclusive territory or market.

   h. A **license** is the right to use a formula, technique, process, or design.

   i. **Goodwill** is the excess of the cost of a group of assets (usually a business) over the fair market value of the assets individually. (See also paragraph 33.)

31. Research and development involve developing new products, testing existing ones, and doing pure research. According to GAAP, the costs associated with these activities should be charged as expenses in the period incurred.

32. The cost to develop computer software that will be sold or leased to others should be treated as research and development up to the point that a product is deemed technologically feasible (i.e.,

when a detailed working program has been designed). At that point, software production costs should be capitalized and amortized over the estimated useful life of the software, using the straight-line method. However, the cost of software developed for *internal* use may be capitalized in its entirety and amortized over its estimated economic life.

33. *Goodwill,* as the term is used in accounting, refers to a company's ability to earn more than is normal for its particular industry. Goodwill should be recorded only when a company is purchased. It equals the excess of the purchase cost over the fair market value of the net assets if purchased separately. Once it is recorded, goodwill should be amortized over its estimated useful life, not to exceed 40 years.

Supplemental Objective 9: Apply depreciation methods to problems of partial years, revised rates, groups of similar items, special types of capital expenditures, and cost recovery.

34. When an asset is purchased after the beginning of the year or discarded before the end of the year, depreciation should be recorded for only part of the year. The accountant figures the year's depreciation and multiplies this figure by the fraction of the year that the asset was in use.

35. Often, the estimated useful life or residual value is found to be over- or understated after some depreciation has been taken. The accountant then must produce a revised figure for the remaining useful life or remaining depreciable cost. Future depreciation then is calculated by spreading the remaining depreciable cost over the remaining useful life, leaving previous depreciation unchanged.

36. When a company has several plant assets that are similar, it probably uses **group depreciation** rather than individual depreciation. Under group depreciation, the original costs of all similar assets are lumped together in one summary account. Then, depreciation is figured for the group of assets as a whole.

37. Businesses make capital expenditures for plant assets, natural resources, and intangible assets. Capital expenditures also include **additions** (such as a building wing) and **betterments** (such as the installation of an air-conditioning system).

38. **Ordinary repairs** are expenditures necessary to maintain an asset in good operating condition in

order to attain its originally intended useful life. They are charged as expenses in the period in which they are incurred. **Extraordinary repairs** are expenditures that either increase an asset's residual value or lengthen its useful life. They are recorded by debiting Accumulated Depreciation (thereby increasing the asset's carrying value) and crediting Cash or Accounts Payable.

39. Under the **Modified Accelerated Cost Recovery System (MACRS)** each depreciable asset is placed in a category for tax purposes only and depreciated according to percentages and over a period of years established by Congress; estimated useful life and residual value are ignored. MACRS depreciation allows the rapid write-off of tangible assets to reduce current taxes but normally is not acceptable for financial reporting purposes. For example, most property other than real estate is depreciated by a 200 percent declining-balance method. Recovery of the cost of property placed in service after December 31, 1986, is calculated according to MACRS for tax purposes. An exception to asset cost allocation prescribed in the Tax Reform Act of 1986 is that the first $17,500 of equipment costs may be expensed immediately.

A. (LO 3) Depreciation Expense, Asset Name XX (amount allocated)
         Accumulated Depreciation, Asset Name XX (amount allocated)
             To record depreciation for the period (review of
             entry introduced in Chapter 3)

B. (LO 5) Depreciation Expense, Machinery XX (amount allocated)
         Accumulated Depreciation, Machinery XX (amount allocated)
             To record depreciation up to date of disposal

C. (LO 5) Accumulated Depreciation, Machinery XX (existing balance)
        Loss on Disposal of Machinery XX (carrying value)
         Machinery XX (purchase price)
             Discarded machine no longer used in the business

D. (LO 5) Cash XX (proceeds on sale)
        Accumulated Depreciation, Machinery XX (existing balance)
         Machinery XX (purchase price)
             Sale of machine for carrying value; no gain or loss

E. (LO 5) Cash XX (proceeds on sale)
        Accumulated Depreciation, Machinery XX (existing balance)
        Loss on Sale of Machinery XX (CV minus cash)
         Machinery XX (purchase price)
             Sale of machine at less than carrying value (CV);
             loss recorded

F. (LO 5) Cash XX (proceeds on sale)
        Accumulated Depreciation, Machinery XX (existing balance)
         Gain on Sale of Machinery XX (cash minus CV)
         Machinery XX (purchase price)
             Sale of machine at more than carrying value (CV);
             gain recorded

G. (LO 6) Regarding the topic of exchanges of plant assets, the journal
        entries are all very similar (see entry H). The amounts, however,
        depend on a variety of factors, among them the similarity or
        dissimilarity of assets exchanged and the purpose of the entry
        (financial accounting or income tax). In addition, gains and
        losses sometimes are recognized, sometimes not. Please see
        your textbook for a thorough explanation.

H. (LO 6) Machinery (new) XX (see text)
        Accumulated Depreciation, Machinery XX (existing balance)
         Machinery (old) XX (purchase price)
         Cash XX (payment required)
             Exchange of machines—cost of old machine and its
             accumulated depreciation removed from the records,
             and new machine recorded at list price. (Note: If gain
             or loss must be recognized, it would be credited or
             debited, respectively.)

I. (LO 7) Depletion Expense, Coal Deposits   XX (amount allocated)
              Accumulated Depletion, Coal Deposits   XX (amount allocated)
                   To record depletion of coal mine

J. (SO 9) Capital expenditures typically are debited to an asset account
              (such as Buildings or Equipment), and revenue expenditures
              typically are debited to an expense account (such as Repair
              Expense). An exception to these rules is for extraordinary repairs,
              as shown in K.

K. (SO 9) Accumulated Depreciation, Machinery   XX (amount of repair)
              Cash   XX (amount of repair)
                   Extraordinary repair to machinery

SELF-TEST

Test your knowledge of the chapter by choosing the best answer for each of the following items.

1. Which of the following is *not* a characteristic of all long-term assets?
   a. Used in operation of business
   b. Possess physical substance
   c. Useful life of more than a year
   d. Not for resale

2. Which of the following would *not* be included in the cost of land?
   a. Cost of paving the land for parking
   b. Assessment from local government for sewer
   c. Cost of clearing an unneeded building from the land
   d. Commission to real estate agent

3. Which of the following most appropriately describes depreciation?
   a. Allocation of cost of plant asset
   b. Decline in value of plant asset
   c. Gradual obsolescence of plant asset
   d. Physical deterioration of plant asset

4. Assuming a useful life of six years, which of the following methods would result in the most depreciation in the first year?
   a. Cannot tell from data given
   b. Double-declining-balance
   c. Production
   d. Straight-line

5. The sale of equipment costing $16,000, with accumulated depreciation of $13,400 and sale price of $4,000, would result in a
   a. gain of $4,000.
   b. gain of $1,400.
   c. loss of $1,400.
   d. loss of $12,000.

6. A truck that cost $16,800 and on which $12,600 of accumulated depreciation has been recorded was disposed of on January 2, the first business day of the year. Assume the truck was traded for a similar truck having a price of $19,600, that a $2,000 trade-in was allowed, and that the balance was paid in cash. Following APB rules, the amount of the gain or loss recognized on this transaction would be
   a. $2,200 gain.
   b. $2,200 loss.
   c. $2,000 gain.
   d. no gain or loss recognized.

7. Which of the following items is not classified as a natural resource?
   a. Timber land
   b. Gas reserve
   c. Goodwill
   d. Oil well

8. According to generally accepted accounting principles, the proper accounting treatment for the cost of a trademark that management feels will retain its value indefinitely is to
   a. amortize the cost over a period not to exceed forty years.
   b. amortize the cost over five years.
   c. carry the cost of the asset indefinitely.
   d. write the cost off immediately.

9. According to generally accepted accounting principles, the proper accounting treatment of the cost of most research and development expenditures is to
   a. amortize the cost over a period not to exceed forty years.
   b. amortize the cost over five years.
   c. carry the cost as an asset indefinitely.
   d. write the cost off immediately as an expense.

10. Reliable Insurance Company has many items of office equipment in its home office. Rather than compute depreciation on each item individually, the company may combine like items in one account and use
    a. statistical depreciation.
    b. combined depreciation.
    c. group depreciation.
    d. direct charge off.

TESTING YOUR KNOWLEDGE

Matching*

Match each term with its definition by writing the appropriate letter in the blank.

_____ 1. Long-term assets (fixed assets)

_____ 2. Depreciation

_____ 3. Obsolescence

_____ 4. Franchise

_____ 5. Residual value (salvage or disposal value)

_____ 6. Accelerated method

_____ 7. Straight-line method

_____ 8. Production method

_____ 9. Full costing

_____ 10. Double-declining-balance method

_____ 11. Group depreciation

_____ 12. Natural resources

_____ 13. Depletion

_____ 14. Amortization

_____ 15. Modified Accelerated Cost Recovery System (MACRS)

_____ 16. Capital expenditure

_____ 17. Revenue expenditure

_____ 18. Patent

_____ 19. Copyright

_____ 20. Leasehold

_____ 21. Trademark

_____ 22. Successful efforts accounting

a. The exclusive right to make a particular product or use a specific process for 17 years

b. Using one depreciation rate for several similar items

c. The allocation of an intangible asset's cost to the periods benefited by the asset

d. Payment for the right to use property

e. Assets to be used in the business for more than one year

f. The allocation of the cost of a tangible asset to the periods benefited by the asset

g. An expenditure for services needed to maintain and operate plant assets (an expense)

h. The depreciation method under which cost allocation is based on units, not time

i. The exclusive right to publish literary, musical, or artistic materials or computer programs for the author's life plus 50 years

j. The accelerated depreciation method based on twice the straight-line rate

k. A depreciation method used for tax purposes only

l. The estimated value of an asset on the disposal date

m. An expenditure for the purchase or expansion of long-term assets (an asset)

n. One reason for an asset's limited useful life

o. Assets in the form of valuable substances that can be extracted and sold

p. An identifying symbol or name for a product or service that can be used only by its owner

q. The method of accounting for oil and gas that immediately writes off the cost of dry wells

r. The depreciation method that charges equal depreciation each year

s. The exclusive right to sell a product within a certain territory

t. The practice of charging the highest depreciation in the first year and decreasing depreciation each year thereafter

u. The allocation of a natural resource's cost to the periods over which the resource is consumed

v. The method of accounting for oil and gas that capitalizes the cost of dry wells

---

*Note to student: The matching quiz might be completed more efficiently by starting with the definition and searching for the corresponding term.

Short Answer

Use the lines provided to answer each item.

1. Distinguish between an addition and a betterment.

   _____

   _____

   _____

   _____

2. When a plant asset is sold for cash, under what unique circumstance would no gain or loss be recorded?

   _____

   _____

3. List four pieces of information necessary to compute the depletion expense of an oil well for a given year.

   _____

   _____

   _____

   _____

4. Distinguish between an ordinary and an extraordinary repair.

   _____

   _____

   _____

   _____

5. For each asset category, provide the accounting term for the allocation of its cost to the periods benefited.

Category	Term for Cost Allocation
Intangible assets	_____
Plant and equipment	_____
Natural resources	_____

6. Plant assets have limited useful lives for two reasons. What are they?

   _____

   _____

True-False

Circle T if the statement is true, F if it is false. Please provide explanations for the false answers, using the blank lines at the end of the section.

T F 1. Land is not subject to depreciation.

T F 2. The loss recorded on a discarded asset is equal to the carrying value of the asset at the time it is discarded.

T F 3. Land held for speculative reasons is not classified as property, plant, and equipment.

T F 4. Depreciation is a process of valuation, not allocation.

T F 5. Depreciation for a machine can be calculated by having an appraiser determine to what extent the machine has worn out.

T F 6. When land is purchased for use as a plant site, its cost should include the cost of clearing and draining the land.

T F 7. Each type of depreciable asset should have its own accumulated depreciation account.

T F 8. Estimated useful life in years is irrelevant when applying the production method of depreciation.

T F 9. Under the straight-line method, if depreciation expense is $1,000 in the first year, it will be $2,000 in the second year.

T F 10. When the estimated useful life of an asset is revised after some depreciation has been taken, the accountant should not go back to previous years to make corrections.

T F 11. For financial accounting purposes, both gains and losses on the exchange of dissimilar assets are recognized in the accounting records.

T F **12.** In an asset's last year of depreciation, accelerated depreciation generally results in less net income than does straight-line depreciation.

T F **13.** Depreciable cost equals cost minus accumulated depreciation.

T F **14.** Estimated useful life and residual value are ignored when applying MACRS depreciation.

T F **15.** A copyright is a name or symbol that can be used only by its owner.

T F **16.** If, by mistake, ordinary maintenance is capitalized instead of being charged as an expense, net income for the period would be overstated.

T F **17.** A betterment is an example of a revenue expenditure.

T F **18.** Recording an extraordinary repair leaves the carrying value of the asset unchanged.

T F **19.** When a machine is sold for less than its carrying value, one of the debits is to Loss on Sale of Machinery and one of the credits is to Accumulated Depreciation, Machinery.

T F **20.** *Capital expenditure* is another term for expense.

T F **21.** For income tax purposes, neither gains nor losses are recognized on the exchange of similar plant assets.

T F **22.** When a plant asset is sold during a year, depreciation expense need not be brought up to date and recorded.

T F **23.** In determining the number of years over which to amortize intangible assets, useful life is far more important than legal life.

T F **24.** As accumulated depreciation increases, carrying value decreases.

T F **25.** Goodwill should not be recorded unless it has been purchased.

T F **26.** Research and development costs should be capitalized when they can be associated with a specific new product.

T F **27.** The full-costing method capitalizes the cost of both successful and dry wells.

T F **28.** A long-term asset's carrying value should be reduced when its value is deemed impaired.

Circle the letter of the best answer.

1. A building and land are purchased for a lump-sum payment of $66,000. How much should be allocated to land if the land is appraised at $20,000 and the building at $60,000?
   a. $22,000
   b. $20,000
   c. $16,500
   d. $13,750

2. The expired cost of a plant asset is called its
   a. accumulated depreciation.
   b. carrying value.
   c. depreciable cost.
   d. residual value.

3. Which depreciation method, when applied to an asset in its first year of use, results in the greatest depreciation charge?
   a. Declining-balance
   b. Production
   c. Straight-line
   d. Impossible to determine without more information

4. When a certain machine was purchased, its estimated useful life was 20 years. However, after it had been depreciated for 5 years, the company decided that it originally had overestimated the machine's useful life by 3 years. What should be done?
   a. Go back and adjust depreciation for the first 5 years.
   b. Depreciate the remainder of the depreciable cost over the next 15 years.
   c. Depreciate the remainder of the depreciable cost over the next 12 years.
   d. Both a and b

5. According to GAAP, intangible assets should never be amortized over more than
   a. 5 years.
   b. 17 years.
   c. 40 years.
   d. 50 years.

6. Land improvements
   a. should be included in the cost of land.
   b. are subject to depreciation.
   c. should be deducted from the cost of land.
   d. should be charged as an expense in the year purchased.

7. A machine that cost $9,000 with a carrying value of $2,000 is sold for $1,700, and an entry is made. Which of the following is true about the entry?
   a. Accumulated Depreciation is debited for $2,000.
   b. Machinery is credited for $2,000.
   c. Loss on Sale of Machinery is credited for $300.
   d. Accumulated Depreciation is debited for $7,000.

8. Which of the following is *not* a revenue expenditure?
   a. Ordinary maintenance of a machine
   b. Replacing an old roof with a new one
   c. The installation of new light bulbs
   d. A tire repair on a company truck

9. Charging a depreciable item as an expense, instead of capitalizing it, results in
   a. overstated total assets.
   b. understated net income for the succeeding period.
   c. overstated depreciation expense for the succeeding period.
   d. understated net income for the period.

10. Overestimating the number of barrels that can be pumped from an oil well over its lifetime results in
    a. understating net income each year.
    b. understating depletion cost per unit each year.
    c. overstating depletion expense each year.
    d. understating total assets each year.

11. The cost of developing computer software that will be sold or leased to others should be
    a. expensed up to the point that the product is technologically feasible.
    b. capitalized in its entirety and amortized over 40 years.
    c. expensed once the product is deemed to be technologically feasible.
    d. expensed in its entirety when incurred.

12. Which of the following normally is charged as an expense in the period of expenditure?
    a. Goodwill
    b. Leaseholds
    c. Leasehold improvements
    d. Research and development costs

APPLYING YOUR KNOWLEDGE

Exercises

1. A machine that cost $26,000 had an estimated useful life of five years and a residual value of $2,000 when purchased on January 2, 20x1. Fill in the amount of depreciation expense for 20x2, as well as the accumulated depreciation and carrying value of the machine as of December 31, 20x2, under both of the listed methods.

	Depreciation Expense for 20x2	Accumulated Depreciation as of 12/31/x2	Carrying Value as of 12/31/x2
a. Straight-line	$ _____	$ _____	$ _____
b. Double-declining-balance	$ _____	$ _____	$ _____

2. A machine that was to produce a certain type of toy was purchased for $35,000 on April 30, 20xx. The machine was expected to produce 100,000 toys during the ten years that the company expected to keep the machine. The company estimated that it then could sell the machine for $5,000. Using the production method, calculate the depreciation expense in 20xx, when the machine produced 7,500 toys.

3. Classify each of the following expenditures as a capital or revenue expenditure by placing a **C** or an **R** next to each item.

_____ **a.** Replacement of the roof on a building

_____ **b.** Replacement of the battery in a company vehicle

_____ **c.** The cost of painting the executive offices

_____ **d.** Installation of aluminum siding on a building

_____ **e.** Replacement of the motor in a machine

_____ **f.** The cost to repair an air-conditioning unit

_____ **g.** The cost to install a piece of machinery

_____ **h.** The addition of a building wing

_____ **i.** The tune-up of a company vehicle

4. On January 2, 20xx, Sacramento Enterprises traded in, along with $15,500 in cash, a machine that cost $25,000 and had a carrying value of $8,000, for a new machine with a retail price of $23,000. The machines are similar in nature. Prepare the journal entry that Sacramento would make to conform to GAAP, as well as the entry that would conform to income tax rulings. Use the journal provided.

General Journal				
Date		Description	Debit	Credit

5. In 20xx, Georgia Coal Company purchased a coal mine for $800,000. It is estimated that 2 million tons of coal can be extracted from the mine. In the space provided, prepare Georgia's adjusting entry for December 31, 20xx, to reflect the extraction and sale of 100,000 tons during the year.

General Journal				
Date		Description	Debit	Credit

CHAPTER 11 LONG-TERM LIABILITIES

REVIEWING THE CHAPTER

Objective 1: Identify the management issues related to issuing long-term debt.

1. Long-term liabilities are obligations that are expected to be settled beyond one year or the normal operating cycle, whichever is longer. Exactly how management finances its operations is vital to a business's survival. The management issues related to issuing long-term debt are (a) whether or not to have long-term debt, (b) how much long-term debt to have, and (c) what types of long-term debt to have.

2. To finance long-term assets, research and development, and other activities of long-run benefit, corporations must obtain funds that can be used for many years. This may be accomplished by issuing stock or by issuing long-term debt in the form of bonds, notes, mortgages, and leases. There are both advantages and disadvantages to issuing long-term debt, as explained below.

3. One advantage of issuing long-term debt is that common stockholders retain their level of control, since bondholders and other creditors do not have voting rights. Another advantage is that interest on debt is tax-deductible to the issuing corporation, thus lowering the tax burden. A third advantage is the **financial leverage** or *trading on the equity* that results from issuing debt. That is, if earnings on the funds obtained exceed the interest incurred, then earnings (and earnings per share) that accrue to the common stockholders will increase.

4. There are some disadvantages to issuing long-term debt, however. First, the more debt that is issued, the more periodic interest that must be paid. Similarly, the principal amount *must* be paid at maturity. Default on either interest or principal could force the business into bankruptcy. Another disadvantage is that if the interest incurred on the funds obtained exceeds the related earnings, then the attempt at financial leverage has backfired.

5. The use of debt financing varies widely across industries. One common measure of the risk (of default) undertaken by a company issuing debt is the **interest coverage ratio,** which is calculated as follows:

$$\frac{\text{Income Before Taxes} + \text{Interest Expense}}{\text{Interest Expense}}$$

The higher the interest coverage ratio (measured in "times"), the lower the company's risk of default on interest payments.

Objective 2: Identify and contrast the major characteristics of bonds.

6. Corporations frequently issue long-term **bonds** or notes to raise funds. The holders of these bonds or notes are creditors of the corporation. They are entitled to periodic interest, plus the principal of the debt on some specified date. As is true for all creditors, their claims for interest and principal take priority over stockholders' claims.

7. When bonds are issued, the corporation executes a contract with the bondholders called a **bond indenture.** In addition, the company issues **bond certificates** as evidence of its debt to the bondholders. A **bond issue** is made up of the total value of bonds issued at one time. Bonds are usually issued with a face value that is some multiple of $1,000, and carry a variety of features.

   a. **Secured bonds** give the bondholders a claim to certain assets of the company upon default. **Unsecured bonds** (also called *debenture bonds*) are issued on the general credit of the company.

   b. When all the bonds of an issue mature on the same date, they are called **term bonds.** When the bonds mature over several maturity dates, they are called **serial bonds.**

   c. When **registered bonds** are issued, the corporation maintains a record of all bondholders and pays interest by check to the bondholders of record. **Coupon bonds,** on the other hand, entitle the bearer to interest when the detachable coupons are presented at a bank for collection.

8. Bond prices are expressed as a percentage of face value. For example, when bonds with a face value of $100,000 are issued at 97, the company receives $97,000.

Objective 3: Record the issuance of bonds at face value and at a discount or premium.

9. Bonds payable due in the current period should be classified as a current liability only if they will be paid with current assets. In addition, the characteristics of all bonds should be disclosed in the notes to the financial statements.

10. When the **face interest rate** equals the **market interest rate** (also called the *effective interest rate*) for similar bonds on the issue date, the company will probably receive face value for the bonds.

11. Regardless of the issue price, bondholders are entitled to interest, which is based on the face amount. Interest for a period of time is computed by this formula:

$$\text{Interest} = \text{Principal} \times \text{Rate} \times \text{Time}$$

12. When the face interest rate is less than the market interest rate for similar bonds on the issue date, the bonds will probably sell at a **discount** (less than face value).

13. Unamortized Bond Discount appears on the balance sheet as a contra-liability to Bonds Payable. The difference between the two amounts is called the *carrying value* or *present value.* The carrying value increases as the discount is amortized and equals the face value of the bonds at maturity.

14. When the face interest rate is greater than the market interest rate for similar bonds on the issue date, the bonds usually sell at a **premium** (greater than face value). Unamortized Bond Premium is added to Bonds Payable on the balance sheet to produce the carrying value.

15. A separate account should be established for bond issue costs. These costs are spread over the life of the bonds, often through the amortization of a discount (which would be raised) or a premium (which would be lowered).

Objective 4: Use present values to determine the value of bonds.

16. Theoretically, the value of a bond is equal to the sum of the present values of (a) the periodic interest payments and (b) the single payment of principal at maturity. The discount rate used is based on the current market rate of interest.

Objective 5a: Use the straight-line and effective interest methods to amortize bond discounts.

17. When bonds are issued at a discount or premium, the interest payments do *not* equal the (true) total interest cost. Instead, total interest cost equals (a) interest payments over the life of the bond plus (b) the original discount amount, or minus (c) the original premium amount.

18. A **zero coupon bond** is a promise to pay a fixed amount at maturity, with no periodic interest payments. Investor earnings consist of the large discount upon issue, which in turn is amortized by the issuing corporation over the life of the bond.

19. A discount on bonds payable is considered an interest charge that must be amortized (spread out) over the life of the bond. Amortization is generally recorded on the interest payment dates, using either the straight-line method or the effective interest method.

20. Under the **straight-line method** of amortization, the amount to be amortized each interest period equals the bond discount divided by the number of interest payments during the life of the bond.

21. The effective interest method of amortization is more difficult to apply than the straight-line method but must be used instead when the results differ significantly.

22. To apply the **effective interest method** when a discount is involved, the market rate or effective rate of interest for similar securities when the bonds were issued must first be determined. This interest rate (halved for semiannual interest) is multiplied by the existing carrying value of the bonds for each interest period to obtain the bond interest expense to be recorded. The actual interest paid is then subtracted from the bond interest expense recorded to obtain the discount amortization for the period. Because the unamortized discount is now less, the carrying value is now greater. This new carrying value is applied to the next period, and the same amortization procedure is repeated.

Objective 5b: Use the straight-line and effective interest methods to amortize bond premiums.

23. Amortization of a premium acts as an offset against interest paid in determining the interest expense to be recorded. Under the straight-line method, the premium to be amortized in each period equals the bond premium divided by the number of interest payments during the life of the bond.

24. The effective interest method is applied to bond premiums in the same way that it is applied to bond discounts. The only difference is that the amortization for the period is computed by subtracting the bond interest expense recorded from actual interest paid (the reverse is done for amortizing a discount).

Objective 6: Account for bonds issued between interest dates and make year-end adjustments.

25. When bonds are issued between interest dates, the interest that has accrued since the last interest date is collected from the investor upon issue. It is then returned to the investor (along with the interest earned) on the next interest date.

26. When the accounting period ends between interest dates, the accrued interest and the proportionate discount or premium amortization must be recorded.

Objective 7: Account for the retirement of bonds and the conversion of bonds into stock.

27. **Callable bonds** are bonds that may be retired by the corporation before the maturity date. The action of retiring a bond issue before its maturity date is called **early extinguishment of debt**. When the market rate for bond interest drops, a company may want to call its bonds and substitute debt with a lower interest rate. When bonds are called (for whatever reason), an entry is needed to eliminate Bonds Payable and any unamortized premium or discount, and to record the payment of cash at the **call price**. In addition, an extraordinary gain or loss on the retirement of the bonds would be recorded. (Extraordinary items will be explained fully in Chapter 13.)

28. **Convertible bonds** are bonds that can be exchanged for other securities (usually common stock) at the option of the bondholder. When a bondholder converts his or her bonds into common stock, the common stock is recorded by the company at the carrying value of the bonds. Specifically, the entry eliminates Bonds Payable and any unamortized discount or premium, and records common stock and paid-in capital in excess of par value. No gain or loss is recorded.

29. A corporation might issue convertible bonds (a) because investors, as a result, will accept a lower rate of interest, (b) to avoid a shift in control, since bondholders do not have voting rights, (c) to benefit from the tax-deductibility of the bond interest, (d) in the hopes that the resultant earnings will exceed the interest cost, and (e) to achieve a certain financial flexibility.

Objective 8: Explain the basic features of mortgages payable, installment notes payable, long-term leases, and pensions and other postretirement benefits as long-term liabilities.

30. A **mortgage** is a long-term debt secured by real property, usually payable in equal monthly installments. Upon payment of an installment, both Mortgage Payable and Mortgage Interest Expense are debited, and Cash is credited. Each month, the interest portion of the payment decreases, while the principal portion of the payment increases.

31. The principal and interest on long-term notes are either payable on one maturity date or due in periodic payments. The latter notes are known as **installment notes payable** and are commonly used by businesses to finance the purchase of equipment. The installment payments can be structured to include either (a) accrued interest plus equal amounts of principal or (b) accrued interest plus increasing amounts of principal. The former method results in decreasing payments, whereas the latter method produces equal payments. The effective interest calculation would be applied in either case.

32. A lease is a contract that allows a business or individual to use an asset for a specific length of time in return for periodic payments. A **capital lease** is so much like a sale (as determined by certain criteria) that it should be recorded by the lessee as an asset (to be depreciated) and a related liability. An **operating lease** is a lease that does not meet the criteria for capital leases; each monthly lease payment should be charged to Rent Expense.

33. A **pension plan** is a program whereby a company agrees to pay benefits to its employees after they retire. Benefits to retirees are usually paid out of a **pension fund.** Pension plans are classified as defined contribution plans or defined benefit plans. **Other postretirement benefits,** such as health care, should be estimated and accrued while the employee is still working (in accordance with the matching rule).

A. (LO 3) Cash   XX (amount received)
        Bonds Payable   XX (face value)
          Sold bonds at face value

B. (LO 3) Bond Interest Expense   XX (amount incurred)
        Cash (or Interest Payable)   XX (amount paid or due)
          Paid (or accrued) interest to bondholders

C. (LO 3) Cash   XX (amount received)
        Unamortized Bond Discount   XX (amount of discount)
        Bonds Payable   XX (face value)
          Sold bonds at a discount

D. (LO 3) Cash   XX (amount received)
        Unamortized Bond Premium   XX (amount of premium)
        Bonds Payable   XX (face value)
          Sold bonds at a premium

E. (LO 5a) Bond Interest Expense   XX (amount incurred)
        Unamortized Bond Discount   XX (amount amortized)
        Cash (or Interest Payable)   XX (amount paid or due)
          Paid (or accrued) interest to bondholders and
          amortized the discount

F. (LO 5b) Bond Interest Expense   XX (amount incurred)
        Unamortized Bond Premium   XX (amount amortized)
        Cash (or Interest Payable)   XX (amount paid or due)
          Paid (or accrued) interest to bondholders and
          amortized the premium

G. (LO 6) Cash   XX (amount received)
        Bond Interest Expense   XX (accrued amount)
        Bonds Payable   XX (face value)
          Sold bonds at face value plus accrued interest
          (see entry H)

H. (LO 6) Bond Interest Expense   XX (six months' amount)
        Cash (or Interest Payable)   XX (amount paid or due)
          Paid (or accrued) semiannual interest on bonds issued
          in G

I. (LO 6) The year-end accrual for bond interest expense is identical
        to entry E for discounts and entry F for premiums, except that
        in both cases Interest Payable is credited instead of Cash.

J. (LO 6) Bond Interest Expense   XX (amount incurred)
        Interest Payable   XX (amount accrued)
        Unamortized Bond Premium   XX (amount amortized)
        Cash   XX (amount paid)
          Paid semiannual interest including interest
          previously accrued, and amortized the
          premium for the period since the end of
          the fiscal year

K. (LO 7) Bonds Payable   XX (face value)
           Unamortized Bond Premium   XX (current credit balance)
           Loss on Retirement of Bonds (Extraordinary)   XX (see explanation)
               Cash   XX (amount paid)
                   Retired bonds at a loss; the loss equals the excess of
                   the call price over the carrying value

L. (LO 7) Bonds Payable   XX (face value)
           Unamortized Bond Premium   XX (current credit balance)
               Cash   XX (amount paid)
               Gain on Retirement of Bonds (Extraordinary)   XX (see explanation)
                   Retired bonds at a gain; the gain equals
                   the excess of the carrying value over the
                   call price

M. (LO 7) Bonds Payable   XX (face value)
           Unamortized Bond Premium   XX (current credit balance)
               Common Stock   XX (par value)
               Paid-in Capital in Excess of Par Value, Common   XX (excess of par)
                   Converted bonds payable into common stock
                   (Note: No gain or loss recorded; also, an unamortized
                   bond discount would have been credited in the entry,
                   if appropriate.)

N. (LO 8) Mortgage Payable   XX (principal)
           Mortgage Interest Expense   XX (interest)
               Cash   XX (monthly payment)
                   Made monthly mortgage payment

O. (LO 8) Cash   XX (amount received)
               Notes Payable   XX (amount borrowed)
                   Borrowed on a long-term installment note

P. (LO 8) Notes Payable   XX (principal)
           Interest Expense   XX (interest)
               Cash   XX (installment payment)
                   Installment payment on note

Q. (LO 8) Equipment Under Capital Lease   XX (present value)
               Obligations Under Capital Lease   XX (present value)
                   To record capital lease contract

R. (LO 8) Depreciation Expense, Equipment Under
               Capital Lease   XX (amount allocated)
                   Accumulated Depreciation, Equipment Under
                       Capital Lease   XX (amount allocated)
                       To record depreciation expense on capital lease

S. (LO 8) Interest Expense   XX (amount incurred)
           Obligations Under Capital Lease   XX (amount reduced)
               Cash   XX (amount paid)
                   Made payment on capital lease

SELF-TEST

Test your knowledge of the chapter by choosing the best answer for each of the following items.

1. It is advantageous for a company to use financial leverage when
   a. it can earn more in assets than it pays in interest.
   b. it can earn less in assets than it pays in interest.
   c. its debt to equity ratio is very high.
   d. it needs to conserve cash.

2. A bond indenture is
   a. a bond on which interest payments are past due.
   b. a bond that is secured by specific assets of the issuing corporation.
   c. an agreement between the issuing corporation and the bondholders.
   d. a bond that is unsecured.

3. If the market rate of interest is lower than the face interest rate on the date of issuance, the bonds will
   a. sell at a discount.
   b. sell at a premium.
   c. sell at face value.
   d. not sell until the face interest rate is adjusted.

4. The current value of a bond can be determined by calculating the present value of the
   a. face value of the bond.
   b. interest payments.
   c. interest payments plus any discount or minus any premium.
   d. interest payments plus the face value of the bond.

5. When the straight-line method is used to amortize a bond discount, the interest expense for an interest period is calculated by
   a. deducting the amount of discount amortized for the period from the amount of cash paid for interest during the period.
   b. adding the amount of discount amortized for the period to the amount of cash paid for interest during the period.
   c. multiplying the face value of the bonds by the face interest rate.
   d. multiplying the carrying value of the bonds by the effective interest rate.

6. The total interest cost on a 9 percent, ten-year, $1,000 bond that is issued at 95 is
   a. $50.
   b. $140.
   c. $900.
   d. $950.

7. Metis Corporation issued a ten-year, 10 percent bond payable in 20x4 at a premium. During 20x5, the company's accountant failed to amortize any of the bond premium. The omission of the premium amortizaton
   a. does not affect the net income reported for 20x5.
   b. causes the net income for 20x5 to be overstated.
   c. causes the net income for 20x5 to be understated.
   d. causes retained earnings at the end of 20x5 to be overstated.

8. The Wang Corporation has authorized a bond issue with interest payment dates of January 1 and July 1. If the bonds are sold at the face amount on March 1, the cash Wang receives is equal to the face amount of the bonds
   a. plus the interest accrued from March 1 to July 1.
   b. plus the interest accrued from January 1 to March 1.
   c. minus the interest accrued from March 1 to July 1.
   d. minus the interest accrued from January 1 to March 1.

9. Bonds that contain a provision that allows the holders to exchange the bonds for other securities of the issuing corporation are called
   a. secured bonds.
   b. callable bonds.
   c. debenture bonds.
   d. convertible bonds.

10. Which of the following is most likely a capital lease?
   a. A five-year lease on a new building
   b. A two-year lease on a truck with an option to renew for one more year
   c. A five-year lease on a computer with an option to buy for a small amount at the end of the lease
   d. A monthly lease on a building that can be canceled with ninety days' notice

TESTING YOUR KNOWLEDGE

*Matching**

Match each term with its definition by writing the appropriate letter in the blank.

_____ 1. Bonds

_____ 2. Bond indenture

_____ 3. Secured bonds

_____ 4. Debentures

_____ 5. Term bonds

_____ 6. Serial bonds

_____ 7. Registered bonds

_____ 8. Coupon bonds

_____ 9. Callable bonds

_____ 10. Bond discount

_____ 11. Bond premium

_____ 12. Effective interest method

_____ 13. Capital lease

_____ 14. Operating lease

_____ 15. Convertible bonds

_____ 16. Pension plan

_____ 17. Pension fund

_____ 18. Bond certificate

_____ 19. Early extinguishment of debt

_____ 20. Zero coupon bonds

_____ 21. Financial leverage (trading on the equity)

a. Unsecured bonds

b. A lease that amounts to a sale

c. Bonds that may be retired by the company before maturity

d. Borrowing for the financial benefit of stockholders

e. The difference between face value and a lower amount paid for bonds

f. Bonds with detachable forms that are redeemed for interest

g. A true lease, recorded with debits to Rent Expense

h. Proof of a company's debt to a bondholder

i. Long-term debt instruments

j. Bonds whose owners receive interest by check directly from the company

k. The retirement of bonds prior to maturity

l. The amortization method based on carrying value

m. The difference between face value and a greater amount paid for bonds

n. A program whereby a company agrees to pay benefits to its employees when they retire

o. Bonds that mature on one specific date

p. The source of benefits that are paid to retirees

q. Bonds that are backed by certain assets

r. Bonds that may be exchanged for common stock

s. Bonds that mature in installments

t. Bonds whose holders receive no periodic interest, but that are issued at a large discount

u. The contract between the bondholder and the corporation

Note to student: The matching quiz might be completed more efficiently by starting with the definition and searching for the corresponding term.

Short Answer

Use the lines provided to answer each item.

1. Distinguish between the terms *debenture* and *indenture.*

   _____

   _____

   _____

   _____

2. Under what circumstances would a premium probably be received on a bond issue?

   _____

   _____

   _____

   _____

3. What is the formula for computing interest for a period of time?

   _____

   _____

   _____

4. When valuing a bond, what two components are added together to determine the present value of the bond?

   _____

   _____

5. State three advantages of issuing long-term debt rather than common stock.

   _____

   _____

   _____

   _____

   _____

   _____

True-False

Circle T if the statement is true, F if it is false. Please provide explanations for the false answers, using the blank lines at the end of the section.

T F   1. Bondholders are owners of a corporation.

T F   2. Financial leverage is also known as trading on the equity.

T F   3. Bond interest can be paid only when declared by the board of directors.

T F   4. Bonds with a lower interest rate than the market rate (for similar bonds) will probably sell at a discount.

T F   5. When a bond premium is amortized, the bond interest expense recorded is greater than the cash paid.

T F   6. When the effective interest method is used to amortize a bond discount, the amount amortized increases each year.

T F   7. When bonds are issued between interest dates, Bond Interest Expense is debited for accrued interest since the last interest date.

T F   8. As a bond premium is amortized, the carrying value of bonds payable decreases.

T F   9. When bonds are issued at a discount, the total interest cost to the issuing corporation equals the interest payments minus the bond discount.

T F 10. When bonds are retired, all of the premium or discount associated with the bonds must be canceled.

T F **11.** When the effective interest method is used to amortize a premium on bonds payable, the premium amortized decreases each year.

T F **12.** When bonds are issued at a premium, the total interest cost to the issuing corporation equals the interest payments minus the bond premium.

T F **13.** Under operating leases, assets should be recorded at the present value of future lease payments.

T F **14.** Pension expense is usually difficult to measure because it is based on many estimates, such as employee life expectancy and employee turnover.

T F **15.** When bonds are converted into stock, a gain or loss should be recorded.

T F **16.** Bond issue costs should be amortized over the life of the bonds.

T F **17.** Postretirement health care benefits should be expensed while the employee is still working.

T F **18.** A disadvantage of issuing long-term debt is the increased risk of default.

T F **19.** A low interest coverage ratio indicates a low risk of default on interest payments.

_____

_____

_____

_____

_____

_____

_____

_____

_____

_____

_____

_____

_____

Multiple Choice

Circle the letter of the best answer.

1. Assume that $900,000 of 5 percent bonds are issued (at face value) two months before the next semiannual interest date. Which of the following statements correctly describes the journal entry?
   a. Cash is debited for $800,000.
   b. Cash is debited for $807,500.
   c. Bond Interest Expense is credited for $7,500.
   d. Bond Interest Expense is credited for $15,000.

2. As a mortgage is paid off, the
   a. principal portion of the fixed payment increases.
   b. interest portion of the fixed payment increases.
   c. principal and interest portions do not change each interest period.
   d. monthly payments increase.

3. Unamortized Bond Premium is presented on the balance sheet as a(n)
   a. long-term asset.
   b. stockholders' equity account.
   c. deduction from Bonds Payable.
   d. addition to Bonds Payable.

4. When the interest dates on a bond issue are May 1 and November 1, the adjusting entry to record bond interest expense on December 31 might include a
   a. debit to Interest Payable.
   b. credit to Cash.
   c. credit to Unamortized Bond Discount.
   d. credit to Bond Interest Expense.

5. Under the effective interest method, as a discount is amortized each period, the
   a. amount amortized decreases.
   b. interest expense recorded increases.
   c. interest paid to bondholders increases.
   d. bonds' carrying value decreases.

6. Which of the following would probably be considered an operating lease?
   a. A 6-year lease on equipment with an option to renew for another 6 years
   b. A 5-year lease on machinery, cancelable at the end of the lease period by the lessor
   c. A 40-year lease on a building, equal to its useful life
   d. A 7-year lease on a company vehicle with an option to buy the vehicle for $1 at the end of the lease period

7. A $200,000 bond issue with a carrying value of $195,000 is called at 102 and retired. Which of the following statements about the journal entry prepared is true?
   a. An extraordinary gain of $5,000 is recorded.
   b. An extraordinary loss of $4,000 is recorded.
   c. An extraordinary loss of $9,000 is recorded.
   d. No gain or loss is recorded.

8. A company has $600,000 in bonds payable with an unamortized premium of $12,000. If one-third of the bonds are converted to common stock, the carrying value of the bonds payable will decrease by
   a. $196,000.
   b. $200,000.
   c. $204,000.
   d. $208,000.

APPLYING YOUR KNOWLEDGE

Exercises

1. A corporation issues $600,000 of 7 percent, 10-year bonds at 98½ on one of its semiannual interest dates. Assuming straight-line amortization, answer each of the following questions.
    a. What is the amount of the bond discount? $_____
    b. How much interest is paid on the next interest date? $_____
    c. How much bond interest expense is recorded on the next interest date? $_____
    d. After 3 years, what is the carrying value of the bonds? $_____

2. A corporation issues $500,000 of 7 percent, 20-year bonds at 110. Interest is paid semiannually, and the effective interest method is used for amortization. Assume that the market rate for similar investments is 6 percent and that the bonds are issued on an interest date.
    a. What amount was received for the bonds? $_____

    b. How much interest is paid each interest period? $_____
    c. How much bond interest expense is recorded on the first interest date? $_____
    d. How much of the premium is amortized on the first interest date? $_____
    e. What is the carrying value of the bonds after the first interest date? $_____

3. A corporation issued $600,000 of 8 percent, 10-year bonds at 106. In the space provided, calculate the total interest cost.

4. On December 31, 20x1, Kramer Company borrows $50,000 on a 10 percent installment note, to be paid annually over 5 years. In the journal provided on the next page, prepare the entry to record the note, as well as the December 31, 20x2, and December 31, 20x3, entries to record the first two annual payments. Assume that the principal is paid in equal installments and that the interest on the unpaid balance accrues annually.

General Journal				
Date		Description	Debit	Credit

5. Assume the same facts and requirements as in Exercise 4 on page 146, except that payments are made in equal installments of $13,190.

		General Journal		
Date		Description	Debit	Credit

Crossword Puzzle
for Chapters 10 and 11

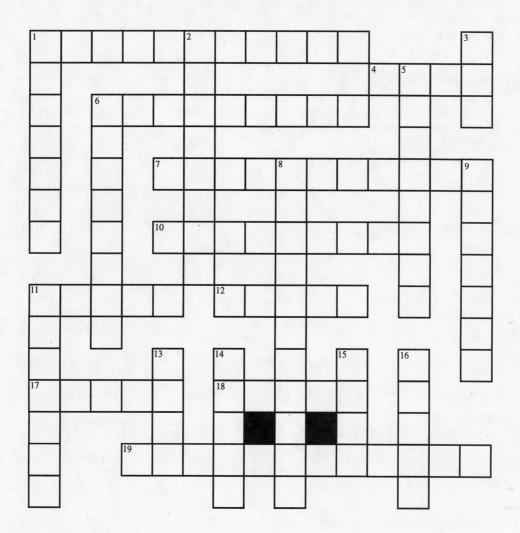

ACROSS

1. Contract for retirement income (2 words)
4. Depreciation estimate
6. Registered symbol or brand name
7. Note settled in a series of payments
10. Exclusive right to a market
11. Buys back (bonds) before maturity
12. Residual _____
17. Sale (of bonds)
18. Use another's property for a fee
19. Bonds, for example (2 words)

DOWN

1. Opposite of discount
2. Routine (repair)
3. _____ present value
5. _____ coverage ratio
6. Possessing physical substance
8. Depreciation method
9. Exchange (2 words)
11. _____ expenditure
13. _____ coupon bonds
14. Long-term asset account (abbr.)
15. Bonds with one maturity date
16. Older term for long-term assets

CHAPTER 12 CONTRIBUTED CAPITAL

REVIEWING THE CHAPTER

Objective 1: Identify and explain the management issues related to contributed capital.

1. A **corporation** is a business organization authorized by the state to conduct business and is a separate legal entity from its owners. It is the dominant form of American business because it is able to gather large amounts of capital.

2. The management of contributed capital, critical to the financing of a corporation, includes the issues of (a) managing under the corporate form of business, (b) using equity financing, (c) determining dividend policies, and (d) evaluating performance using return on equity. These issues will be addressed in the paragraphs to follow.

3. The corporate form of business has several advantages over the sole proprietorship and partnership. It is a separate legal entity and offers limited liability to the owners. It also offers ease of capital generation and ease of transfer of ownership. Other advantages are the lack of mutual agency in a corporation and its continuous existence. In addition, a corporate form of business allows centralized authority and responsibility and professional management.

4. The corporate form of business also has several disadvantages when compared with the sole proprietorship and partnership. It is subject to greater government regulation and **double taxation** (the corporation's income is subject to income taxes and its stockholders are taxed on any dividends). The limited liability of the owners can limit the amount a small corporation can borrow. In addition, separation of ownership and control may allow management to make harmful decisions.

5. Ownership in a corporation is evidenced by a document called a **stock certificate.** A stockholder sells stock by endorsing the stock certificate and sending it to the corporation's secretary or its transfer agent. The secretary or transfer agent is responsible for transferring the corporation's stock, maintaining stockholders' records, and preparing a list of stockholders for stockholders' meetings and for the payment of dividends. In addition, corporations often hire an **underwriter,** an intermediary between the corporation and the investing public, to help in their **initial public offering (IPO)** of capital stock. A corporation in this instance is said to be "going public."

6. The articles of incorporation (of a corporate charter) specify the **authorized stock,** or the maximum number of shares that the corporation is allowed to issue. **Par value** is the legal value of a share of stock. **Legal capital** equals the number of shares issued times the par value; it is the minimum amount that can be reported as contributed capital.

7. A **dividend** is a distribution of assets by a corporation to its stockholders, normally in cash. Dividends are usually stated as a specified dollar amount per share of stock and are declared by the board of directors (with the advice of senior management).

8. One may evaluate the amount of dividends received by referring to the **dividends yield,** which is calculated as follows:

$$\frac{\text{Dividends per Share}}{\text{Market Price per Share}}$$

Expressed as a percentage, the dividends yield measures the return, in terms of dividends, per share of stock.

9. The **price/earnings (P/E) ratio,** on the other hand, measures investors' confidence in the company's future. It is calculated as follows:

$$\frac{\text{Market Price per Share}}{\text{Earnings per Share}}$$

A price/earnings ratio of 15 times, for example, means that investors are confident enough in the company to pay $15 per share of stock for every dollar of earnings accruing to one share.

10. A number of factors affect the decision to pay dividends. Such factors include the extent of profitable operations, the expected volatility of earnings, and the actual amount of cash available for dividend payments.

11. One measure of management's performance is the **return on equity,** calculated as follows:

$$\frac{\text{Net Income}}{\text{Average Stockholders' Equity}}$$

Expressed as a percentage, the return on equity is affected by such management decisions as the issuance of stock and the acquisition of treasury stock.

Objective 2: Define start up and organization costs and state their effects on financial reporting.

12. The costs of forming a corporation, called **start up and organization costs,** include incorporation fees, attorneys' fees, stock-printing costs, accountants' fees, and other costs necessary for corporate formation. Such costs must be expensed when incurred.

Objective 3: Identify the components of stockholders' equity.

13. In a corporation's balance sheet, the owners' claims to the business are called stockholders' equity. The stockholders' equity section is divided into two parts: contributed capital (the stockholders' investments) and retained earnings (earnings that have remained in the business).

14. When only one type of stock is issued, it is called **common stock.** A second type of stock, called preferred stock, also can be issued. Because common stockholders' claim to assets on liquidation ranks behind that of creditors and preferred stockholders, common stock is considered the **residual equity** of a corporation.

15. **Issued stock** consists of shares that have been sold to stockholders. **Outstanding stock** consists of shares that have been issued, but not repurchased, by the issuing corporation. Treasury stock consists of shares bought back and being held by the corporation.

Objective 4: Account for cash dividends.

16. Dividends usually are stated as a specified dollar amount per share of stock and are declared by the board of directors. The **date of declaration** is the date the board of directors formally declares a dividend, specifying that the owners of the stock on the **date of record** will receive the dividends on the **date of payment.** After the date of record, stock is said to be **ex-dividend** (without dividend rights). A **liquidating dividend** is the return of contributed capital to the stockholders. It normally is paid when a company is going out of business or is reducing its operations.

17. When cash dividends are declared, Cash Dividends Declared is debited and Cash Dividends Payable is credited; when they are paid, Cash Dividends Payable is debited and Cash is credited. The Cash Dividends Declared account is closed to Retained Earnings at the end of the year. No journal entry is made on the date of record.

Objective 5: Identify the characteristics of preferred stock, including the effect on distribution of dividends.

18. Holders of **preferred stock** are given preference over common shareholders on dividend declaration and liquidation. Each share of preferred stock entitles its owner to a dividend each year. This dividend is a specific dollar amount or percentage of par value. Preferred stockholders receive their dividends before common stockholders receive anything. Once the preferred stockholders have received the annual dividends to which they are entitled, however, the common stockholders generally receive the remainder.

19. In addition, preferred stock can be (a) cumulative or noncumulative, (b) convertible or nonconvertible, and (c) callable. It usually has no voting rights.

a. If the stock is **cumulative preferred stock** and the preferred stockholders do not receive the full amount of their annual dividend, the unpaid amount is carried over to the next year. Unpaid back dividends are called **dividends in arrears** and should be disclosed either on the balance sheet or in a note to the financial statements. When the stock is **noncumulative preferred stock,** unpaid dividends are not carried over to the next period.

b. An owner of **convertible preferred stock** has the option to exchange each share of preferred stock for a set number of shares of common stock.

c. Most preferred stocks are **callable preferred stocks,** which means that the corporation has the right to buy the stock back at a specified call or redemption price. If the owner so desires, convertible preferred stock could alternatively be converted to common stock.

Objective 6: Account for the issuance of stock for cash and other assets.

20. Capital stock may or may not have a par value, depending on the specifications in the charter. When par value stock is issued, the Capital Stock account is credited for the legal capital (par value), and any excess is recorded as Paid-in Capital in Excess of Par Value. In the stockholders' equity section of the balance sheet, the entire amount is labeled Total Contributed Capital. On rare occasions, stock is issued at a discount (less than par value), requiring a debit to Discount on Capital Stock.

21. **No-par stock** is stock for which a par value has not been established. It can be issued with or without a stated value. **Stated value,** which is established by the board of directors, is the legal capital for a share of no-par stock. The total stated value is recorded in the Capital Stock account. Any amount received in excess of stated value is recorded as Paid-in Capital in Excess of Stated Value. If no stated value is set, the entire amount received is legal capital and is credited to Capital Stock.

22. Sometimes stock is issued in exchange for assets or for services received. This kind of transaction should be recorded at the fair market value of the stock. If the stock's fair market value cannot be determined, the fair market value of the assets or services received should be used.

Objective 7: Account for treasury stock.

23. **Treasury stock** is common or preferred stock that has been issued and reacquired by the issuing company. That is, it is issued but no longer outstanding. Treasury stock is purchased (a) to distribute to employees through stock option plans, (b) to maintain a favorable market for the company's stock, (c) to increase earnings per share, (d) to use in purchasing other companies, and (e) to prevent a hostile takeover of the company.

24. Treasury stock can be held indefinitely, reissued, or canceled, and has no rights until it is reissued. Treasury stock, the last item in the stockholders' equity section of the balance sheet, appears as a deduction from the total of contributed capital and retained earnings.

25. When treasury stock is purchased, its account is debited for the purchase cost. It may be reissued at cost, above cost, or below cost. When cash received from a reissue exceeds the cost, the difference is credited to Paid-in Capital, Treasury Stock. When cash received is less than cost, the difference is debited to Paid-in Capital, Treasury Stock (and Retained Earnings if needed). In no case should a gain or loss be recorded.

26. When treasury stock is retired, all the contributed capital associated with the retired shares must be removed from the accounts. When less is paid than was contributed originally, the difference is credited to Paid-in Capital, Retirement of Stock. When more is paid, the difference is debited to Retained Earnings.

Objective 8: Account for the exercise of stock options.

27. A **stock option plan** is an agreement whereby corporate employees can purchase a certain quantity of the company's stock at a certain price for a certain period of time. If the plan allows virtually all employees to purchase stock at the existing market price, then the journal entry on issue resembles the entry made when stock is sold to outsiders. However, if only certain employees (usually management) are allowed to purchase the corporation's stock in the future at a fixed price, the plan is said to be compensatory.

28. On the grant date, the amount by which the estimated fair value of the options (covered in a more advanced course) exceeds the option price is either (a) recorded as compensation expense over the grant period, or (b) reported in the notes to the financial statements. Most companies are expected to choose the latter approach, which would also require disclosure of the impact on income and earnings per share of not recording compensation expense.

A. (LO 4) Cash Dividends Declared   XX (amount declared)
              Cash Dividends Payable   XX (amount to be paid)
                  Declaration of a cash dividend to common or
                  preferred stockholders

B. (LO 4) Cash Dividends Payable   XX (amount paid)
              Cash   XX (amount paid)
                  Payment of cash dividends declared in A above

C. (LO 6) Cash   XX (amount invested)
              Common Stock   XX (legal capital amount)
                  Issued par value common stock for par value

D. (LO 6) Cash   XX (amount invested)
              Common Stock   XX (legal capital amount)
              Paid-in Capital in Excess of Par Value, Common   XX (excess of par)
                  Issued par value common stock for amount in excess
                  of par value

E. (LO 6) Cash   XX (amount invested)
              Common Stock   XX (legal capital amount)
                  Issued no-par common stock (no stated value
                  established)

F. (LO 6) Cash   XX (amount invested)
              Common Stock   XX (legal capital amount)
               Paid-in Capital in Excess of Stated Value, Common   XX (excess of stated value)
                  Issued no-par common stock with stated value for
                  amount in excess of stated value

G. (LO 6) Start up and Organization Expense   XX (fair market value of services)
              Common Stock   XX (par value)
               Paid-in Capital in Excess of Par Value, Common   XX (excess of par)
                  Issued par value common stock for incorporation
                  services

H. (LO 6) Land   XX (fair market value of stock)
              Common Stock   XX (par value)
               Paid-in Capital in Excess of Par Value, Common   XX (excess of par)
                  Issued par value common stock with a market value
                  in excess of par value for a piece of land

I. (LO 7) Treasury Stock, Common   XX (cost)
              Cash   XX (amount paid)
                  Acquired shares of the company's common stock

J. (LO 7) Cash   XX (amount received)
              Treasury Stock, Common   XX (cost)
                  Reissued shares of treasury stock at cost

K. (LO 7) Cash   XX (amount received)

                   Treasury Stock, Common   XX (cost)

                   Paid-in Capital, Treasury Stock   XX ("gain")

                      Sale of shares of treasury stock at amount above cost

L. (LO 7) Cash   XX (amount received)

                   Paid-in Capital, Treasury Stock   XX ("loss")

                   Retained Earnings (only if needed)   XX ("loss")

                      Treasury Stock, Common   XX (cost)

                      Sale of shares of treasury stock at amount below cost

M. (LO 7) Common Stock   XX (par value)

                   Paid-in Capital in Excess of Par Value, Common   XX (excess of par)

                   Retained Earnings (only if needed)   XX (premium paid)

                      Treasury Stock, Common   XX (cost)

                      Retirement of treasury stock; cost exceeded original

                      investment amount

N. (LO 7) If the treasury stock in M had been retired for an amount less than the original investment amount, then instead of Retained Earnings being debited for the excess paid, Paid-in Capital, Retirement of Stock would be credited for the difference.

O. (LO 8) Cash   XX (amount invested)

                   Common Stock   XX (par value)

                   Paid-in Capital in Excess of Par Value, Common   XX (excess of par)

                      Issued par value common stock under employee

                      stock option plan

SELF-TEST

Test your knowledge of the chapter by choosing the best answer for each of the following items.

1. One disadvantage of the corporate form of business is
   a. government regulation.
   b. centralized authority and responsibility.
   c. the corporation being a separate legal entity.
   d. continuous existence.

2. The start up and organization costs of a corporation should
   a. be recorded and maintained as an intangible asset for the life of the corporation.
   b. be recorded as an intangible asset and amortized over a reasonable length of time.
   c. be written off as an expense when incurred.
   d. not be incurred before the state grants the corporation its charter.

3. All of the following normally are found in the stockholders' equity section of a corporate balance sheet *except*
   a. paid-in capital in excess of par value.
   b. retained earnings.
   c. cash dividends payable.
   d. common stock.

4. The board of directors of the Hui Corporation declared a cash dividend on January 18, 20x8, to be paid on February 18, 20x8, to shareholders holding stock on February 2, 20x8. Given these facts, February 2, 20x8 is the
   a. date of declaration.
   b. date of record.
   c. payment date.
   d. ex-dividend date.

5. The journal entry to record the declaration of a cash dividend
   a. reduces assets.
   b. increases liabilities.
   c. increases total stockholders' equity.
   d. does not affect total stockholders' equity.

6. Dividends in arrears are dividends on
   a. noncumulative preferred stock that have not been declared for some specific period of time.
   b. cumulative preferred stock that have been declared but have not been paid.
   c. cumulative preferred stock that have not been declared for some specific period of time.
   d. common stock that can never be declared.

7. The par value of common stock represents the
   a. amount entered into the corporation's Common Stock account when shares are issued.
   b. exact amount the corporation receives when the stock is issued.
   c. liquidation value of the stock.
   d. stock's market value.

8. The Paid-in Capital in Excess of Stated Value account is used when
   a. the par value of capital stock is greater than the stated value.
   b. capital stock is sold at an amount greater than stated value.
   c. the market value of the stock rises above its stated value.
   d. the number of shares issued exceeds the stock's stated value.

9. Which of the following is properly deducted from stockholders' equity?
   a. Treasury stock
   b. Retained earnings
   c. Dividends in arrears
   d. Paid-in capital in excess of par value

10. A plan under which employees are allowed to purchase shares of stock in a company at a specified price is called a stock
    a. option plan.
    b. subscription plan.
    c. dividend plan.
    d. compensation plan.

TESTING YOUR KNOWLEDGE

*Matching**

Match each term with its definition by writing the appropriate letter in the blank.

_____ 1. Corporation

_____ 2. Start up and organization costs

_____ 3. Issued stock

_____ 4. Authorized stock

_____ 5. Outstanding stock

_____ 6. Common stock

_____ 7. Preferred stock

_____ 8. Dividends in arrears

_____ 9. Par value

_____ 10. No-par stock

_____ 11. Stated value

_____ 12. Treasury stock

_____ 13. Ex-dividend

_____ 14. Liquidating dividend

_____ 15. Convertible preferred stock

_____ 16. Callable preferred stock

_____ 17. Cumulative preferred stock

_____ 18. Stock option plan

_____ 19. Stock certificate

_____ 20. Residual equity

a. Unpaid back dividends

b. Descriptive of common stockholders' ownership in a corporation

c. Without dividend rights

d. The amount of legal capital of a share of no-par stock

e. Stock that is presently held by stockholders

f. The dominant form of business in the United States

g. The type of stock whose holders have prior claim over common stockholders to dividends

h. Issued stock that has been reacquired by the corporation

i. Stock whose unpaid dividends "carry over" to future years until paid

j. Proof of ownership in a corporation

k. Expenditures necessary to form a corporation

l. The maximum amount of stock that a corporation may issue

m. The name of the stock when only one type of stock has been issued

n. Stock that may or may not have a stated value

o. The legal value for stock that is stated in the charter

p. Stock that has been sold to stockholders, and may or may not have been bought back by the corporation

q. Stock that may be bought back at the option of the issuing corporation

r. An agreement whereby certain employees may purchase stock at a fixed price

s. The return of contributed capital to a corporation's stockholders

t. Preferred stock that an investor may exchange for common stock

---

Note to student: The matching quiz might be completed more efficiently by starting with the definition and searching for the corresponding term.

Short Answer

Use the lines provided to answer each item.

1. List eight advantages of the corporate form of business.

   _____

   _____

   _____

   _____

   _____

   _____

   _____

   _____

2. List four disadvantages of the corporate form of business.

   _____

   _____

   _____

   _____

3. Name the two major portions of the stockholders' equity section of a balance sheet.

   _____

   _____

4. Preferred shareholders are given preference over common shareholders under what two circumstances?

   _____

   _____

5. Under what circumstance would a corporation have more shares of stock issued than outstanding?

   _____

   _____

   _____

6. What is the difference between treasury stock and unissued stock?

   _____

   _____

   _____

   _____

True-False

Circle T if the statement is true, F if it is false. Please provide explanations for the false answers, using the blank lines at the end of the section.

T F 1. Corporate income is taxed twice, at the corporate level and at the individual level (when it is distributed as dividends).

T F 2. The concept of legal capital was established to protect the corporation's stockholders.

T F 3. Ordinarily, creditors cannot attach the personal assets of the corporation's stockholders.

T F 4. Start up and organization costs must be charged as expenses in the year the corporation is formed.

T F 5. Contributed capital consists of capital stock plus paid-in capital in excess of par (stated) value.

T F 6. A transfer agent keeps records of stock transactions.

T F **7.** Preferred stock cannot be both convertible and cumulative.

T F **8.** Dividends in arrears do not exist when preferred stock is noncumulative.

T F **9.** The worth of a share of stock can be measured by its par value.

T F **10.** The purchase of treasury stock reduces total assets and total stockholders' equity.

T F **11.** Preferred stockholders are guaranteed annual dividends; common stockholders are not.

T F **12.** Preferred stock is considered the residual equity of a corporation.

T F **13.** The amount of compensation in connection with a stock option plan is measured on the date the option is exercised.

T F **14.** On the date a dividend is paid, total assets and total stockholders' equity decrease.

T F **15.** Dividends in arrears should appear as a liability on the balance sheet.

T F **16.** Treasury Stock is listed on the balance sheet as an asset.

T F **17.** When a corporation sells stock to the investing public, it often engages the services of an underwriter.

T F **18.** When treasury stock is sold at more than its cost, Gain on Sale of Treasury Stock is credited.

T F **19.** The higher the market price per share of stock, the lower the dividends yield.

T F **20.** The purchase of treasury stock by a corporation will decrease its return on equity.

T F **21.** The higher the price/earnings ratio, the higher is investors' confidence in a company's future.

Multiple Choice

Circle the letter of the best answer.

1. When treasury stock is reissued below cost, all of the following may be true *except*
   a. Retained Earnings is debited.
   b. Treasury Stock is credited.
   c. Paid-in Capital, Treasury Stock is debited.
   d. Loss on Reissue of Treasury Stock is debited.

2. The purchase of treasury stock does *not* affect
   a. the amount of stock outstanding.
   b. the amount of stock issued.
   c. total assets.
   d. total stockholders' equity.

3. Which of the following statements is true?
   a. Outstanding shares plus issued shares equal authorized shares.
   b. Unissued shares plus outstanding shares equal authorized shares.
   c. Authorized shares minus unissued shares equal issued shares.
   d. Unissued shares minus issued shares equal outstanding shares.

4. Dace Corporation has outstanding 1,000 shares of $100 par value, 7 percent noncumulative preferred stock, and 20,000 shares of $10 par value common stock. Last year, the company paid no dividends; this year, it distributed $40,000 in dividends. What portion of this $40,000 should common stockholders receive?
   a. $0
   b. $2,800
   c. $26,000
   d. $33,000

5. Which of the following is *not* a characteristic of corporations in general?
   a. Separation of ownership and management
   b. Ease of transfer of ownership
   c. Double taxation
   d. Unlimited liability of stockholders

6. On which of the following dates is a journal entry made?
   a. Date of record
   b. Date of payment
   c. Date of declaration
   d. Both **b** and **c**

7. Stock is said to be "ex-dividend" after
   a. it has been sold to another party.
   b. the date of record.
   c. the date of payment.
   d. the date of declaration.

8. When callable preferred stock is called and surrendered, the stockholder is *not* entitled to
   a. a call premium.
   b. the par value of the stock.
   c. any dividends in arrears.
   d. the market value of the stock.

APPLYING YOUR KNOWLEDGE

Exercises

1. In the journal provided, prepare the entries for the
   following transactions.

Jan.   1   Paid $8,000 in legal and incorporation fees to
form Jade Corporation.

Feb.   9   Issued 5,000 shares of $100 par value common stock at $115 per share.

Apr. 12   Exchanged 2,000 shares of 4 percent, no-par
preferred stock, which had a stated value of
$100 per share, for a building with a market
value of $240,000. The market value of the
stock cannot be determined.

June 23   Declared a $4 per share dividend on the preferred stock, to be paid on July 8. The date of
record is July 1.

July   8   Paid the dividend declared on June 23.

Dec. 20   The corporation's president exercised her option to purchase 200 shares of $100 par value
common stock at $110 per share. The market
price on that date was $130 per share.

	General Journal			
Date		**Description**	**Debit**	**Credit**

Contributed Capital

2. Singh Corporation began operation on August 10, 20x1, by issuing 50,000 shares of $10 par value common stock at $50 per share. As of January 1, 20x3, its capital structure was the same. For each of the following sets of facts for January 20x3, prepare the proper entry in the journal provided. In all cases, assume sufficient cash and retained earnings.

Jan. 12 The corporation purchases 5,000 shares of stock from the stockholders at $60 per share.

20 The corporation reissues 2,000 shares of treasury stock at $65 per share.

27 The corporation reissues another 2,000 shares of treasury stock at $58 per share.

31 The corporation retires the remaining 1,000 treasury shares.

		General Journal		
Date		**Description**	**Debit**	**Credit**

3. McKeney Corporation paid no dividends in its first two years of operations. In its third year, it paid $51,000 in dividends. For all three years, there have been 1,000 shares of 6 percent, $100 par value cumulative preferred stock, and 5,000 shares of $10 par value common stock outstanding. How much of the $51,000 in dividends goes to

  a. preferred stockholders? $ _____

  b. common stockholders? $ _____

4. Assume the same facts as in Exercise 3 at the left, except that McKeney's preferred stock is *noncumulative*. How much of the $51,000 in dividends goes to

  a. preferred stockholders? $ _____

  b. common stockholders? $ _____

CHAPTER 13 THE CORPORATE INCOME STATEMENT AND THE STATEMENT OF STOCKHOLDERS' EQUITY

REVIEWING THE CHAPTER

Objective 1: Identify the issues related to evaluating the quality of a company's earnings.

1. The most commonly used predictors of a company's performance are expected changes in earnings per share and in return on equity. Because net income is a component of both these ratios, the **quality of earnings** must be good if the measure is to be valid. The quality of earnings is affected by (a) the accounting methods and estimates the company's management chooses and (b) the nature of nonoperating items on the income statement.

2. A different net income figure results, for example, when different estimates and procedures for dealing with uncollectible accounts, inventory, depreciation, depletion, and amortization are chosen. In general, the method that produces a lower, or more conservative, figure also produces a better quality of earnings. In addition, nonoperating and nonrecurring items, such as discontinued operations, extraordinary gains and losses, and the effects of accounting changes, can impair comparability if the financial analyst refers only to the bottom-line figure. Fortunately, generally accepted accounting principles require that the significant accounting policies are both explained (in the notes to the financial statements) and applied consistently wherever possible.

Objective 2: Prepare a corporate income statement.

3. Corporate income statements should present **comprehensive income**—the change in a company's equity during a period from sources other than owners and includes net income, change in unrealized investment gains and losses, and other items affecting equity. This approach to the measurement of income has resulted in several items being added to the income statement—discontinued operations, extraordinary items, and accounting changes. In addition, earnings per share figures must be disclosed.

Objective 3: Show the relationships among income taxes expense, deferred income taxes, and net of taxes.

4. Corporate taxable income is determined by subtracting allowable business deductions from includable gross income. Tax rates currently range from a 15 percent to a 39 percent marginal rate.

5. Computing income taxes for financial reporting differs from computing income taxes due the government for the same accounting period. This difference is caused by the fact that financial reporting income is governed by generally accepted accounting principles, whereas taxable income is governed by the Internal Revenue Code.

6. When income for financial reporting differs materially from taxable income, the **income tax allocation** technique should be used. Under this method, the difference between the current tax expense and income tax expense is debited or credited to an account called **Deferred Income Taxes.** Adjustments to this account must be made in light of legislated changes in income tax laws and regulations in the current year.

7. Deferred income taxes are the result of temporary differences in the treatment of certain items (such as depreciation) for tax and financial reporting purposes. They are classified as current or noncurrent, depending upon the classification of the related asset or liability that created the temporary difference.

8. Certain income statement items must be reported **net of taxes** to avoid distorting net operating income. These items are discontinued operations, extraordinary gains and losses, and accounting changes.

Objective 4: Describe the disclosure on the income statement of discontinued operations, extraordinary items, and accounting changes.

9. The results of operations for the period and any gains or losses from the **discontinued operations** of a segment of a business should be disclosed (net of taxes) after income from continuing operations. A **segment** is defined as a separate major line of business or class of customer.

10. An **extraordinary item** is an event that is unusual and occurs infrequently. Extraordinary items that are material in amount should be disclosed separately on the income statement (net of taxes) after discontinued operations.

11. Extraordinary gains and losses arise from such events as natural disasters, theft, the passage of a new law, the takeover of property by a foreign government, and the early retirement of debt.

12. A company can change from one accounting principle to another (e.g., from FIFO to LIFO) only if it can justify the new method as better accounting practice. The change must be disclosed in the financial statements. The **cumulative effect of an accounting change** on prior years (net of taxes) should appear on the income statement after extraordinary items.

Objective 5: Compute earnings per share.

13. Readers of financial statements use the earnings per share figure to judge a company's perform-

ance, to estimate its future earnings and to compare it with other companies. Earnings per share figures should be disclosed for (a) income from continuing operations, (b) income before extraordinary items and the cumulative effect of accounting changes, (c) the cumulative effect of accounting changes, and (d) net income. These figures should appear on the face of the income statement.

14. A company that has issued no securities that are convertible into common stock has a **simple capital structure.** In this case, only **basic earnings per share** would be presented, the calculation of which is

$$\frac{\text{Net Income} - \text{Nonconvertible Preferred Dividends}}{\text{Weighted-Average Common Shares Outstanding}}$$

15. A company that has issued securities that can be converted into common stock has a **complex capital structure. Potentially dilutive securities,** such as stock options and convertible preferred stocks or bonds, are so-named because they have the potential to decrease earnings per share. In this case, a dual presentation of basic and **diluted earnings per share** is required. The latter figure shows the maximum potential effect of dilution on the common stockholders' ownership position.

Objective 6: Prepare a statement of stockholders' equity.

16. The **statement of stockholders' equity** can be used in place of the statement of retained earnings. It is a labeled computation of the changes in the stockholders' equity accounts during the accounting period. It contains all the components of the statement of retained earnings, as well as a summary of the period's stock transactions.

17. **Retained earnings** are the profits that a corporation has earned since its beginning, minus any losses, dividends declared, or transfers to contributed capital. Ordinarily, Retained Earnings has a credit balance. When a debit balance exists, the corporation is said to have a **deficit.** Retained earnings are not the same as cash or any other asset, but simply an intangible representation of earnings "plowed back into the business."

18. Retained earnings can be unrestricted or restricted. Unrestricted retained earnings dictate the asset amount (if available) that can be distributed to stockholders as dividends. A **restriction on retained earnings** dictates the asset amount that must be retained in the business for other

purposes. Retained earnings are restricted for contractual or legal reasons, or by voluntary actions of the board of directors. Restrictions on retained earnings are disclosed most commonly in the notes to the financial statements.

Objective 7: Account for stock dividends and stock splits.

19. A **stock dividend** is a proportional distribution of shares of stock to a corporation's stockholders. Stock dividends are declared to (a) give evidence of the company's success without paying a cash dividend, (b) reduce a stock's market price, (c) allow a nontaxable distribution, and (d) increase the company's permanent capital. The result of a stock dividend is the transfer of a part of retained earnings to contributed capital. For a small stock dividend (less than 20 to 25 percent), the market value of the shares distributed is transferred from retained earnings. For a large stock dividend (greater than 20 to 25 percent), the par or stated value is transferred. A stock dividend does not change total stockholders' equity or any individual's proportionate equity in the company.

20. A **stock split** is an increase in the number of shares of stock outstanding, with a corresponding decrease in the par or stated value of the stock. For example, a 3 for 1 split on 40,000 shares of $30 par value would result in the distribution of 80,000 additional shares. (That is, someone who owned one share now would own three shares.) The par value would be reduced to $10. A stock split does not increase the number of shares authorized; nor does it affect the balances in stockholders' equity.

21. The purpose of a stock split is to improve the stock's marketability by pushing its market price down. In the example above, if the stock was selling for $180 per share, a 3 for 1 split probably would cause the market price to fall to about $60 per share. A memorandum entry should be made for a stock split, disclosing the decrease in par or stated value as well as the increase in the number of shares of stock outstanding.

Objective 8: Calculate book value per share.

22. The **book value** of a share of stock equals the net assets represented by one share of a company's stock. If the company has common stock only, the book value per share is arrived at by dividing stockholders' equity by the number of outstanding and distributable shares. When the company also has preferred stock, the call value of the preferred stock plus any dividends in arrears are deducted from stockholders' equity in computing the **book value per share** of common stock.

Summary of Journal Entries Introduced in Chapter 13

A. (LO 3)   Income Taxes Expense   XX (amount per GAAP)
     Income Taxes Payable   XX (currently payable)
     Deferred Income Taxes   XX (eventually payable)
       To record estimated current and deferred income taxes

B. (LO 7)   Stock Dividends Declared   XX (amount transferred)
     Common Stock Distributable   XX (par value amount)
     Paid-in Capital in Excess of Par Value, Common XX (excess of par)
       Declared a stock dividend on common stock

C. (LO 7)   Common Stock Distributable   XX (par value amount)
     Common Stock   XX (par value amount)
       Distribution of a stock dividend

Test your knowledge of the chapter by choosing the best answer for each of the following items.

1. The balance of the Retained Earnings account represents
   a. an excess of revenues over expenses for the most current operating period.
   b. the profits of a company since its inception, less any losses, dividends to stockholders, or transfers to contributed capital.
   c. cash set aside for specific future uses.
   d. cash available for daily operations.

2. A corporation should account for the declaration of a 3 percent stock dividend by
   a. transferring from retained earnings to contributed capital an amount equal to the market value of the dividend shares.
   b. transferring from retained earnings to contributed capital an amount equal to the legal capital represented by the dividend shares.
   c. making only a memorandum entry in the general journal.
   d. transferring from retained earnings to contributed capital whatever amount the board of directors deems appropriate.

3. Which of the following increases the number of shares of common stock outstanding?
   a. A stock split
   b. A restriction on retained earnings
   c. Treasury stock
   d. A cash dividend

4. When retained earnings are restricted, total retained earnings
   a. increase.
   b. decrease.
   c. may increase or decrease.
   d. are unaffected.

5. The purpose of a statement of stockholders' equity is to
   a. summarize the changes in the components of stockholders' equity over the accounting period.
   b. disclose the computation of book value per share of stock.
   c. budget for the transactions expected to occur during the forthcoming period.
   d. replace the statement of retained earnings.

6. All of the following elements of a corporation's common stock can be determined from the accounting records *except*
   a. par value.
   b. stated value.
   c. book value.
   d. market value.

7. Which of the following items appears on the corporate income statement before income from continuing operations?
   a. Income from operations of a discontinued segment
   b. Income taxes expense
   c. The cumulative effect of a change in accounting principle
   d. An extraordinary gain

8. When there is a difference in the timing of revenues and expenses for accounting and for income tax purposes, it is usually necessary to
   a. prepare an adjusting entry.
   b. adjust figures on the corporate tax return.
   c. perform income tax allocation procedures.
   d. do nothing because the difference is a result of two different sets of rules.

9. A loss due to discontinued operations should be reported on the income statement
   a. before both extraordinary items and the cumulative effect of an accounting change.
   b. before the cumulative effect of an accounting change and after extraordinary items.
   c. after both extraordinary items and the cumulative effect of an accounting change.
   d. after the cumulative effect of an accounting change and before extraordinary items.

10. Which of the following would be involved in the computation of earnings per common share for a company with a simple capital structure?
    a. Common shares authorized
    b. Dividends declared on nonconvertible preferred stock
    c. The shares of nonconvertible preferred stock outstanding
    d. Treasury shares

TESTING YOUR KNOWLEDGE

*Matching**

Match each term with its definition by writing the appropriate letter in the blank.

_____ 1. Retained earnings

_____ 2. Deficit

_____ 3. Statement of stockholders' equity

_____ 4. Income tax allocation

_____ 5. Simple capital structure

_____ 6. Complex capital structure

_____ 7. Discontinued operations

_____ 8. Comprehensive income

_____ 9. Stock dividend

_____ 10. Stock split

_____ 11. Restricted retained earnings

_____ 12. Segments

_____ 13. Potentially dilutive securities

_____ 14. Extraordinary item

_____ 15. Earnings per share

_____ 16. Accounting change

_____ 17. Book value per share

a. An unusual and infrequent gain or loss

b. The makeup of a corporation that has issued convertible securities

c. A negative figure for retained earnings

d. Distinct parts of business operations

e. A summary of the changes in stockholders' equity accounts during the period

f. The net assets represented by one share of a company's stock

g. The change in a company's equity during a period from sources other than owners, including net income, change in unrealized investment gains and losses, and other items affecting equity

h. Use of a different but more appropriate accounting method

i. A proportional distribution of stock to a corporation's stockholders

j. The profits that a corporation has earned since its inception, minus any losses, dividends declared, or transfers to contributed capital

k. A measure of net income earned for each share of common stock

l. A corporate stock maneuver in which par or stated value is changed

m. The makeup of a corporation that has not issued convertible securities

n. The income statement section immediately before extraordinary gains or losses

o. The technique to reconcile accounting income and taxable income

p. The quantity of assets that are not available for dividends

q. Options and convertible preferred stocks that could lower the earnings per share figure

---

Note to student: The matching quiz might be completed more efficiently by starting with the definition and searching for the corresponding term.

Short Answer

Use the lines provided to answer each item.

1. List three ways in which the Retained Earnings account can be reduced.

   _____

   _____

   _____

2. What are the two major distinctions between a stock dividend and a stock split?

   _____

   _____

   _____

   _____

3. What two conditions must be met for an item to qualify as extraordinary?

   _____

   _____

4. Number the following items to indicate their order of appearance on an income statement:

   _____ Cumulative Effect of Accounting Change

   _____ Revenues

   _____ Extraordinary Gains and Losses

   _____ Net Income

   _____ Discontinued Operations

   _____ Income from Continuing Operations

True-False

Circle T if the statement is true, F if it is false. Please provide explanations for the false answers, using the blank lines at the end of the section.

T F **1.** If an extraordinary gain of $20,000 has occurred, it should be reported net of taxes at more than $20,000.

T F **2.** A restriction on retained earnings represents cash set aside for a special purpose.

T F **3.** The book value of a share of common stock decreases when dividends are declared.

T F **4.** After a stock dividend is distributed, each stockholder owns a greater percentage of the corporation.

T F **5.** The market value of a stock on the date a small stock dividend is declared has no bearing on the journal entry.

T F **6.** The main purpose of a stock split is to reduce the stock's par value.

T F **7.** A gain on the sale of a plant asset qualifies as an extraordinary item.

T F **8.** Extraordinary items should appear on the statement of stockholders' equity.

T F **9.** The effect of a change from straight-line depreciation to accelerated depreciation should be reported on the income statement immediately after extraordinary items.

T F **10.** Common Stock Distributable is a current liability on the balance sheet.

T F **11.** Both basic and diluted earnings per share data should be provided for a corporation with a complex capital structure.

T F 12. If taxable income always equaled accounting income, there would be no need for income tax allocation.

T F 13. The quality of earnings is affected by the existence of an extraordinary item on the income statement.

T F 14. Potentially dilutive securities are included in the calculation of basic earnings per share.

T F 15. Stock Dividends Declared is closed to Retained Earnings at the end of the accounting period.

_____

_____

_____

_____

_____

_____

_____

_____

_____

_____

_____

_____

_____

_____

_____

_____

_____

_____

_____

_____

Multiple Choice

Circle the letter of the best answer.

1. Which of the following has no effect on retained earnings?
   a. Stock split
   b. Stock dividend
   c. Cash dividend
   d. Net loss

2. A company with 10,000 shares of common stock outstanding distributed a 10 percent stock dividend and then split its stock 4 for 1. How many shares are now outstanding?
   a. 2,750
   b. 41,000
   c. 44,000
   d. 55,000

3. When retained earnings are restricted, which of the following statements is true?
   a. Total retained earnings increase.
   b. The company is no longer limited in the amount of dividends it can pay.
   c. Total retained earnings are reduced.
   d. Total stockholders' equity remains the same.

4. On the date that a stock dividend is distributed,
   a. Common Stock Distributable is credited.
   b. Cash is credited.
   c. Retained Earnings remains the same.
   d. no entry is made.

5. The effect of an accounting change should appear on
   a. the income statement.
   b. the balance sheet.
   c. the statement of stockholders' equity.
   d. no financial statement.

6. Cohen Corporation had 60,000 shares of common stock outstanding from January 1 to October 1, and 40,000 shares outstanding from October 1 to December 31. What is the weighted-average number of shares used to calculate earnings per share?
   a. 45,000 shares
   b. 50,000 shares
   c. 55,000 shares
   d. 100,000 shares

7. If retained earnings were $70,000 on January 1, 20xx, and $100,000 on December 31, 20xx, and if cash dividends of $15,000 were declared and paid during the year, net income for the year must have been
   a. $30,000.
   b. $45,000.
   c. $55,000.
   d. $85,000.

8. Which of the following would *not* appear on a statement of stockholders' equity?
   a. Conversion of preferred stock into common stock
   b. Dividends declared
   c. Discontinued operations
   d. Purchase of treasury stock

9. A corporation has issued only one type of stock and wants to compute book value per share. It needs all the information below *except*
   a. retained earnings.
   b. the current year's dividends.
   c. total contributed capital.
   d. total shares outstanding and distributable.

10. Retained earnings
    a. are the same as cash.
    b. are the amount invested by stockholders in a corporation.
    c. equal cumulative profits, less losses and dividends declared and transfers to contributed capital.
    d. are not affected by revenues and expenses.

11. The quality of a company's earnings may be affected by
    a. the countries in which the company operates.
    b. the choice of independent auditors.
    c. the industry in which the company operates.
    d. the accounting methods used by the company.

APPLYING YOUR KNOWLEDGE

Exercises

1. For each of the following sets of facts, prepare the
proper entry in the journal provided.

Sept. 1 Piat Corporation begins operations by issuing 10,000 shares of $100 par value common
stock at $120 per share.

Mar. 7 A 5 percent stock dividend is declared. The
market price of the stock is $130 per share on
March 7.

   30 This is the date of record for the stock dividend.

Apr. 13 The stock dividend is distributed.

General Journal				
Date		Description	Debit	Credit

2. A company has $100,000 in operating income before taxes. It also had an extraordinary loss of $30,000 when lightning struck one of its warehouses. The company must pay a 40 percent tax on all items. Complete the partial income statement in good form.

Operating Income Before Taxes	$100,000

3. Crown Corporation had taxable income of $40,000, $40,000, and $80,000 in 20x1, 20x2, and 20x3, respectively. Its income for accounting purposes was $60,000, $30,000, and $70,000 for 20x1, 20x2, and 20x3, respectively. The difference between taxable income and accounting income was due to $30,000 in expenses that were deductible in full for tax purposes in 20x1 but were expensed one-third per year for accounting purposes. Make the correct journal entry to record income taxes in each of the three years. Assume a 40 percent tax rate.

General Journal				
Date		**Description**	**Debit**	**Credit**

4. Drumheller Corporation's balance sheet as of December 31, 20xx, includes the following information regarding stockholders' equity:

Contributed Capital		
Preferred Stock, $50 par value, 7% cumulative, 4,000 shares authorized, issued, and outstanding		$200,000
Common Stock, no-par, 30,000 shares authorized, issued, and outstanding		360,000
Paid-in Capital in Excess of Par Value, Preferred		40,000
Total Contributed Capital		$600,000
Retained Earnings		80,000
Total Stockholders' Equity		$680,000

Dividends in arrears total $28,000.

In the space that follows, compute the book value per share of both preferred stock and common stock.

5. Throughout 20xx, Sacchi Corporation had 10,000 shares of common stock outstanding, as well as 30,000 shares of nonconvertible preferred stock. Net income for the year was $50,000, preferred dividends totaled $20,000, and common dividends totaled $5,000. In the space below, calculate basic earnings per share.

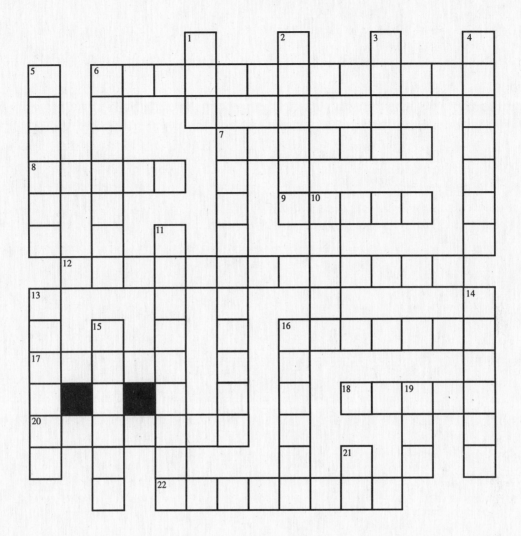

ACROSS

6. All-inclusive income
7. Dividends in _____
8. A legal capital designation (hyphenated)
9. Corporate stock maneuver
12. Unusual and infrequent (event)
16. Portion of business operations
17. Buy and sell investments
18. _____ earnings per share
20. Cancelled, as treasury stock
22. Ex-_____

DOWN

1. First-time public stock issue, for short
2. Stock units
3. Financial statement reader
4. Negative retained earnings
5. Mutual _____
6. Capital structure type
7. Maximum number of shares allowed to be issued
10. _____/earnings ratio
11. Type of stock
13. _____ on equity
14. Equity securities
15. Time value of money multiplier
16. Stock value for 8-Across
19. Overseer of publicly-owned corporations (abbr.)
21. Paid-_____ Capital

The Corporate Income Statement and the Statement of Stockholders' Equity

CHAPTER 14 THE STATEMENT OF CASH FLOWS

REVIEWING THE CHAPTER

Objective 1: Describe the statement of cash flows, and define *cash* **and** *cash equivalents.*

1. The **statement of cash flows** is considered a major financial statement, as are the income statement, balance sheet, and statement of stockholders' equity. The statement of cash flows, however, provides much information and answers certain questions that the other three statements do not. Its presentation is required by the FASB.

2. The statement of cash flows shows the effect on **cash** and cash equivalents of the operating, investing, and financing activities of a company for an accounting period. **Cash equivalents** are short-term, highly liquid investments such as money market accounts, commercial paper (short-term notes), and U.S. Treasury bills. Short-term investments (marketable securities) are *not* considered cash equivalents.

Objective 2: State the principal purposes and uses of the statement of cash flows.

3. The principal purpose of the statement of cash flows is to provide information about a company's cash receipts and cash payments during an accounting period. This goal is in accordance with the FASB's "Statement of Financial Accounting Concepts No. 1," which states that financial statements should provide investors and creditors with information regarding the business's cash flows. The statement of cash flows' secondary purpose is to provide information about a company's operating, investing, and financing activities during the period.

4. Investors and creditors can use the statement of cash flows to assess such things as the company's ability to generate positive future cash flows, ability to pay its liabilities, ability to pay dividends, and need for additional financing. In addition, management can use the statement of cash flows (among other things) to assess the debt-paying ability of the business, determine dividend policy, and plan for investing and financing needs.

Objective 3: Identify the principal components of the classifications of cash flows, and state the significance of noncash investing and financing transactions.

5. The statement of cash flows categorizes cash receipts and cash payments as operating, investing, and financing activities.
   a. **Operating activities** include receiving cash from customers from the sale of goods and services, receiving interest and dividends on loans and investments, receiving cash from the sale of trading securities, and making cash payments for wages, goods and services, interest, taxes, and purchases of trading securities.
   b. **Investing activities** include purchasing and selling long-term assets and marketable securities (other than trading securities or cash

equivalents) as well as making and collecting on loans to other entities.

c. **Financing activities** include issuing and buying back capital stock as well as borrowing and repaying loans on a short- or long-term basis (i.e., issuing bonds and notes). Dividends paid would also be included in this category, but repayment of accounts payable or accrued liabilities would not.

6. The statement of cash flows should include a separate schedule of **noncash investing and financing transactions,** involving only long-term assets, long-term liabilities, or stockholders' equity. Transactions such as the issuance of a mortgage for land or the conversion of bonds into stock represent simultaneous investing and financing activities that do not, however, result in an inflow or outflow of cash.

Objective 4: Analyze the statement of cash flows.

7. The statement of cash flows can be analyzed by examining certain relationships. Two such cash-flow relationships, or measures, are cash-generating efficiency and free cash flow.

8. **Cash-generating efficiency,** which focuses on net cash flows from operating activities, is the ability of a company to generate cash from its current or continuing operations. It may be expressed as cash flow yield, cash flows to sales, or cash flows to assets.

a. **Cash flow yield** equals net cash flows from operating activities divided by net income (or income from continuing operations). A cash flow yield of 2.0 times, for example, means that operating activities have generated twice as much cash flow as net income.

b. **Cash flows to sales** equals net cash flows from operating activities divided by net sales. A ratio of 5.7 percent, for example, means that operating cash flows of 5.7 cents have been generated for every dollar of net sales.

c. **Cash flows to assets** equals net cash flows from operating activities divided by average total assets. A ratio of 4.8 percent, for example, means that operating cash flows of 4.8 cents have been generated for every dollar of average total assets.

9. **Free cash flow** is a measure of cash remaining from operating activities after providing for certain commitments. It equals net cash flows from operating activities minus dividends minus net

capital expenditures (purchases minus sales of plant assets). A *positive* free cash flow means that the company has met its cash commitments and has cash remaining to reduce debt or expand further. A *negative* free cash flow means that the company will have to sell investments, borrow money, or issue stock to continue at its planned levels.

10. As is true with all financial statement ratios, the trends in the cash-generating efficiency and free cash flow over several years should be examined to analyze a company's cash flows.

Objective 5: Use the indirect method to determine cash flows from operating activities.

11. In the formal statement of cash flows, individual cash inflows from operating, investing, and financing activities are shown separately in their respective categories. To prepare the statement, one needs to examine a comparative balance sheet, the current income statement, and additional information about transactions affecting noncurrent accounts during the period. The four steps in statement preparation are (1) determining cash flows from operating activities, (2) determining cash flows from investing activities, (3) determining cash flows from financing activities, and (4) presenting the information obtained in the first three steps in the form of a statement of cash flows.

12. Cash flows from operating activities result from converting accrual-basis net income to a cash basis and may be determined using either the **direct method** or the **indirect method.**

13. Under the indirect method, the net cash flows from operating activities is determined by taking net income and adding or deducting items that do not affect cash flow from operations. Items to add include depreciation expense, amortization expense, depletion expense, losses, decreases in certain current assets (accounts receivable, inventory, and prepaid expenses), and increases in certain current liabilities (accounts payable, accrued liabilities, and income taxes payable). Items to deduct include gains, increases in certain current assets (see above), and decreases in certain current liabilities (see above). The direct and indirect methods produce the same results and are both considered GAAP. The FASB, however, recommends use of the direct method accompanied by a separate schedule (the indirect method) reconciling net income to net cash flows.

Objective 6a: Determine cash flows from investing activities.

14. When determining cash flows from investing and financing activities, the objective is to explain the change in the appropriate account balances from one year to the next. As previously stated, investing activities focus on the purchase and sale of long-term assets and short-term investments (other than trading securities or cash equivalents).
    a. Under the indirect approach, gains and losses from the sale of the above assets should be deducted from and added back to, respectively, net income to arrive at net cash flows from operating activities.
    b. Under the direct approach, gains and losses are simply ignored in determining net cash flows from operating activities.
    c. Under both approaches, the full cash proceeds are entered into the Cash Flows from Investing Activities section of the statement of cash flows.

Objective 6b: Determine cash flows from financing activities.

15. Financing activities focus on certain liability and stockholders' equity accounts and include short- and long-term borrowing (notes and bonds) and repayment, issuance and repurchase of capital stock, and payment of dividends. Changes in the Retained Earnings account are explained in the statement of cash flows, for the most part, through analyses of net income and dividends declared.

Objective 7: Use the indirect method to prepare a statement of cash flows.

16. The only difference between the direct and indirect methods of preparing a statement of cash flows is in the structure of the Cash Flows from Operating Activities section. Exhibit 4 of your textbook presents a completed statement of cash flows using the indirect method. As already explained, the essence of the indirect approach is the conversion of net income into net cash flows from operating activities.

Supplemental Objective 8: Prepare a work sheet for the statement of cash flows.

17. A work sheet for preparing the statement of cash flows is especially useful in complex situations. Using the indirect approach, it essentially allows for the systematic analysis of all changes in the balance sheet accounts.

18. Exhibit 5 of your textbook presents the format of a completed work sheet. In preparing the work sheet, five steps should be followed.
    a. Enter all balance sheet accounts into the Description column, listing all debit accounts before credit accounts.
    b. Enter all end-of-prior-period amounts and end-of-current-period amounts in the appropriate columns, and foot. The total debits should equal the total credits in each column.
    c. In the bottom portion of the work sheet, write the captions Cash Flows from Operating Activities, Cash Flows from Investing Activities, and Cash Flows from Financing Activities, leaving sufficient space between sections to enter data.
    d. Analyze the change in each balance sheet account, using the income statement and information on other transactions that affect noncurrent accounts during the period. Then enter the resulting debits and credits in the Analysis of Transactions columns, labeling each entry with a key letter corresponding to a reference list of changes.
    e. Foot the top and bottom portions of the Analysis of Transactions columns. The top portion should balance immediately, but the bottom portion should balance only when the net increase or decrease in cash is entered (credited for an increase or debited for a decrease). The changes in cash entered into the top and bottom of the work sheet must equal each other and should be labeled with the same key letter.

Supplemental Objective 9: Use the direct method to determine cash flows from operating activities and prepare a statement of cash flows.

19. Under the direct method, the net cash flows from operating activities is determined by taking cash receipts from sales, adding interest and dividends received, and deducting cash payments for purchases, operating expenses, interest, and income taxes. (See the table on page 180.)

20. Exhibit 7 of your textbook presents a completed statement of cash flows that has incorporated the direct method. When the direct method is used, a schedule explaining the difference between reported net income and cash flows from operating activities must be provided.

Formulas to Determine Cash Flows from Operating Activities under the Direct Method

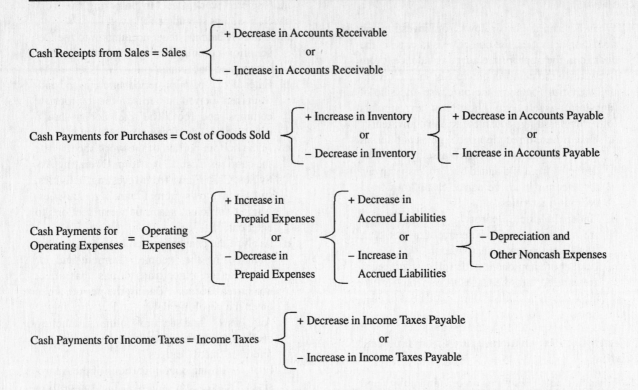

Cash Receipts from Sales = Sales
{
+ Decrease in Accounts Receivable
or
– Increase in Accounts Receivable
}

Cash Payments for Purchases = Cost of Goods Sold
{
+ Increase in Inventory
or
– Decrease in Inventory
}
{
+ Decrease in Accounts Payable
or
– Increase in Accounts Payable
}

Cash Payments for Operating Expenses = Operating Expenses
{
+ Increase in Prepaid Expenses
or
– Decrease in Prepaid Expenses
}
{
+ Decrease in Accrued Liabilities
or
– Increase in Accrued Liabilities
}
{
– Depreciation and Other Noncash Expenses
}

Cash Payments for Income Taxes = Income Taxes
{
+ Decrease in Income Taxes Payable
or
– Increase in Income Taxes Payable
}

Test your knowledge of the chapter by choosing the best answer for each of the following items.

1. Cash equivalents include
   a. three-month Treasury bills.
   b. short-term investments.
   c. accounts receivable.
   d. long-term investments.

2. The primary purpose of the statement of cash flows is to provide information
   a. regarding the results of operations for a period of time.
   b. regarding the financial position of a company as of the end of an accounting period.
   c. about a company's operating, investing, and financing activities during an accounting period.
   d. about a company's cash receipts and cash payments during an accounting period.

3. Which of the following is supplemental to the statement of cash flows?
   a. Operating activities
   b. Investing activities
   c. Significant noncash transactions
   d. Financing activities

4. Which of the following would be classified as an operating activity on the statement of cash flows?
   a. Declared and paid a cash dividend
   b. Issued long-term notes for plant assets
   c. Paid interest on a long-term note
   d. Purchased a patent

5. Which of the following would be classified as an investing activity on the statement of cash flows?
   a. Declared and paid a cash dividend
   b. Issued long-term notes for plant assets
   c. Paid interest on a long-term note
   d. Purchased a patent

6. Which of the following would be classified as a financing activity on the statement of cash flows?
   a. Declared and paid a cash dividend
   b. Issued long-term notes for plant assets
   c. Paid interest on a long-term note
   d. Purchased a patent

7. On the statement of cash flows, the net amount of the major components of cash flow will equal the increase or decrease in
   a. cash and accounts receivable.
   b. working capital.
   c. cash and cash equivalents.
   d. very short-term investments.

8. Cash flow yield is expressed in terms of
   a. dollars.
   b. times.
   c. a percentage.
   d. days.

9. A basic feature of the work sheet approach to preparing the statement of cash flows is that entries are made on the work sheet to
   a. be used for reference for later entry in the general journal.
   b. adjust the cash amount to an accrual basis.
   c. explain the changes in income statement accounts.
   d. explain the changes in balance sheet accounts.

10. The direct method of preparing the operating activities section of the statement of cash flows differs from the indirect method in that it
   a. starts with the net income figure.
   b. lists the changes in current asset accounts in the operating section.
   c. begins with cash from customers, which is revenues adjusted for the change in accounts receivable.
   d. lists significant noncash transactions.

TESTING YOUR KNOWLEDGE

Matching*

Match each term with its definition by writing the appropriate letter in the blank.

_____ 1. Statement of cash flows

_____ 2. Cash equivalents

_____ 3. Operating activities

_____ 4. Investing activities

_____ 5. Financing activities

_____ 6. Noncash investing and financing transactions

_____ 7. Direct method

_____ 8. Indirect method

_____ 9. Cash-generating efficiency

_____ 10. Free cash flow

a. The items placed at the bottom of the statement of cash flows in a separate schedule

b. Net cash flows from operating activities minus dividends minus net capital expenditures

c. In determining cash flows from operations, the procedure that starts with the figure for net income

d. A measure expressed as cash flow yield, cash flows to sales, or cash flows to assets

e. The statement of cash flows section that deals mainly with stockholders' equity accounts and borrowing

f. The financial report that explains the change in cash during the period

g. The statement of cash flows section that deals with long-term assets and marketable securities other than trading securities or cash equivalents

h. In determining cash flows from operations, the procedure that adjusts each income statement item from an accrual basis to a cash basis

i. The statement of cash flows section that most closely relates to net income (loss)

j. Short-term, highly liquid investments

Short Answer

Use the lines provided to answer each item.

1. Give two examples of noncash investing and financing transactions.

_____

_____

_____

_____

2. When the statement of cash flows is prepared under the indirect method, why are depreciation, amortization, and depletion expense added back to net income to determine cash flows from operating activities?

_____

_____

_____

_____

Note to student: The matching quiz might be completed more efficiently by starting with the definition and searching for the corresponding term.

3. Which sections of the statement of cash flows are prepared identically under the direct and indirect methods?

_____

_____

_____

_____

4. List three examples of cash equivalents.

_____

_____

_____

True-False

Circle T if the statement is true, F if it is false. Please provide explanations for the false answers, using the blank lines at the end of the section.

T F 1. The statement of cash flows is a major financial statement required by the FASB.

T F 2. Payment on an account payable is considered a financing activity.

T F 3. The proceeds from the sale of available-for-sale securities would be considered an investing activity, whether the investments are classified as short-term or long-term.

T F 4. To calculate cash payments for purchases, the cost of goods sold must be known, along with the changes in inventory and accounts payable during the period.

T F 5. Under the indirect method, a decrease in prepaid expenses would be added to net income in determining net cash flows from operating activities.

T F 6. The schedule of noncash investing and financing transactions might include line items for depreciation, depletion, and amortization recorded during the period.

T F 7. In the Analysis of Transactions columns of the bottom portion of a statement of cash flows work sheet, Retained Earnings is credited and Dividends Paid debited for dividends paid during the period.

T F 8. In the Cash Flows from Operating Activities section of a statement of cash flows work sheet, the items that are credited in the Analysis of Transactions columns must be deducted from net income in the statement of cash flows.

T F 9. A net positive figure for cash flows from investing activities implies that the business is generally expanding.

T F 10. The issuance of common stock for cash would be disclosed in the financing activities section of the statement of cash flows.

T F 11. Under the indirect method, a loss on the sale of buildings would be deducted from net income in the operating activities section of the statement of cash flows.

T F 12. To calculate cash payments for operating expenses, operating expenses must be modified by (among other items) depreciation, which is treated as an add-back.

T F 13. Cash obtained by borrowing is considered a financing activity, whether the debt is classified as short-term or long-term.

T F 14. The purchase of land in exchange for the issuance of common stock in effect represents simultaneous investing and financing activities.

T F 15. It is possible for the direct and indirect methods to produce different net-change-in-cash figures on a statement of cash flows.

T F 16. Free cash flow does not include a deduction for dividends because dividend payment is never required.

_____

_____

_____

_____

_____

_____

_____

_____

_____

_____

_____

_____

_____

_____

_____

_____

_____

_____

_____

_____

_____

_____

_____

_____

_____

_____

Multiple Choice

Circle the letter of the best answer.

1. How would interest and dividends received be included on a statement of cash flows that employs the indirect method?
   a. Included as components of net income in the operating activities section
   b. Deducted from net income in the operating activities section
   c. Included in the investing activities section
   d. Included in the financing activities section
   e. Included in the schedule of noncash investing and financing transactions

2. How would a gain on the sale of investments be disclosed on a statement of cash flows that employs the indirect method?
   a. Added to net income in the operating activities section
   b. Deducted from net income in the operating activities section
   c. Included in the investing activities section
   d. Included in the financing activities section
   e. Included in the schedule of noncash investing and financing transactions

3. How would an increase in accounts payable be disclosed on a statement of cash flows that employs the indirect method?
   a. Added to net income in the operating activities section
   b. Deducted from net income in the operating activities section
   c. Included in the investing activities section
   d. Included in the financing activities section
   e. Included in the schedule of noncash investing and financing transactions

4. How would the purchase of a building by incurring a mortgage payable be disclosed on a statement of cash flows that employs the indirect method?
   a. Added to net income in the operating activities section
   b. Deducted from net income in the operating activities section
   c. Included in the investing activities section
   d. Included in the financing activities section
   e. Included in the schedule of noncash investing and financing transactions

5. How would dividends paid be disclosed on a statement of cash flows that employs the indirect method?
   a. Added to net income in the operating activities section
   b. Deducted from net income in the operating activities section
   c. Included in the investing activities section
   d. Included in the financing activities section
   e. Included in the schedule of noncash investing and financing transactions

6. How would an increase in inventory be disclosed on a statement of cash flows that employs the indirect method?
   a. Added to net income in the operating activities section
   b. Deducted from net income in the operating activities section
   c. Included in the investing activities section
   d. Included in the financing activities section
   e. Included in the schedule of noncash investing and financing transactions

7. All of the following represent cash flows from operating activities *except* cash
   a. payments for income taxes.
   b. receipts from sales.
   c. receipts from the issuance of stock.
   d. payments for purchases.

8. When net income is recorded (debited) in the Analysis of Transactions columns of a statement of cash flows work sheet, which item is credited?
   a. Cash
   b. Income summary
   c. Net increase in cash
   d. Retained earnings

9. Brooks Corporation had cash sales of $30,000 and credit sales of $70,000 during the year, and the Accounts Receivable account increased by $14,000. Cash receipts from sales totaled
   a. $70,000.
   b. $86,000.
   c. $100,000.
   d. $114,000.

10. The calculations of cash flow yield, cash flows to sales, and cash flows to assets are all based upon
    a. net cash flows from financing activities.
    b. net increase or decrease in cash.
    c. net cash flows from operating activities.
    d. net cash flows from investing activities.

APPLYING YOUR KNOWLEDGE

Exercises

1. Use the following information to calculate the items below.

Accounts Payable, Jan. 1, 20xx	$ 47,000
Accounts Payable, Dec. 31, 20xx	54,000
Accounts Receivable, Jan. 1, 20xx	32,000
Accounts Receivable, Dec. 31, 20xx	22,000
Accrued Liabilities, Jan. 1, 20xx	17,000
Accrued Liabilities, Dec. 31, 20xx	11,000
Cost of Goods Sold for 20xx	240,000
Depreciation Expense for 20xx	20,000
Income Taxes Expense for 20xx	33,000
Income Taxes Payable, Jan. 1, 20xx	4,000
Income Taxes Payable, Dec. 31, 20xx	6,000
Inventory, Jan. 1, 20xx	86,000
Inventory, Dec. 31, 20xx	74,000
Operating Expenses for 20xx	70,000
Prepaid Expenses, Jan. 1, 20xx	2,000
Prepaid Expenses, Dec. 31, 20xx	3,000
Sales for 20xx	350,000

a. Cash payments for operating expenses =

$ _____

b. Cash receipts from sales =

$ _____

c. Cash payments for income taxes =

$ _____

d. Cash payments for purchases =

$ _____

e. Net cash flows from operating activities =

$ _____

2. For 20x7, Perta Corporation had average total assets of $800,000, net sales of $900,000, net income of $60,000, net cash flows from operating activities of $120,000, dividend payments of $30,000, purchases of plant assets of $75,000, and sales of plant assets of $40,000. Using this information, compute the following cash flow measures.

a. Cash flow yield = _____ times

b. Cash flows to sales = _____ %

c. Cash flows to assets = _____ %

d. Free cash flow = $ _____

3. Use the following information to complete Connector Corporation's statement of cash flows work sheet on the next page for the year ended December 31, 20x9. Make sure to use the key letters in the Analysis of Transactions columns to refer to the following explanation list:

a. Net income for 20x9 was $22,000.

b–d. These key letters record changes in current assets and current liabilities.

e. Sold plant assets that cost $30,000 with accumulated depreciation of $10,000, for $24,000.

f. Purchased plant assets for $62,000.

g. Recorded depreciation expense of $26,000 for 20x9.

h. Converted bonds payable with a $10,000 face amount into common stock.

i. Declared and paid dividends of $12,000.

x. This key letter codes the change in cash.

	Account Balances 12/31/x8	Analysis of Transactions for 20x9		Account Balance 12/31/x9
		Debit	Credit	
Debits				
Cash	35,000			29,000
Accounts Receivable	18,000			21,000
Inventory	83,000			72,000
Plant Assets	200,000			232,000
Total Debits	336,000			354,000
Credits				
Accumulated Depreciation	40,000			56,000
Accounts Payable	27,000			19,000
Bonds Payable	100,000			90,000
Common Stock	150,000			160,000
Retained Earnings	19,000			29,000
Total Credits	336,000			354,000
Cash Flows from Operating Activities				
Cash Flows from Investing Activities				
Cash Flows from Financing Activities				
Net Decrease in Cash				

Connector Corporation
Work Sheet for the Statement of Cash Flows
For the Year Ended December 31, 20x9

CHAPTER 15 FINANCIAL STATEMENT ANALYSIS

REVIEWING THE CHAPTER

Objective 1: Describe and discuss the objectives of financial statement analysis.

1. **Financial statement analysis** comprises all the techniques employed by users of financial statements to show important relationships in the financial statements.

2. The users of financial statements are classified as either internal or external. The main internal user is management. The main external users are creditors and investors. Both creditors and investors will probably acquire a **portfolio,** or group of loans or investments, which allows the creditors and investors to average both the returns and the risks.

3. Creditors and investors use financial statement analysis (a) to assess past performance and current position and (b) to assess future potential and the risk related. Information about the past and present is very helpful in making projections about the future. Moreover, the easier it is to predict future performance, the less risk is involved. The lower risk means that the investor or creditor will require a lower expected rate of return.

Objective 2: Describe and discuss the standards for financial statement analysis.

4. Decision makers assess performance by means of (a) rule-of-thumb measures, (b) analysis of past performance of the company, and (c) comparison with industry norms.
   a. Rule-of-thumb measures for key financial ratios are helpful but should not be the only basis for making a decision. For example, a company may report high earnings per share but may lack sufficient current assets to pay current debts.
   b. The past performance of a company can help show trends. The skill lies in the analyst's ability to predict whether a trend will continue or will reverse itself.
   c. Comparing a company's performance with the performance of other companies in the same industry is helpful, but there are three limitations to using industry norms as standards. First, no two companies are exactly the same. Second, many companies, called **diversified companies,** or *conglomerates,* operate in many unrelated industries, so that comparison is hard. (However, the FASB requirement to report financial information by segments has been somewhat helpful.) Third, different companies may use different acceptable accounting procedures for recording similar items.

Objective 3: State the sources of information for financial statement analysis.

5. The chief sources of information about publicly held corporations are reports published by the company, SEC reports, business periodicals, and credit and investment advisory services.
   a. A corporation's annual report provides useful financial information. It includes the following sections: (1) management's analysis of the past year's operations, (2) the financial statements, (3) the notes to the statements, including the

company's principal accounting procedures, (4) the auditors' report, and (5) a five- or ten-year summary of operations.

b. **Interim financial statements** may indicate significant changes in a company's earnings trend. They consist of limited financial information for less than a year (usually quarterly).

c. Publicly held corporations are required to file with the SEC an annual report (Form 10-K), a quarterly report (Form 10-Q), and a current report of significant events (Form 8-K). These reports are available to the public and are a valuable source of financial information.

d. Financial analysts obtain information from such sources as *The Wall Street Journal, Forbes, Barron's, Fortune,* the *Financial Times,* Moody's, Standard & Poor's, Dun & Bradstreet, and Robert Morris Associates.

Objective 4: Apply horizontal analysis, trend analysis, and vertical analysis to financial statements.

6. The most common tools and techniques of financial analysis are horizontal analysis, trend analysis, vertical analysis, and ratio analysis.

a. Comparative financial statements show the current and prior year's information side by side to aid in financial statement analysis. In **horizontal analysis,** absolute and percentage changes in specific items from one year to the next are shown. The first of the two years being considered is called the **base year,** and the percentage change is computed by dividing the amount of the change by the base-year amount.

b. **Trend analysis** is the same as horizontal analysis, except that percentage changes are calculated for several consecutive years. For percentage changes to be shown over several years, **index numbers** must be used against which changes in related items are measured.

c. In **vertical analysis,** the percentage relationship of individual items on the statement to a total within the statement (e.g., cost of goods sold as a percentage of net sales) is presented. The result is a **common-size statement.** On a common-size balance sheet, total assets and total liabilities and stockholders' equity would each be labeled 100 percent. On a common-size income statement, sales or revenues would be labeled 100 percent. Common-size statements may be presented in comparative form to show information both within the period and between periods and to make comparisons between companies.

Objective 5: Apply ratio analysis to financial statements in a comprehensive evaluation of a company's financial situation.

7. In **ratio analysis,** certain relationships (ratios) between financial statement items are determined and then compared with those of prior years or other companies. Ratios provide information about a company's liquidity, profitability, long-term solvency, cash flow adequacy, and market strength. The most common ratios are shown in the table on the next page.

Ratio	Components	Use or Meaning
Liquidity Ratios		
Current ratio	$\dfrac{\text{Current Assets}}{\text{Current Liabilities}}$	Measure of short-term debt-paying ability
Quick ratio	$\dfrac{\text{Cash + Marketable Securities + Receivables}}{\text{Current Liabilities}}$	Measure of short-term debt-paying ability
Receivable turnover	$\dfrac{\text{Net Sales}}{\text{Average Accounts Receivable}}$	Measure of relative size of accounts receivable balance and effectiveness of credit policies
Average days' sales uncollected	$\dfrac{\text{Days in Year}}{\text{Receivable Turnover}}$	Measure of average time taken to collect receivables
Inventory turnover	$\dfrac{\text{Cost of Goods Sold}}{\text{Average Inventory}}$	Measure of relative size of inventory
Average days' inventory on hand	$\dfrac{\text{Days in Year}}{\text{Inventory Turnover}}$	Measure of average days taken to sell inventory
Payables turnover	$\dfrac{\text{Cost of Goods Sold} \pm \text{Change in Inventory}}{\text{Average Accounts Payable}}$	Measure of relative size of accounts payable
Average days' payable	$\dfrac{\text{Days in Year}}{\text{Payables Turnover}}$	Measure of average days to pay accounts payable

(**Note:** The term **operating cycle** means the time it takes to sell and collect for products sold. It equals average days' inventory on hand plus average days' sales uncollected.)

Ratio	Components	Use or Meaning
Profitability Ratios		
Profit margin	$\dfrac{\text{Net Income}}{\text{Net Sales}}$	Measure of net income produced by each dollar of sales
Asset turnover	$\dfrac{\text{Net Sales}}{\text{Average Total Assets}}$	Measure of how efficiently assets are used to produce sales
Return on assets	$\dfrac{\text{Net Income}}{\text{Average Total Assets}}$	Measure of overall earning power or profitability
Return on equity	$\dfrac{\text{Net Income}}{\text{Average Stockholders' Equity}}$	Measure of profitability of stockholders' investments
Long-Term Solvency Ratios		
Debt to equity ratio	$\dfrac{\text{Total Liabilities}}{\text{Stockholders' Equity}}$	Measure of capital structure and leverage
Interest coverage ratio	$\dfrac{\text{Income Before Income Taxes + Interest Expense}}{\text{Interest Expense}}$	Measure of creditors' protection from default on interest payments
Cash Flow Adequacy Ratios		
Cash flow yield	$\dfrac{\text{Net Cash Flows from Operating Activities}}{\text{Net Income}}$	Measure of ability to generate operating cash flows in relation to net income
Cash flows to sales	$\dfrac{\text{Net Cash Flows from Operating Activities}}{\text{Net Sales}}$	Measure of ability of sales to generate operating cash flows
Cash flows to assets	$\dfrac{\text{Net Cash Flows from Operating Activities}}{\text{Average Total Assets}}$	Measure of ability of assets to generate operating cash flows
Free cash flow	Net Cash Flows from Operating Activities – Dividends – Net Capital Expenditures	Measure of cash generated or cash deficiency after providing for commitments
Market Strength Ratios		
Price/earnings (P/E) ratio	$\dfrac{\text{Market Price per Share}}{\text{Earnings per Share}}$	Measure of investor confidence in a company
Dividends yield	$\dfrac{\text{Dividends per Share}}{\text{Market Price per Share}}$	Measure of current return to an investor in a stock

Financial Statement Analysis

SELF-TEST

Test your knowledge of the chapter by choosing the best answer for each of the following items.

1. A general rule in choosing among alternative investments is the greater the risk taken, the
   a. greater the return required.
   b. lower the profits expected.
   c. lower the potential expected.
   d. greater the price of the investment.

2. Which of the following is the most useful in evaluating whether a company has improved its position in relation to its competitors?
   a. Rule-of-thumb measures
   b. Past performance of the company
   c. Past and current performances of the company
   d. Industry averages

3. One of the best places to look for early signals of change in a company's profitability is the
   a. interim financial statements.
   b. year-end financial statements.
   c. annual report sent to stockholders.
   d. annual report sent to the SEC.

4. Cash flow yield equals net cash flows from operating activities divided by
   a. average stockholders' equity.
   b. net income.
   c. average total assets.
   d. net sales.

5. In trend analysis, each item is expressed as a percentage of the
   a. net income figure.
   b. retained earnings figure.
   c. base year figure.
   d. total assets figure.

6. In a common-size balance sheet for a wholesale company, the 100% figure is
   a. merchandise inventory.
   b. total current assets.
   c. total property, plant, and equipment.
   d. total assets.

7. The best way to study the changes in financial statements between two years is to prepare
   a. common-size statements.
   b. a trend analysis.
   c. a horizontal analysis.
   d. a ratio analysis.

8. A common measure of liquidity is
   a. return on assets.
   b. profit margin.
   c. inventory turnover.
   d. interest coverage.

9. Asset turnover is most closely related to
   a. profit margin and return on assets.
   b. profit margin and debt to equity.
   c. interest coverage and debt to equity.
   d. earnings per share and profit margin.

10. Which of the following describes the computation of the interest coverage ratio?
    a. Net income minus interest expense divided by interest expense
    b. Net income plus interest expense divided by interest expense
    c. Income before income taxes plus interest expense divided by interest expense
    d. Net income divided by interest expense

TESTING YOUR KNOWLEDGE

*Matching**

Match each term with its definition by writing the appropriate letter in the blank.

_____ 1. Financial statement analysis

_____ 2. Portfolio

_____ 3. Diversified companies (conglomerates)

_____ 4. Interim financial statements

_____ 5. Horizontal analysis

_____ 6. Base year

_____ 7. Trend analysis

_____ 8. Index number

_____ 9. Vertical analysis

_____ 10. Common-size statement

_____ 11. Ratio analysis

_____ 12. Operating cycle

a. The time it takes to sell and collect for products sold

b. A group of investments or loans

c. The determination of certain relationships between financial statement items

d. A financial statement expressed in terms of percentages, the result of vertical analysis

e. Limited financial information for less than a year (usually quarterly)

f. The first year being considered when horizontal analysis is used

g. Techniques used to show important relationships in financial statements

h. A presentation of the percentage change in specific items over several years

i. A number used in trend analysis to show change in related items from one year to another

j. A presentation of absolute and percentage changes in specific items from one year to the next

k. A presentation of the percentage relationships of individual items on a statement to a total within the statement

l. Companies that operate in many unrelated industries

Short Answer

Use the lines provided to answer each item.

1. List four ratios that measure profitability.

_____

_____

_____

_____

2. Briefly distinguish between horizontal and vertical analysis.

_____

_____

_____

_____

_____

Note to student: The matching quiz might be completed more efficiently by starting with the definition and searching for the corresponding term.

3. List the three methods by which decision makers assess performance.

_____

_____

_____

4. Why is it wiser to acquire a portfolio of small investments rather than one large investment?

_____

_____

_____

5. List four measures of cash flow adequacy.

_____

_____

_____

_____

True-False

Circle T if the statement is true, F if it is false. Please provide explanations for the false answers, using the blank lines at the end of the section.

T F **1.** Horizontal analysis is possible for both an income statement and a balance sheet.

T F **2.** Common-size financial statements show dollar changes in specific items from one year to the next.

T F **3.** A company with a 2.0 current ratio will experience a decline in the current ratio when a short-term liability is paid.

T F **4.** Inventory is not included in computing the quick ratio.

T F **5.** Inventory turnover equals average inventory divided by cost of goods sold.

T F **6.** The price/earnings ratio must be computed before earnings per share can be determined.

T F **7.** When computing the return on equity, interest expense must be added back to net income.

T F **8.** When a company has no debt, its return on assets equals its return on equity.

T F **9.** The lower the debt to equity ratio, the riskier the situation.

T F **10.** Receivable turnover measures the time it takes to collect an average receivable.

T F **11.** A low interest coverage would be cause for concern for a company's bondholders.

T F **12.** Average days' inventory on hand is a liquidity ratio.

T F **13.** Dividends yield is a profitability ratio.

T F **14.** On a common-size income statement, net income is given a label of 100 percent.

T F **15.** Interim financial statements may serve as an early signal of significant changes in a company's earning trend.

T F **16.** Probably the best source of financial news is *The Wall Street Journal*.

T F **17.** Return on assets equals the profit margin times asset turnover.

T F **18.** The higher the payables turnover, the longer the average days' payable.

_____

_____

_____

_____

_____

_____

_____

_____

_____   _____

_____   _____

_____   _____

_____   _____

_____   _____

_____   _____

_____   _____

Multiple Choice

Circle the letter of the best answer.

1. Which of the following is a measure of long-term solvency?
   a. Current ratio
   b. Interest coverage
   c. Asset turnover
   d. Profit margin

2. Short-term creditors would probably be *most* interested in which of the following ratios?
   a. Current ratio
   b. Average days' inventory on hand
   c. Debt to equity ratio
   d. Quick ratio

3. Net income is irrelevant in computing which of the following ratios?
   a. Cash flow yield
   b. Return on assets
   c. Asset turnover
   d. Return on equity

4. A high price/earnings ratio indicates
   a. investor confidence in high future earnings.
   b. that the stock is probably overvalued.
   c. that the stock is probably undervalued.
   d. little investor confidence in high future earnings.

5. Index numbers are used in
   a. trend analysis.
   b. ratio analysis.
   c. vertical analysis.
   d. common-size statements.

6. The main internal user of financial statements is
   a. the SEC.
   b. management.
   c. investors.
   d. creditors.

7. Comparing performance with industry norms is complicated by
   a. the existence of diversified companies.
   b. the use of different accounting procedures by different companies.
   c. the fact that companies in the same industry usually differ in some respect.
   d. all of the above.

8. A low receivable turnover indicates that
   a. few customers are defaulting on their debts.
   b. the company's inventory is moving very slowly.
   c. the company is making collections from its customers very slowly.
   d. a small proportion of the company's sales are credit sales.

9. In a common-size income statement, net income is labeled
   a. 0 percent.
   b. the percentage that net income is in relation to sales.
   c. the percentage that net income is in relation to operating expenses.
   d. 100 percent.

10. Which of the following measures equals cash generated or cash deficiency after providing for commitments?
    a. Cash flows to assets
    b. Cash flow yield
    c. Free cash flow
    d. Cash flows to sales

APPLYING YOUR KNOWLEDGE

Exercises

1. Complete the horizontal analysis for the comparative income statements shown here. Round percentages to the nearest tenth of a percent.

	20x1	20x2	Increase (Decrease) Amount	Percentage
Sales	$200,000	$250,000		
Cost of Goods Sold	120,000	144,000		
Gross Margin	$ 80,000	$106,000		
Operating Expenses	50,000	62,000		
Income Before Income Taxes	$ 30,000	$ 44,000		
Income Taxes	8,000	16,000		
Net Income	$ 22,000	$ 28,000		

2. The following is financial information for Solian Corporation for 20xx. Current assets consist of cash, accounts receivable, marketable securities, and inventory. Assume no change in inventory.

Average accounts receivable	$100,000
Average (and ending) inventory	180,000
Cost of goods sold	350,000
Current assets, Dec. 31	500,000
Current liabilities, Dec. 31	250,000
Market price, Dec. 31, on 21,200 shares	40/share
Net income	106,000
Net sales	600,000
Average stockholders' equity	480,000
Average total assets	880,000
Net cash flows from operating activities	75,000
Accounts payable	50,000

Compute the following ratios as of December 31. Round off to the nearest tenth of a whole number for **a–l** and **o–p,** to the nearest hundredth of a whole number in **m** and **n.**

a. Current ratio = _____

b. Quick ratio = _____

c. Inventory turnover = _____

d. Average days' inventory on hand = _____

e. Return on assets = _____

f. Return on equity = _____

g. Receivable turnover = _____

h. Average days' sales uncollected = _____

i. Profit margin = _____

m. Asset turnover = _____

j. Cash flow yield = _____

n. Price/earnings ratio = _____

k. Cash flows to sales = _____

o. Payables turnover = _____

l. Cash flows to assets = _____

p. Average days' payable = _____

CHAPTER 16 INTERNATIONAL ACCOUNTING AND LONG-TERM INVESTMENTS

REVIEWING THE CHAPTER

Objective 1: Define *exchange rate* and record transactions that are affected by changes in foreign exchange rates.

1. When businesses expand internationally (called **multinational** or **transnational corporations**), two accounting problems arise. (a) The financial statements of foreign subsidiaries involve different currencies. These must be translated into domestic currency by means of an **exchange rate.** (b) The foreign financial statements are not necessarily prepared in accordance with domestic generally accepted accounting principles.

2. Purchases and sales with foreign countries pose no accounting problem for the domestic company when the domestic currency is being used. However, when the transaction involves foreign currency, the domestic company should record an **exchange gain or loss.** This exchange gain or loss reflects the change in the exchange rate from the transaction date to the date of payment.

3. When financial statements are prepared between the transaction date and the date of payment, GAAP requires that an unrealized gain or loss must be recorded if the exchange rate has changed.

Objective 2: Describe the restatement of a foreign subsidiary's financial statements in U.S. dollars.

4. A foreign subsidiary that a parent company controls should be included in the parent company's consolidated financial statements. The subsidiary's financial statements must therefore be restated into the parent's **reporting currency.** The method of **restatement** depends on the foreign subsidiary's **functional currency**—that is, the currency with which it transacts most of its business.

5. There are two basic types of foreign operations. Type I subsidiaries are self-contained within a foreign country. Their financial statements must be restated from the functional currency (local currency in this case) to the reporting currency. Type II subsidiaries are simply an extension of the parent's operations. Their financial statements must be restated from the local currency to the functional currency (which in this case is the same as the reporting currency).

6. When a Type I subsidiary operates in a country where there is hyperinflation (more than 100 percent cumulative inflation over three years), it is treated as a Type II subsidiary, with the functional currency being the U.S. dollar.

Objective 3: Describe the progress toward international accounting standards.

7. At present, there are *some* recognized worldwide standards of accounting. To their credit, the International Accounting Standards Committee (IASC) and the International Federation of Accountants (IFAC) *have* made much progress in setting up these international accounting standards. Despite the efforts of these bodies, however, there are still

serious inconsistencies in financial statements among countries, and comparison remains a difficult task. Obstacles to setting international standards include disagreement (among countries) on the goals of financial statements, differences in regulatory laws and governments, inconsistent accounting procedures, and varying influences of the tax laws on financial reporting. More and more countries, however, are recognizing the importance of uniform international accounting standards in conducting international trade.

Objective 4: Identify the classifications of long-term investments in bonds and stocks.

8. **Insider trading** is the practice of buying or selling shares of a publicly held company based on information not yet known by the public. Though not illegal in all countries, insider trading is considered a crime in the United States. Suspected offenders are investigated by the SEC.

9. Long-term investments in bonds are recorded at cost including commissions. When the bonds are purchased between interest dates, the investor must also pay for the accrued interest (which will be returned to the investor on the next interest payment date).

10. Most long-term bond investments are classified as **available-for-sale securities** because investors usually sell before the securities mature. Such securities are valued at fair (market) value. Long-term bond investments are classified as **held-to-maturity securities** when an early sale is *not* intended. Such securities are valued at cost, adjusted by discount or premium amortization.

11. All long-term investments in the stock of other companies are recorded at cost. After purchase, the accounting treatment depends on the extent of influence exercised by the investing company. If the investing company can affect the operating and financing policies of the investee, even though it owns 50 percent or less of the investee's voting stock, it has **significant influence.** If the investing company can decide the operating and financing policies of the investee because it owns more than 50 percent of the investee's voting stock, it has **control.**

12. The extent of influence exercised over another company is often difficult to measure accurately. However, unless there is evidence to the contrary, long-term investments in stock are classified as (a) noninfluential and noncontrolling (generally less than 20 percent ownership), (b) influential but noncontrolling (generally 20 to 50 percent ownership), and (c) controlling (over 50 percent ownership).

Objective 5: Apply the cost adjusted to market method and the equity method as appropriate in accounting for long-term investments.

13. The cost adjusted to market method should be used in accounting for noninfluential and noncontrolling investments. The equity method should be used in accounting for all other (that is, influential or controlling) investments. In addition, consolidated financial statements should usually be prepared when a controlling relationship exists.

   a. Under the **cost adjusted to market method,** the investor credits Dividend Income as dividends are received. In addition, the securities are recorded on the balance sheet and in comprehensive income disclosures at the lower of cost or market. Unrealized Loss on Long-Term Investments is debited and Allowance to Adjust Long-Term Investments to Market is credited for the excess of total cost over total market. For available-for-sale equity securities, the Unrealized Loss on Long-Term Investments appears in the stockholders' equity section of the balance sheet as a negative amount (and as a component of other comprehensive income), and the Allowance to Adjust Long-Term Investments to Market appears in the asset section as a contra account to Long-Term Investments. An adjusting entry opposite to the one described above would be made when market value relative to cost has increased.

   b. Under the **equity method,** the investor records investment income as a debit to the Investment account and a credit to an Investment Income account. The amount recorded is the investee's periodic net income times the investor's ownership percentage. When the investor receives a cash dividend, the Cash account is debited and the Investment account is credited. All long-term investments in stock are initially recorded at cost, regardless of the method to account for subsequent transactions.

14. When a company has a controlling interest in another company, the investor is called the **parent company** and the investee is called the **subsidiary.** Companies in such a relationship must prepare **consolidated financial statements** (combined statements of the parent and its subsidiaries). The purchase method (described below) or the pooling of interests method (the subject of a more advanced accounting course) is used.

Objective 6: Explain when to prepare consolidated financial statements, and describe the uses of such statements.

15. Consolidated financial statements should be prepared when an investing company has legal and effective control over another company (more than 50 percent ownership). With few exceptions, the financial statements of all majority-owned subsidiaries must be consolidated with the parent company's financial statements for external reporting purposes. Consolidated financial statements are useful because they present a financial picture of the entire economic entity. Some businesses also present separate statements for their finance subsidiaries in their annual report.

16. The **purchase method** is required to account for business combinations effected with cash, debt, or preferred stock. The pooling of interests method, used when a business combination is effected through an exchange of common stock, has been recommended for virtual elimination by the FASB.

17. When consolidated financial statements are prepared, **eliminations** must be made on the consolidating work sheet for intercompany items. Among those items that must be eliminated are intercompany receivables, payables, sales, purchases, interest income, and interest expense, as well as the investment in the subsidiary company. In addition, under the purchase method, the entire stockholders' equity section of the subsidiary is eliminated. These eliminations appear only on the work sheet and not in the accounting records or on the consolidated financial statements.

Objective 7a: Prepare the consolidated balance sheet at acquisition date for a purchase at book value.

18. Under the purchase method, the parent records the investment at the purchase cost.
    a. When the book value of the net assets purchased equals their purchase cost, the assets and liabilities acquired should appear at cost on the consolidated balance sheet. No goodwill should be recorded.
    b. The stockholders' equity section of the subsidiary at acquisition is not included on the consolidated balance sheet.
    c. When less than 100 percent of the subsidiary has been purchased, the **minority interest** (outside ownership) must be disclosed on the consolidated balance sheet, either as a component of stockholders' equity or by itself between long-term liabilities and stockholders' equity.

Objective 7b: Prepare the consolidated balance sheet at acquisition date for a purchase at other than book value.

19. If the purchase cost exceeds the book value of the net assets purchased, the extra amount should be allocated to the assets and liabilities acquired when consolidated financial statements are being prepared. The allocation should be based on fair market values at the date of acquisition. Any unassigned excess should be recorded as **goodwill** (or *goodwill from consolidation*) in the consolidated financial statements.

20. When the book value of the net assets purchased exceeds their purchase cost, the book value of the subsidiary's long-term assets (other than marketable securities) should be reduced proportionately until the extra amount is eliminated.

Objective 8: Prepare a consolidated income statement.

21. Intercompany items must be eliminated when preparing a consolidated income statement. They are (a) intercompany purchases and sales, (b) intercompany income and expenses on loans, receivables, or bond indebtedness, and (c) other intercompany income and expenses.

A. (LO 1)   Accounts Receivable, foreign company   XX (amount billed)
                   Sales   XX (amount billed)
                        Credit sale made, fixed amount billed in
                        foreign currency, recorded in U.S. dollars

B. (LO 1)   Cash   XX (amount received)
                   Exchange Gain or Loss   XX (the difference)
                   Accounts Receivable, foreign company   XX (amount billed)
                        Received payment in foreign currency,
                        exchange loss arose from weakening of
                        foreign currency in relation to U.S. dollar

C. (LO 1)   Purchases   XX (amount billed)
                   Accounts Payable, foreign company   XX (amount billed)
                        Credit purchase made, fixed amount billed
                        in foreign currency

D. (LO 1)   Accounts Payable, foreign company   XX (amount billed)
                   Exchange Gain or Loss   XX (the difference)
                   Cash   XX (amount paid)
                        Made payment in foreign currency,
                        exchange gain arose from weakening of foreign
                        currency in relation to U.S. dollar

E. (LO 1)   Note: When a U.S. company transacts business entirely
                   in U.S. dollars, no exchange gain or loss will occur. Those
                   simple journal entries illustrated in your textbook are not
                   duplicated here.

F. (LO 1)   Note: At year end, an adjusting entry must be made
                   for any unrealized exchange gains or losses on
                   outstanding receivables or payables that are to be
                   settled in a foreign currency.

G. (LO 5)   Long-Term Investments   XX (purchase price)
                   Cash   XX (purchase price)
                        Purchased long-term investment in stock

H. (LO 5)   Unrealized Loss on Long-Term Investments   XX (amount of decline)
                   Allowance to Adjust Long-Term Investments to
                   Market   XX (amount of decline)
                        To record reduction of long-term investment
                        to market

I.   (LO 5)   Cash   XX (amount received)
                   Loss on Sale of Investments   XX (the difference)
                   Long-Term Investments   XX (purchase price)
                        To record sale of shares of stock (Note: had a
                        gain on sale arisen, Gain on Sale of Investment
                        would have been credited)

J. (LO 5) Cash   XX (amount received)

       Dividend Income   XX (amount received)

          Receipt of cash dividend; cost adjusted to
market method assumed

K. (LO 5) Allowance to Adjust Long-Term Investments to Market   XX (amount of recovery)

       Unrealized Loss on Long-Term Investments   XX (amount of recovery)

          To record the adjustment in long-term investment
so it is reported at market (market still below cost)

L. (LO 5) Investment in XYZ Corporation   XX (amount paid)

       Cash   XX (amount paid)

          Investment in XYZ Corporation common stock

M. (LO 5) Investment in XYZ Corporation   XX (equity percentage of income)

       Income, XYZ Corporation Investment   XX (equity percentage of income)

          Recognition of percentage of income reported
by investee; equity method assumed

N. (LO 5) Cash   XX (amount received)

       Investment in XYZ Corporation   XX (amount received)

          Cash dividend received; equity method
assumed

O. (LO 7a) Investment in XYZ Corporation   XX (book value)

       Cash   XX (amount paid)

          Purchase of 100 percent of XYZ Corporation
at book value

P. (LO 7a) Common Stock (subsidiary)   XX (current balance)

       Retained Earnings (subsidiary)   XX (current balance)

          Investment in XYZ Corporation   XX (current balance)

          Work sheet entry to eliminate intercompany
investment at acquisition date, subsidiary
wholly owned

Q. (LO 7a) Common Stock (subsidiary)   XX (current balance)

       Retained Earnings (subsidiary)   XX (current balance)

          Investment in XYZ Corporation   XX (current balance)

          Minority Interest   XX (equity percentage)

          Work sheet entry to eliminate intercompany
investment at acquisition date, subsidiary less
than 100 percent owned

R. (LO 7b) Other Assets   XX (excess allocated)

       Goodwill   XX (excess allocated)

       Common Stock (subsidiary)   XX (current balance)

       Retained Earnings (subsidiary)   XX (current balance)

          Investment in XYZ Corporation   XX (current balance)

          Work sheet entry to eliminate intercompany
investment at acquisition date; cost exceeds
book value

S. (LO 7b) Payables   XX (intercompany amount)
                 Receivables   XX (intercompany amount)
                     Work sheet entry to eliminate intercompany
                     receivables and payables (entry described but
                     not illustrated in text)

T. (LO 8) Sales   XX (intercompany amount)
                 Cost of Goods Sold (Purchases)   XX (intercompany amount)
                     Work sheet entry to eliminate intercompany
                     sales and purchases

U. (LO 8) Interest Income (Other Revenue)   XX (intercompany amount)
                 Interest Expense (Other Expense)   XX (intercompany amount)
                     Work sheet entry to eliminate intercompany
                     interest

SELF-TEST

Test your knowledge of the chapter by choosing the best answer for each of the following items.

1. A U.S. company makes a credit purchase in U.S. dollars from a company in England and pays in U.S. dollars during a time when the value of the pound rises from $1.70 to $1.75. Which of the following situations is true for the U.S. company?
   a. Neither an exchange gain nor an exchange loss has occurred.
   b. An exchange gain has occurred.
   c. An exchange loss has occurred.
   d. More information is needed.

2. A U.S. company makes a purchase on credit from a company in England. It is billed in pounds and pays when the exchange rate has risen from $1.70 per pound at the date of purchase to $1.75 per pound at the date of payment. Which of the following situations is true for the U.S. company?
   a. Neither an exchange gain nor an exchange loss has occurred.
   b. An exchange gain has occurred.
   c. An exchange loss has occurred.
   d. More information is needed.

3. The currency of the place where a subsidiary carries on most of its business is called the
   a. functional currency.
   b. home currency.
   c. subsidiary currency.
   d. reporting currency.

4. Which of the following is true with regard to adherence to uniform accounting standards by companies of different nations?
   a. Tax laws have usually not hindered the development of universally acceptable accounting standards.
   b. Efforts are being made by several international accounting organizations to identify areas of agreement in accounting standards.
   c. No progress has been made in harmonizing international accounting standards.
   d. Most countries follow FASB pronouncements.

5. The ability to affect the operating and financial policies of a company whose shares are owned, even if the investor company holds less than 50 percent of the voting stock, is known as
   a. noninfluential.
   b. noncontrolling.
   c. control.
   d. significant influence.

6. When the equity method is used to account for a long-term investment in stock of another company, the carrying value of the investment is affected by
   a. an excess of market price over cost.
   b. neither earnings nor dividends of the investee.
   c. earnings and dividends of the investee.
   d. a decline in the market value of the stock.

7. Consolidated financial statements are useful because
   a. they are much more detailed than the statements for the individual companies.
   b. minority shareholders need the consolidated information in order to make good investment decisions.
   c. the parent and subsidiaries comprise a single legal entity, and the financial statements should reflect that fact.
   d. investors of the parent company want a clear financial picture of the total economic entity.

8. Which of the following items would *not* require an eliminating entry during preparation of consolidated financial statements?
   a. Amount owed by subsidiary to parent
   b. Amount owed by parent to subsidiary
   c. Short-term investments
   d. Investment in subsidiary

9. B Company buys all the stock of C Company for $634,000. C Company has contributed capital of $404,000 and retained earnings of $160,000, and assets are fairly valued. The consolidated financial statements would contain
   a. minority interest and goodwill.
   b. goodwill but not minority interest.
   c. minority interest but not goodwill.
   d. neither minority interest nor goodwill.

10. In preparing consolidated financial statements, all of the following commonly require elimination entries except
   a. intercompany sales and purchases.
   b. intercompany interest expense and income.
   c. stockholders' equity of parent.
   d. stockholders' equity of subsidiary.

TESTING YOUR KNOWLEDGE

Matching*

Match each term with its definition by writing the appropriate letter in the blank.

_____ 1. Cost adjusted to market method

_____ 2. Equity method

_____ 3. Parent company

_____ 4. Subsidiary

_____ 5. Consolidated financial statements

_____ 6. Purchase method

_____ 7. Significant influence

_____ 8. Minority interest

_____ 9. Control

_____ 10. Eliminations

_____ 11. Restatement

_____ 12. Exchange rate

_____ 13. Reporting currency

_____ 14. Functional currency

_____ 15. Multinational (transnational) corporation

_____ 16. Insider trading

a. A business that operates in more than one country

b. The method used to account for noninfluential and noncontrolling investments

c. Buying and selling stock based on information not yet public

d. The consolidation method used when the parent owns more than 50 percent of the subsidiary's voting stock and did not acquire it through an exchange of stock

e. The type of money in which a given set of consolidated financial statements is presented

f. The method used to account for influential but noncontrolling investments

g. A company that is controlled by another company

h. Expressing one currency in terms of another

i. A company that has a controlling interest in another company

j. Combined statements of the parent and its subsidiaries

k. Usually, ownership of 20 to 50 percent of another company's voting stock

l. Ownership of more than 50 percent of the voting stock of another corporation

m. The type of money with which a company transacts most of its business

n. Entries that appear on a consolidated work sheet

o. The value of one currency in terms of another

p. Outside ownership of a subsidiary

*Note to student: The matching quiz might be completed more efficiently by starting with the definition and searching for the corresponding term.

Short Answer

Use the lines provided to answer each item.

1. List the three classifications for long-term investments in stocks (in terms of level of ownership), as well as the method that should be used after purchase to account for each investment.

Classification

_____

_____

_____

Method

_____

_____

_____

2. Briefly explain the accounting treatment for dividends received under the cost adjusted to market method and under the equity method.

_____

_____

_____

_____

3. Under what circumstance should goodwill be recorded on a consolidated balance sheet?

_____

_____

_____

4. Why must certain items be eliminated when consolidated financial statements are prepared?

_____

_____

_____

_____

_____

5. Under what circumstances would a company record an exchange gain or loss?

_____

_____

_____

_____

True-False

Circle T if the statement is true, F if it is false. Please provide explanations for the false answers, using the blank lines at the end of the section.

T F   1. When one company has an influential but noncontrolling interest in another company, it would use the equity method to account for the investment.

T F   2. Under the cost adjusted to market method, the investor records investment income for a percentage (based on percentage ownership) of the investee's periodic net income.

T F   3. When one company owns at least 20 percent of another company, consolidated financial statements should be prepared.

T F   4. When consolidated financial statements are prepared, the parent's investment on the subsidiary must be eliminated.

T F   5. Under the purchase method of consolidation, the subsidiary's earnings for the entire year of acquisition are included on the consolidated financial statements.

T F   6. Under the equity method, the investor records a cash dividend by debiting Cash and crediting the Investment account.

T F   7. Minority interest should be reported as an asset on the consolidated balance sheet.

T F **8.** Goodwill from consolidation does not appear on the unconsolidated balance sheet of the parent or subsidiary, but may appear on the consolidated balance sheet.

T F **9.** When Company A transacts business with foreign Company B in the currency of Company A, Company A will not record an exchange gain or loss even if the exchange rate has changed between the transaction date and the date of payment.

T F **10.** Given the data in question **9,** Company B should record an exchange gain or loss.

T F **11.** When a given exchange rate remains constant over a period of time, no transaction involving the two currencies will result in an exchange gain or loss over that period.

T F **12.** The calculation of net income should include any unrealized exchange gains and losses that arose during the period.

T F **13.** When preparing consolidated financial statements, purchases of goods and services from outsiders should be eliminated.

T F **14.** When the book value of the net assets purchased equals their purchase cost, the assets and liabilities purchased should appear at cost on the consolidated balance sheet.

T F **15.** Long-term bonds treated as held-to-maturity investments are accounted for at fair (market) value.

Multiple Choice

Circle the letter of the best answer.

1. The journal entry to record the receipt of a dividend under the cost adjusted to market method would include a
   a. debit to the Investment account.
   b. credit to Dividend Income.
   c. debit to Goodwill.
   d. credit to the Investment account.

2. When the book value of the net assets purchased exceeds their purchase cost,
   a. goodwill exists.
   b. the entire excess should appear as negative goodwill in the consolidated balance sheet.
   c. the subsidiary's long-term assets should be increased until the extra amount is eliminated.
   d. the subsidiary's long-term assets should be reduced until the extra amount is eliminated.

3. The elimination of an intercompany investment cannot include a
   a. debit to the Investment account.
   b. debit to Goodwill.
   c. debit to Retained Earnings.
   d. credit to minority interest.

4. The unconsolidated financial statements of a parent company may not include
   a. purchases from its subsidiary.
   b. goodwill from consolidation.
   c. an account reflecting the investment in its subsidiary.
   d. purchases from outsiders.

5. Which of the following items would not be eliminated when consolidated financial statements are prepared, assuming that the subsidiary is 100 percent owned?
   a. The subsidiary's capital stock
   b. The parent's investment in the subsidiary
   c. Interest owed to the subsidiary from the parent
   d. Profit on goods sold by the subsidiary to outsiders

6. Petersly Company uses the cost adjusted to market method to account for its three long-term investments. The total cost of the investments is $95,000, and the total market value of the investments at the end of 20xx is $60,000. The account Allowance to Adjust Long-Term Investments to Market has a credit balance of $10,000 before the 20xx adjusting entry is made. The year-end adjusting entry for 20xx would include a
   a. debit to Unrealized Loss on Long-Term Investments for $35,000.
   b. debit to Allowance to Adjust Long-Term Investments to Market for $10,000.
   c. credit to Allowance to Adjust Long-Term Investments to Market for $60,000.
   d. debit to Unrealized Loss on Long-Term Investments for $25,000.

7. For available-for-sale equity securities, the account Unrealized Loss on Long-Term Investments appears
   a. as a note only.
   b. on the balance sheet as a contra-asset account.
   c. on the income statement as a loss.
   d. on the balance sheet as a contra-stockholders' equity account, and as a component of other comprehensive income.

8. When an American company purchases goods from France and the transaction involves francs, what would the American company record on the date of payment if the value of the franc declined relative to the dollar between the purchase date and the payment date?
   a. An unrealized exchange gain
   b. An exchange loss
   c. An exchange gain
   d. No exchange gain or loss

APPLYING YOUR KNOWLEDGE

Exercises

1. Texona Corporation purchased 80 percent of the common stock of Trahan Corporation for $165,000. Trahan's stockholders' equity included common stock of $60,000 and retained earnings of $90,000. On the lines provided, show the debits, credits, and amounts for the eliminating entry that would be made on the work sheet for consolidating the balance sheets of Texona and Trahan. Assume that up to $10,000 of any excess of cost over carrying value is allocated to the building purchased.

Account Debited	Amount	Account Credited	Amount
_____	$ _____	_____	$ _____
_____	_____	_____	_____
_____	_____		
	_____		

2. Glenn Corporation owns 15 percent of the voting stock of Tewa Company and 30 percent of the voting stock of Rorris Company. Both are long-term investments. During a given year, Tewa paid total dividends of $80,000 and earned $110,000, and Rorris paid total dividends of $50,000 and earned $65,000. In the journal, prepare Glenn's entries to reflect the above facts. Leave the date column empty, as no dates have been specified.

General Journal				
Date		Description	Debit	Credit

3. Rilke Corporation, an American company, sold merchandise on credit to a Mexican company for 100,000 pesos. On the sale date, the exchange rate was $.05 per peso. On the date of receipt, the value of the peso had declined to $.045. Prepare the entries in the journal to record Rilke's Corporation's sale and receipt of payment. Leave the date column empty, as no dates have been specified.

	General Journal			
Date		**Description**	**Debit**	**Credit**

Crossword Puzzle
for Chapters 14, 15, and 16

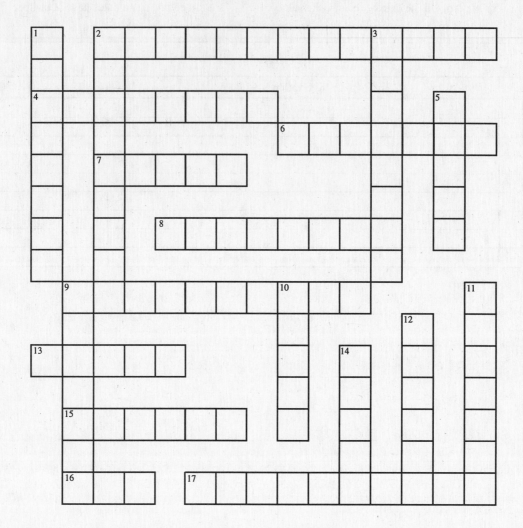

ACROSS

2. Ratio indicating investor confidence in a company (2 words)
4. Analysis resulting in 9-Across
6. Quarterly financial statement, e.g.
7. Statement of cash _____
8. Financial statement examination
9. Statement showing percentage relationships (hyphenated)
13. _____ analysis, a variation of horizontal analysis
15. Method to account for long-term investments
16. An operating-activity outflow
17. Analysis involving dollar and percentage changes

DOWN

1. Interest _____ ratio
2. Group of investments or loans
3. An operating-activity inflow or outflow
5. Dividends _____
9. With 14-Down, a measure of liquidity
10. Number used in 13-Across
11. Majority ownership of voting stock
12. Method for 7-Across
14. See 9-Down

APPENDIX A THE MERCHANDISING WORK SHEET AND CLOSING ENTRIES

REVIEWING THE APPENDIX

1. Under the periodic inventory system, the objectives of dealing with inventory at the end of the period are to (a) remove the beginning balance from the Merchandise Inventory account, (b) enter the ending balance into the Merchandise Inventory account, and (c) enter the beginning inventory as a debit and the ending inventory as a credit to the Income Summary account to help calculate net income.

2. The work sheet for a merchandising company is prepared a bit differently from that of a service company. The main difference is the inclusion of accounts such as Merchandise Inventory, Sales, and Freight In. In addition, work sheet preparation will differ depending upon whether the periodic or the perpetual inventory system is being used.

3. Under the periodic inventory system, beginning inventory appears as a debit in the Income Statement column. Ending inventory appears as a credit in the Income Statement column and as a debit in the Balance Sheet column. A Cost of Goods Sold account will *not* appear on the work sheet, though it will under the perpetual inventory system. Under either inventory system, an Adjusted Trial Balance column may be eliminated if only a few adjustments are necessary.

4. Data for closing entries may be obtained from the completed work sheet. Below is a summary of the closing entries prepared when using a periodic inventory system:

Income Summary XX (sum of credits)
    Merchandise Inventory   XX (beginning amount)
    Sales Returns and Allowances   XX (current debit balance)
    Sales Discounts   XX (current debit balance)
    Purchases   XX (current debit balance)
    Freight In   XX (current debit balance)
    All other expenses   XX (current debit balances)
        Closing entry 1: To close temporary expense and revenue accounts
        with debit balances and to remove the beginning inventory

Merchandise Inventory	XX (ending amount)
Sales	XX (current credit balance)
Purchases Returns and Allowances	XX (current credit balance)
Purchases Discounts	XX (current credit balance)
Income Summary	XX (sum of debits)

Closing entry 2: To close temporary expense and revenue accounts
with credit balances and to establish the ending inventory

| Income Summary | XX (current credit balance) |
| Retained Earnings | XX (net income amount) |

Closing entry 3: To close the Income Summary account

| Retained Earnings | XX (amount declared) |
| Dividends | XX (amount declared) |

Closing entry 4: To close the Dividends account

5. Under the perpetual inventory system, the Merchandise Inventory account is up to date at the end of the accounting period. This occurs because the account is updated whenever there is a purchase, sale, or return. Therefore, Merchandise Inventory is not involved in the closing process. On the work sheet, the Trial balance and Balance Sheet columns both reflect the ending balance.

6. As inventory is sold (under the perpetual inventory system), the cost is transferred from the Merchandise Inventory account to Cost of Goods Sold. Therefore, Cost of Goods Sold will appear on the work sheet and in the closing entries along with all the other expenses.

7. Data for closing entries may be obtained from the completed work sheet. Below is a summary of the closing entries prepared when using a perpetual inventory system:

Income Summary	XX (sum of credits)
Sales Returns and Allowances	XX (current debit balance)
Sales Discounts	XX (current debit balance)
Cost of Goods Sold	XX (current debit balance)
Freight In	XX (current debit balance)
All other expenses	XX (current debit balances)

Closing entry 1: To close temporary expense and revenue accounts
with debit balances

| Sales | XX (current credit balance) |
| Income Summary | XX (sales amount) |

Closing entry 2: To close temporary revenue account with credit balance

| Income Summary | XX (current credit balance) |
| Retained Earnings | XX (net income amount) |

Closing entry 3: To close the Income Summary account

| Retained Earnings | XX (amount declared) |
| Dividends | XX (amount declared) |

Closing entry 4: To close the Dividends account

Exercises

1. The work sheet for Southwest Mart, Inc., has been started, as shown on the next page. Use the following information to complete the work sheet (remember to key the adjustments). Assume use of the periodic inventory system. You will notice that the Adjusted Trial Balance column has been provided, even though it is not absolutely necessary.
   a. Expired rent, $250
   b. Accrued salaries, $500
   c. Depreciation on equipment, $375
   d. Ending merchandise inventory, $620
   e. Accrued income taxes expense, $180

Southwest Mart, Inc.
Work Sheet
For the Month Ended March 31, 20xx

Account Name	Trial Balance		Adjustments		Adjusted Trial Balance		Income Statement		Balance Sheet	
	Debit	Credit	Debit	Credit	Debit	Credit	Debit	Credit	Debit	Credit
Cash	1,000									
Accounts Receivable	700									
Merchandise Inventory	400									
Prepaid Rent	750									
Equipment	4,200									
Accounts Payable		900								
Common Stock		3,000								
Retained Earnings		1,200								
Sales		9,800								
Sales Discounts	300									
Purchases	3,700									
Purchases Returns and Allowances		150								
Freight In	400									
Salaries Expense	3,000									
Advertising Expense	600									
	15,050	15,050								

2. Following are the accounts and data needed to prepare the 20xx closing entries for Harrington Manufacturing Company. Assume a normal account balance for each, as well as use of the *perpetual* inventory system. Use the journal form provided below. Omit explanations.

Cost of Goods Sold	$52,700
Freight In	3,200
General and Administrative Expenses	24,800
Income Taxes Expense	6,500
Sales	244,100
Sales Returns and Allowances	5,300
Selling Expenses	39,400

In addition, dividends of $50,000 were declared and paid during the year.

General Journal				
Date		**Description**	**Debit**	**Credit**

The Merchandising Work Sheet and Closing Entries

APPENDIX B SPECIAL-PURPOSE JOURNALS

REVIEWING THE APPENDIX

1. A company can record all its transactions in the general journal. However, companies with a large number of transactions also use special-purpose journals for efficiency, economy, and control.

2. Most business transactions fall into one of four types, and are recorded in one of four special-purpose journals, as follows:
   a. Sales of merchandise on credit are recorded in the sales journal.
   b. Purchases on credit are recorded in the purchases journal
   c. Receipts of cash are recorded in the cash receipts journal.
   d. Disbursements of cash are recorded in the cash payments journal.

3. The *sales journal,* used only to handle credit sales, saves time because (a) each entry requires only one line; (b) account names need not be written out, since frequently occurring accounts are used as column headings; (c) an explanation is not needed; and (d) only total sales for the month are posted to the Sales account, not each individual sale. Postings are made daily, however, to customer accounts (in the accounts receivable subsidiary ledger). Similar time-saving principles apply to the other special-purpose journals.

4. Most companies that sell to customers on credit keep an accounts receivable record for each customer. In this way the company can determine how much a given customer owes at any time. All customer accounts are filed alphabetically or by account number in the accounts receivable *subsidiary ledger.*

5. The general ledger, however, contains an Accounts Receivable *controlling* (or *control*) *account.* The controlling account is updated at the end of each month and keeps a running total of *all* accounts receivable. Its balance must equal the sum of all the accounts in the accounts receivable subsidiary ledger (as determined through the preparation of a schedule of accounts receivable).

6. Most companies also use an Accounts Payable controlling account and subsidiary ledger, which function much like the Accounts Receivable controlling account and subsidiary ledger.

7. The *purchases journal* is used to record purchases on credit. A single-column purchases journal records the purchases of merchandise only. However, a multicolumn purchases journal will accommodate purchases of more than just merchandise. Only total purchases for the month are posted to the Purchases account; however, postings are made daily to creditor accounts (in the accounts payable subsidiary ledger).

8. All receipts of cash are recorded in the *cash receipts journal.* Typically, a cash receipts journal would include debit columns for Cash, Sales Discounts, and Other (or Sundry) Accounts, and credit columns for Accounts Receivable, Sales, and Other Accounts. Postings to customer accounts and Other Accounts are made on a daily

basis. All column totals, except for Other Accounts, are posted to the general ledger at the end of the month.

9. All payments of cash are recorded in the *cash payments journal*. Typically, a cash payments journal would include debit columns for Accounts Payable and Other Accounts, and credit columns for Cash, Purchases Discounts, and Other Accounts. Postings to credit accounts and Other Accounts are made daily. All column totals, except for Other Accounts, are posted to the general ledger at the end of the month.

10. Transactions that cannot be recorded in a special-purpose journal, such as a return of merchandise bought on account, are recorded in the general journal. Closing entries and adjusting entries are also made in the general journal. Postings are made at the end of each day, and in the case of Accounts Receivable and Accounts Payable, postings are made to both the controlling account and the subsidiary account.

TESTING YOUR KNOWLEDGE

Matching*

Match each term with its definition by writing the appropriate letter in the blank.

_____ **1.** Special-purpose journal

_____ **2.** Subsidiary ledger

_____ **3.** Subsidiary account

_____ **4.** Controlling account

_____ **5.** Schedule of accounts receivable

a. Any journal except the general journal

b. A formal listing of the balances of customers

c. The record of a customer or creditor in a subsidiary ledger

d. Where the customer or creditor accounts are kept

e. Any general ledger account that has a related subsidiary ledger

---

Note to student: The matching quiz might be completed more efficiently by starting with the definition and searching for the corresponding term.

APPLYING YOUR KNOWLEDGE

Exercises

1. In the spaces provided, indicate the symbol of the journal that should be used by Targum Appliance Store.

   S = Sales journal
   P = Purchases journal (single-column)
  CR = Cash receipts journal
  CP = Cash payments journal
   J = General journal

_____ **a.** Goods that had been purchased by Targum on credit are returned.

_____ **b.** Goods that had been purchased by Targum for cash are returned for a cash refund.

_____ **c.** Toasters are purchased on credit by Targum.

_____ **d.** The same toasters are paid for.

_____ **e.** A blender is sold on credit.

_____ **f.** The electric bill is paid.

_____ **g.** Adjusting entries are made.

_____ **h.** Office furniture is purchased by Targum on credit.

_____ **i.** Closing entries are made.

_____ **j.** Targum pays for half of the office furniture.

_____ **k.** A customer pays a bill and receives a discount.

2. Enter the following transactions of Cournoyer Liquidators, Inc., into the cash receipts journal provided below. Complete the Post. Ref. column as though the entries had been posted daily. Also, make the proper posting notations in the journals as though the end-of-month postings had been made. Accounts Receivable is account no. 114, Sales is account no. 411, Sales Discounts is account no. 412, and Cash is account no. 111.

Feb.   3 Received payment of $500 less a 2 percent discount from Don Morris for merchandise previously purchased on credit.

      9 Sold land (account no. 135) for $8,000 cash.

   14 Issued $10,000 more in common stock (account no. 311).

   23 Sue O'Neill paid Cournoyer $150 for merchandise she had purchased on credit.

   28 Cash sales for the month totaled $25,000.

Cash Receipts Journal										Page 1
				Debits			Credits			
Date		Account Debited/Credited	Post. Ref.	Cash	Sales Disc.	Other Accts.	Accts. Receiv.	Sales	Other Accts.	

3. A page from a special-purpose journal is shown below.

Date	Ck. No.	Payee	Account Credited/ Debited	Post. Ref.	Credits			Debits	
					Cash	Purchases Discounts	Other Accounts	Accounts Payable	Other Accounts
May 1	114	DePasquale Supply Co.		✓	784	16		800	
7	115	Monahan Bus Equip.	Office Equipment	167	2,000				2,000
13	116	Celestial News	Advertising Expense	512	350				350
19	117	Denecker Motors		✓	420			420	
					3,554	16		1,220	2,350
					(111)	(413)		(211)	(315)

The following questions relate to this journal.

a. What type of journal is this? _____

_____

b. What error was made in this journal? _____

_____

_____

c. Provide an explanation for the four transactions.

May 1 _____

_____

May 7 _____

_____

May 13 _____

May 19 _____

_____

d. Explain the following:

1. The check marks in the Post. Ref. column

_____

_____

2. The numbers 167 and 512 in the Post. Ref.

column _____

_____

3. The numbers below the column totals ____

_____

_____

_____

_____

_____

_____

_____

APPENDIX C ACCOUNTING FOR UNINCORPORATED BUSINESSES

REVIEWING THE APPENDIX

1. A *sole proprietorship* is a business owned by one person. In accounting, it is considered an entity separate from its owner, but for legal purposes, the owner and proprietorship are considered one and the same (that is, the owner is personally liable for all debts of the business). A cash investment is recorded as a debit to Cash and a credit to the owner's capital account. A cash withdrawal is recorded as a debit to the owner's withdrawals account and a credit to Cash. Closing entries for a sole proprietorship are the same as for a corporation, except that Income Summary is closed to the owner's capital account, as is the owner's withdrawals account (an account that does not exist for a corporation).

2. According to the Uniform Partnership Act, a *partnership* is "an association of two or more persons to carry on as co-owners of a business for profit." Its chief characteristics are as follows:
   a. Voluntary association: Partners choose each other when they form their business.
   b. *Partnership agreement:* Partners may have either an oral or a written agreement.
   c. *Limited life:* Certain events may dissolve the partnership.
   d. *Mutual agency:* Each partner may bind the partnership to outside contracts.
   e. *Unlimited liability:* Each partner is personally liable for all debts of the partnership.
   f. Co-ownership of partnership property: Business property is jointly owned by all partners.
   g. Participation in partnership income: Each partner shares income and losses of the business.

3. The owners' equity section of a partnership's balance sheet is called *partners' equity,* and separate Capital and Withdrawals accounts must be maintained for each partner. When a partner makes an investment, the assets contributed are debited at their fair market value, and the partner's Capital account is credited.

4. The method of distributing partnership income and losses should be specified in the partnership agreement. If the agreement does not mention the distribution of income and losses, the law requires that they be shared equally. The most common methods base distribution on (a) a stated ratio only, (b) a capital balance ratio only, or (c) a combination of salaries, interest on each partner's capital, and the stated ratio. Net income is distributed to partners' equity by debiting Income Summary and crediting each partner's Capital account; the reverse is done for a net loss.

5. When income and losses are based on a stated ratio only, partnership income or loss for the period is multiplied by each partner's ratio (stated as a fraction or percentage) to arrive at each partner's share.

6. When income and losses are based on a *capital balance* ratio only, partnership income or loss for the period is multiplied by each partner's proportion of the capital balance at the beginning of the period.

7. When income and losses are based on salaries, interest, and a stated ratio, a procedure must be followed. First, salaries and interest must be allocated

to the partners regardless of the net income figure for the period. Then, any net income left over after the salaries and interest must be allocated to the partners in the stated ratio. On the other hand, if salaries and interest are greater than net income, the excess must be deducted from each partner's allocation, in the stated ratio.

8. When a partnership is legally dissolved, it loses the authority to continue business as a going concern. *Dissolution* of a partnership occurs on (a) the admission of a new partner, (b) the withdrawal of a partner, or (c) the death of a partner.

9. A new partner can be admitted into a partnership by either (a) purchasing an interest in the partnership from one or more of the original partners or (b) investing assets into the partnership.
   a. When a new partner purchases an interest from another partner, the selling partner's capital account is debited and the buying partner's capital account credited for the interest in the business sold. The purchase price is ignored in making this entry.
   b. When a new partner invests his or her own assets into the partnership, the contributed assets are debited and the new partner's capital account is credited. The amount of the debit and credit may or may not equal the value of the assets. It depends on the value of the business and the method applied. When the partners feel that a share of their business is worth more than the value of the assets being contributed, they generally ask the entering partner to pay them a *bonus*. Under the opposite set of circumstances, a partnership may give the new partner a greater interest in the business than the value of the assets contributed.

10. A partner may withdraw from (leave) a partnership in one of two ways. (a) The partner may take assets from the partnership that are greater than, less than, or equal to his or her capital investment. (b) The partner may sell his or her interest to new or existing partners. In addition, when a partner dies, the partnership is thereby dissolved. Accordingly, certain immediate steps must be taken to settle with the heirs of the deceased partner.

11. *Liquidation* of a partnership is the process of (a) selling partnership assets, (b) paying off partnership liabilities first to outside creditors, then to partners' loans, and (c) distributing the remaining assets to the partners according to their capital balances.

TESTING YOUR KNOWLEDGE

*Matching**

Match each term with its definition by writing the appropriate letter in the blank.

_____ 1. Sole proprietorship

_____ 2. Partnership

_____ 3. Voluntary association

_____ 4. Partnership agreement

_____ 5. Limited life

_____ 6. Mutual agency

_____ 7. Unlimited liability

_____ 8. Dissolution

_____ 9. Liquidation

_____ 10. Partners' equity

a. The sale of partnership assets, and payment to creditors and owners

b. The fact that any change in partners will cause the business to dissolve

c. The power of each partner to enter into contracts that are within the normal scope of the business

d. The balance sheet section that lists the partners' capital accounts

e. A business owned by one person

f. An association of two or more persons to carry on as co-owners of a business for profit

g. Creditors' claims to the partners' personal assets if the partnership cannot pay its debts

h. The end of a partnership as a going concern

i. The specifics of how the partnership is to operate

j. The partners' consent to join one another in forming a partnership

---

Note to student: The matching quiz might be completed more efficiently by starting with the definition and searching for the corresponding term.

APPLYING YOUR KNOWLEDGE

Exercises

1. Partners A, B, and C each receive a $10,000 salary, as well as 5 percent interest on their respective investments of $60,000, $40,000, and $50,000. If they share income and losses in a 3:2:1 ratio, how much net income or loss would be allocated to each under the following circumstances?

   a. A net income of $40,500

   A = $ _____

   B = $ _____

   C = $ _____

   b. A net income of $25,500

   A = $ _____

   B = $ _____

   C = $ _____

   c. A net loss of $4,500

   A = $ _____

   B = $ _____

   C = $ _____

2. Partners G, H, and I have capital balances of $10,000 each, and share income and losses in a 2:2:1 ratio. They agree to allow J to purchase a one-third interest in the business. If they use the bonus method to record the transaction, provide the proper journal entry under each of the following assumptions:

   a. J contributes $12,000 in cash.

   b. J contributes $15,000 in cash.

   c. J contributes $21,000 in cash.

		General Journal		
Date		**Description**	**Debit**	**Credit**

ANSWERS

Chapter 1

Self-Test

1. d (LO 1)		**6.** d (LO 5)	
2. a (LO 2)		**7.** a (LO 5)	
3. b (LO 3)		**8.** d (LO 6)	
4. b (LO 4)		**9.** a (LO 7)	
5. b (LO 5)		**10.** c (LO 8)	

Matching

1. h	**7.** s	**13.** u	**19.** d
2. f	**8.** c	**14.** e	**20.** g
3. o	**9.** j	**15.** l	**21.** a
4. r	**10.** v	**16.** q	**22.** p
5. w	**11.** i	**17.** m	**23.** k
6. n	**12.** b	**18.** t	

Short Answer

1. (LO 6)
   Zeno Corporation
   Income Statement
   For the Year Ended June 30, 20xx
2. (LO 1) Bookkeeping deals only with the mechanical and repetitive recordkeeping process. Accounting involves bookkeeping as well as the design of an accounting system, its use, and the analysis of its output.

3. (LO 8)
   a. *Integrity*—The accountant is honest, regardless of consequences.
   b. *Objectivity*—The accountant is impartial in performing his or her job.
   c. *Independence*—The accountant avoids all relationships or situations that could impair his or her objectivity.

d. *Due care*—The accountant carries out his or her responsibilities with competence and diligence.

4. (LO 2) Management, outsiders with a direct financial interest, and outsiders with an indirect financial interest

5. (LO 1) To earn a satisfactory profit to attract and hold investor capital; to maintain sufficient funds to pay debts as they fall due

6. (LO 6)

Statement

a. Income statement
b. Statement of retained earnings
c. Balance sheet
d. Statement of cash flows

Purpose

a. Measures net income during a certain period
b. Shows how retained earnings changed during the period
c. Shows financial position at a point in time
d. Discloses operating, investing, and financing activities during the period

True-False

1. F (LO 6) It is the balance sheet that shows financial position.
2. F (LO 7) The IRS interprets and enforces tax laws.
3. T (LO 5)
4. T (LO 5)
5. F (LO 5) It indicates that the company has one or more debtors.
6. T (LO 5)
7. F (LO 3) The measurement stage refers to the recording of business transactions.
8. F (LO 6) Dividends are a deduction on the statement of retained earnings.
9. T (LO 7)
10. T (LO 4)
11. T (LO 6)
12. T (LO 6)

13. F (LO 7) That is the GASB's responsibility.
14. F (LO 4) A corporation is managed by its board of directors.
15. T (LO 7)
16. F (LO 5) Net assets equal assets *minus* liabilities.
17. F (LO 6) Balance sheets do not list revenues and expenses.
18. F (LO 3) Nonexchange transactions, such as the accumulation of interest, do exist.
19. T (LO 1)
20. T (LO 6)
21. T (LO 3)
22. F (LO 2) Economic planners have an indirect financial interest in accounting information.
23. T (LO 5)
24. F (LO 1) Cash flow is a measure of liquidity.

Multiple Choice

1. a (LO 6) The answer "Wages Expense" is correct because it is the account title, of the possible choices, that would appear on the income statement. The income statement is the financial statement that reports revenues and expenses.

2. c (LO 7) The SEC (Securities and Exchange Commission) is an agency of the federal government that regulates financial trading. Its role is to help protect the investing public from inaccurate or incomplete information. The SEC requires that certain financial information be made available so that the public will be able to make informed investment decisions.

3. b (LO 4) The stock of a corporation is easily transferred from one investor to another. Corporations are owned through ownership of shares of stock.

4. b (LO 6) The balance sheet is a "snapshot" of the business, in a financial sense, on a given date. The account balances, as they appear on the balance sheet, are a report of the ultimate effect of financial transactions during an accounting period, not a report of the actual transactions.

5. a (LO 7) An audit is used to verify the information presented by the management of a firm in its financial statements. The term "fairness" refers to the ability of users of the financial statements to rely on the information as presented.

6. d (LO 5) Collection on an account receivable is simply an exchange of one asset (the account receivable) for another asset (cash). There is no effect on the accounting equation.

7. d (LO 4) The partners *are* the partnership. There is no separate legal entity in this form of organization. When a partner leaves the partnership, the original partnership is dissolved, although a new partnership may be formed by replacing the exiting partner.

8. a (LO 6) "Assets" is a major heading found on the balance sheet. Accounts Receivable is a type of asset.

9. c (LO 5) The payment of a liability will reduce both sides of the accounting equation equally. The transaction is a reduction in assets and a reduction in liabilities in equal amounts.

10. d (LO 5) The purchase of an asset for cash is an exchange of one asset for another. It is an increase and a decrease, in equal amounts, on one side of the accounting equation. Therefore, it has no effect on total assets, liabilities, or stockholders' equity.

11. b (LO 6) The statement of cash flows does not acknowledge anything called "funding activities."

Exercises

1. (LO 2)
   a. Potential investors need all recent financial statements to assess the future profitability of a company to determine whether they should invest in it.
   b. The principal goal of the SEC is to protect the investing public. Insisting that Moses make its statements public as well as examining the statements for propriety certainly will help the public make decisions regarding Moses.
   c. The bank would have difficulty in determining Moses's ability to repay the loan if it does not have access to Moses's most recent financial statements.
   d. Present stockholders will wish to see the statements in order to decide whether to sell, maintain, or increase their investments.
   e. Management will want to see the statements because the statements should help them pinpoint the weaknesses that caused the year's loss.

2. (LO 5) $35,000

3. (LO 6)

Foster's TV Repair Corporation
Balance Sheet
December 31, 20xx

Assets	
Cash	$ 950
Accounts Receivable	1,500
Equipment	850
Land	1,000
Building	10,000
Truck	4,500
Total Assets	$18,800
Liabilities	
Accounts Payable	$ 1,300
Stockholders' Equity	
Common Stock	14,500
Retained Earnings	3,000
Total Liabilities and Stockholders' Equity	$18,800

4. (LO 5)

Transaction	Cash	Accounts Receivable	Supplies and Equipment	Trucks	Accounts Payable	Common Stock	Retained Earnings
			Assets		**Liabilities**	**Stockholders' Equity**	
a	+$20,000					+$20,000	
b	−650		+$650				
c				+$5,200	+$5,200		
d	+525						+$525
e	−2,600				−2,600		
f		$150					+150
g	−250						−250
h	+150	−150					
i		+20					+20
j	−200						−200
Balance at end of month	$16,975	$20	$650	$5,200	$2,600	$20,000	$245

Solution to Crossword Puzzle
(Chapter 1)

```
     L     F I N A N C I A L
 S O L E       E           U D       C
     S         T       P   D         C
 A S S E T S S     C R E D I T O R
             E     O       T■  R
 B A L A N C E     F       A I C P A
 O   I             I       N     O
 O A C C O U N T I N G           O
 K B         N     A         T A X
 K I     E   B     A             T
 E L I Q U I D I T Y       M I S
 E I     U   A     L             O
 P T     I   S     I             N
 E Y     T   E N T I T Y
 R       Y   D         Y
```

Chapter 2

Self-Test

1. a (LO 1)
2. b (LO 2)
3. d (LO 3)
4. b (LO 3)
5. c (LO 3)

6. a (LO 4)
7. c (LO 4)
8. c (LO 6)
9. a (LO 7)
10. a (LO 5)

Matching

1. k
2. f
3. q
4. o
5. b
6. g
7. a

8. m
9. l
10. s
11. j
12. r
13. e

14. n
15. p
16. h
17. c
18. i
19. d

Short Answer

1. (LO 3) Determine the transaction's effect on the accounts, apply the rules of double entry, make the entry (journalize), post the entry to the ledger, and prepare a trial balance.
2. (LO 1)
   a. July 14
   b. $150
   c. Cash and Accounts Receivable

3. (LO 4) Two examples are the purchase of any asset for cash and the collection of an account receivable.
4. (LO 4) One example is the payment of an account payable.
5. (LO 2) Revenues, expenses, and dividends

True-False

1. F (LO 1) A sale should be recorded when it takes place.
2. T (LO 1)
3. T (LO 2)
4. F (LO 3) The credit side of an account does not imply anything favorable or unfavorable.
5. F (LO 3) Only those accounts with zero balances have equal debits and credits.
6. F (LO 7) One quickly can determine cash on hand by referring to the ledger.
7. T (LO 2)

8. F (LO 2) Notes Payable is the proper account title; the liability is evidenced by the existence of a promissory note.
9. T (LO 2)
10. T (LO 3)
11. F (LO 3) It is possible to have only increases or only decreases in a journal entry.
12. F (LO 6) Journal entries are made before transactions are posted to the ledger.
13. F (LO 6) Liabilities and stockholders' equity accounts are indented only when credited.

14. T (LO 6)

15. T (LO 7)

16. T (LO 7)

17. T (LO 3, 7)

18. F (LO 2) It is a table of contents to the general ledger.

19. F (LO 5) Unearned Revenue has a normal credit balance.

20. F (LO 2) Retained earnings is not cash and should be shown in the stockholders' equity section.

21. T (LO 2)

Multiple Choice

1. c (LO 1) Summarization of accounting data occurs at the end of the accounting cycle. Journal entries are prepared throughout the accounting period.

2. d (LO 4) When a liability is paid, each side of the accounting equation is reduced by the same amount. The transaction results in a reduction in an asset and a corresponding reduction in a liability.

3. c (LO 6) The explanation accompanying a journal entry is a brief statement of reason for the entire transaction. Debits and credits are elements of the recorded transaction. The explanation is entered after all debit and credit entries have been made.

4. d (LO 7) The final step in the posting process is the transfer of the ledger account number to the Post. Ref. column of the general journal. This last step is an indication that all other steps in the process are complete.

5. c (LO 5) If only part of a journal entry has been posted, the omitted information would usually be either a debit or a credit. As a result, total debits would not equal total credits in the general ledger accounts. Therefore, the trial balance would be out of balance.

6. b (LO 4) In the transaction described, the receipt of cash in payment of an account receiv-

able, an exchange of one asset for another has occurred. Therefore, total assets would remain unchanged.

7. a (LO 3) Increasing the Dividends account ultimately causes a reduction in Retained Earnings, a stockholders' equity account. A decrease in stockholders' equity is recorded with a debit.

8. b (LO 2) Of the accounts listed, Prepaid Rent is the only one that is classified as an asset. Unearned Revenue is a liability; Retained Earnings is a stockholders' equity account; and Fees Earned is a revenue account.

9. a (LO 2) Of the accounts listed, only Interest Payable would represent an amount owed.

10. b (LO 4) Unearned Rent would represent a liability on the accounting records of the *lessor.* The question refers to the possible entries of the *lessee,* which include entries into Prepaid Rent, Rent Payable, and Rent Expense.

11. c (LO 5) Sales is a revenue account. Revenues increase with a credit entry, and therefore Sales is referred to as having a *normal credit balance.* Revenues ultimately cause an increase in Retained Earnings, which also has a normal credit balance.

Exercises

1. (LO 6)

\multicolumn{5}{c}{**General Journal**}

Date		Description	Debit	Credit
May	2	Cash	28,000	
		Common Stock		28,000
		To record the stockholders' original investment		
	3	Prepaid Rent	900	
		Cash		900
		Paid 3 months' rent in advance		
	5	Printing Equipment	10,000	
		Photographic Equipment	3,000	
		Cash		2,000
		Accounts Payable		11,000
		Purchased a press and equipment from Mechan Press, Inc.		
	8	No entry		
	9	Cash	1,200	
		Unearned Revenue		1,200
		Received payment in advance from Ebony's Department Store for brochures to be printed		
	11	Printing Supplies	800	
		Notes Payable		800
		Purchased paper from Heritage Paper Co.		
	14	Cash	250	
		Accounts Receivable	250	
		Revenue from Services		500
		Completed job for Franklin Shoes		
	14	Salaries Expense	200	
		Cash		200
		Paid the pressman his weekly salary		
	15	Accounts Payable	1,000	
		Cash		1,000
		Payment on account owed to Mechan Press, Inc.		
	18	Cash	250	
		Accounts Receivable		250
		Franklin Shoes paid its debt in full		
	20	Dividends	700	
		Cash		700
		The board of directors declared and paid a $700 cash dividend		
	24	Utilities Expense	45	
		Accounts Payable		45
		To record electric bill		
	30	Accounts Payable	45	
		Cash		45
		To record payment of electric bill		

2. (LO 3)
  a. debit balance of $1,750
  b. credit balance of $1,000
  c. debit balance of $14,600

3. (LO 7)

General Journal						Page 7
Date		**Description**	**Post. Ref.**	**Debit**	**Credit**
Apr.	3	Cash	11	1,000	
		Revenue from Services	41		1,000
		Received payment from Isham Company for services			
	5	Accounts Payable	21	300	
		Cash	11		300
		Paid Evelyn Supply Company for supplies purchased on March 31 on credit			

Cash								Account No. 11
							Balance	
Date		**Item**	**Post. Ref.**	**Debit**	**Credit**	**Debit**	**Credit**
Apr.	3		J7	1,000		1,000	
	5		J7		300	700	

Accounts Payable								Account No. 21
							Balance*	
Date		**Item**	**Post. Ref.**	**Debit**	**Credit**	**Debit**	**Credit**
Apr.	5		J7	300		300	

Revenue from Services								Account No. 41
							Balance*	
Date		**Item**	**Post. Ref.**	**Debit**	**Credit**	**Debit**	**Credit**
Apr.	5		J7		1,000		1,000

*Previous postings have been omitted, resulting in an improbable debit balance in Accounts Payable.

Chapter 3

Self-Test

1. a	(LO 1)	**6.** c	(LO 4)
2. d	(LO 5)	**7.** b	(LO 5)
3. d	(LO 2)	**8.** a	(LO 4)
4. c	(LO 2)	**9.** d	(SO 7)
5. a	(LO 3)	**10.** c	(LO 6)

Matching

1. i	**6.** q	**11.** a	**16.** j
2. d	**7.** f	**12.** h	**17.** b
3. n	**8.** k	**13.** m	**18.** g
4. r	**9.** e	**14.** p	
5. c	**10.** o	**15.** l	

Short Answer

1. (LO 4) Dividing recorded expenses between two or more accounting periods; dividing recorded revenues between two or more accounting periods; recording unrecorded expenses; and recording unrecorded revenues

2. (LO 2) The matching rule means that revenues should be recorded in the period in which they are earned, and that all expenses related to those revenues also should be recorded in that period.

3. (LO 5) Depreciation is the allocation of the cost of a long-lived asset to the periods benefiting from the asset.

4. (LO 5) Prepaid expenses are expenses paid for in advance; they initially are recorded as assets. Unearned revenues represent payment received in advance of providing goods or services; they initially are recorded as liabilities.

True-False

1. T (LO 5)

2. T (LO 1)

3. F (LO 2) The calendar year lasts specifically from January 1 to December 31.

4. T (LO 2)

5. F (LO 3) Under accrual accounting, the timing of cash exchanges is irrelevant in recording revenues and expenses.

6. F (LO 6) Adjusting entries are made before the financial statements are prepared.

7. T (LO 5)

8. F (LO 5) It is debited for the amount consumed during the period (the amount available during the period less ending inventory).

9. F (LO 5) Accumulated Depreciation (a contra account) has a credit balance, even though it appears in the asset section of the balance sheet.

10. T (LO 5)

11. F (LO 5) Unearned Revenues is a liability account.

12. F (LO 4) The credit is to a liability account.

13. T (LO 6)

14. F (LO 5) If payment has not yet been received, the debit is to Accounts Receivable.

15. T (LO 5)

16. T (LO 3, 4)

Multiple Choice

1. c (LO 5) An adjusting entry normally contains at least one balance sheet account and at least one income statement account. Choice **c** does not, nor does it fit the description for any adjusting entry.

2. b (LO 5) Office Supplies are not considered long-lived assets. The use of office supplies is recorded as an expense. Adjustments to Office Supplies are the result of reconciling the ending inventory of office supplies to a cumulative total in the Office Supplies account. This cumulative total is a result of the addition of office supplies throughout the accounting period to the beginning office supplies inventory balance.

3. b (LO 5) Unearned Fees is used to record the firm's liability for amounts received but not yet earned. The use of this system of recognition is required so that revenue amounts can be represented properly and allocated in the appropriate accounting period. As the revenues are earned, the proper amounts are transferred from liabilities to revenues. Between the time those future revenues were received and the time they actually are earned, one accounting period may have ended and another accounting period begun.

4. a (LO 5) Depreciation is the allocation of the cost of an asset over the expected useful life of that asset. The matching rule requires the allocation of the cost while the asset is in use in the revenue-generating activities of a firm.

5. c (LO 6) Net income is the result of the calculation that nets revenues and expenses. The adjusted trial balance contains summary balances of each general ledger account after adjusting entries have been made.

6. d (LO 5) The adjustment debiting Interest Receivable and crediting Interest Income is required so that interest income for the period is recorded, even though the interest has not been received as yet.

7. a (LO 2) Estimates are involved in the preparation of account balances used to report net income. An example of this kind of estimate is the recording of depreciation expense. Although not exact, the reported net income of one accounting period can be compared with the net income of other accounting periods, providing a basis for conclusions about the firm.

8. d (LO 5) Until such time as Prepaid Rent is expired, and through adjustments is recorded as an expense, it remains an asset on the books of a firm.

9. b (LO 3) The Cash account balance represents a dollar amount at the time the balance sheet is prepared. Cash is *never* involved in the end-of-period adjustments.

10. c (LO 6) After preparation of the trial balance, but before preparation of the adjusted trial balance, an adjusting entry will be made to record office supplies consumed. This entry will reduce the Office Supplies account and increase the Office Supplies Expense account.

Exercises

1. (LO 6)

Excelsior Transit Company
Partial Balance Sheet
December 31, 20x2

Assets

Cash		$ 5,000
Accounts Receivable		3,000
Company Vehicles	$24,000	
Less Accumulated Depreciation,		
Company Vehicles	9,000	15,000
Total Assets		$23,000

2. (LO 5)
   a. $970
   b. $1,750
   c. $450

3. (LO 5)

General Journal				
Date*		Description	Debit	Credit
a.		Supplies Expense	125	
		Supplies		125
		To record supplies consumed during the period		
b.		Wages Expense	2,000	
		Wages Payable		2,000
		To record accrued wages		
c.		Unearned Revenues	600	
		Revenues from Services		600
		To record earned revenues		
d.		Depreciation Expense, Buildings	4,500	
		Accumulated Depreciation, Buildings		4,500
		To record depreciation on buildings		
e.		Advertising Expense	2,000	
		Prepaid Advertising		2,000
		To record advertising used during the year		
f.		Insurance Expense	250	
		Prepaid Insurance		250
		To record insurance expired during the year		
g.		Fees Receivable	2,200	
		Revenues from Services		2,200
		To record revenues earned for which payment has not been received		
h.		Interest Expense	52	
		Interest Payable		52
		To record accrued interest on a note payable		
i.		Income Taxes Expense	21,700	
		Income Taxes Payable		21,700
		To record accrued income tax expense		

*In reality, all of the adjusting entries would be dated December 31.

4. (LO 7)
   a. $6,200 ($1,200 + $8,700 − $3,700)
   b. $35,400 ($900 + $35,000 − $500)
   c. $3,000 ($1,800 + $3,600 − $2,400)

Solution to Crossword Puzzle
(Chapters 2 and 3)

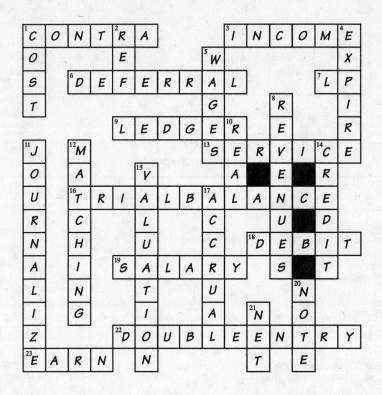

Chapter 4

Self-Test

1. b (LO 2)		**6.** d (SO 8)	
2. c (LO 6)		**7.** c (SO 9)	
3. d (LO 6)		**8.** a (LO 1)	
4. c (LO 6)		**9.** d (LO 4)	
5. b (LO 7)		**10.** b (LO 4)	

Matching

1. h	**6.** e	**11.** r	**16.** d
2. p	**7.** m	**12.** i	**17.** a
3. g	**8.** q	**13.** l	**18.** c
4. o	**9.** b	**14.** s	**19.** f
5. k	**10.** n	**15.** j	

Short Answer

1. (LO 6) Revenue accounts, expense accounts, Income Summary, Dividends
2. (SO 9) Trial Balance, Adjustments, Adjusted Trial Balance, Income Statement, Balance Sheet
3. (LO 7) Assets, liabilities, and stockholders' equity accounts will appear. Revenue and expense accounts, Income Summary, and the Dividends account will not appear.
4. (SO 8) Reversing entries enable the bookkeeper to continue making simple, routine journal entries rather than more complicated ones.
5. (LO 2) The steps should be numbered as follows: 3, 5, 1, 4, 2, 6.

6. (LO 1)
   a. Cost-benefit principle—Benefits must match or exceed the costs.
   b. Control principle—There must be good internal control.
   c. Compatibility principle—It must be a workable system.
   d. Flexibility principle—It must be able to accommodate change.
7. (LO 4) Hardware, software, and personnel

True-False

1. T (SO 9)
2. T (SO 9)
3. T (SO 9)
4. T (SO 10)
5. F (LO 6) Income Summary does not appear on any statement.
6. F (LO 6) Only nominal accounts are closed.

7. T (LO 6)
8. F (LO 6) The Dividends account is closed to Retained Earnings.
9. F (LO 6) When there is a net loss, Income Summary will be credited.
10. T (SO 8)
11. F (SO 9) The work sheet is never published.

12. F (SO 9) The key letter is in the *Adjustments* columns to relate debits and credits of the same entry.

13. T (SO 9)

14. F (LO 7) It will not include the Dividends account, because that account will have a zero balance.

15. F (SO 8) Reversing entries, dated the first day of the new accounting period, serve to simplify the bookkeeping process.

16. T (LO 6)

17. F (LO 4) The CPU (central processing unit) is part of a computer's *hardware.*

18. T (LO 4)

19. T (LO 3)

20. F (LO 5) It is called a *browser.*

Multiple Choice

1. c (LO 7) Of the accounts listed, Retained Earnings is the only account that remains open after the closing procedures are complete at the end of the accounting cycle. The post-closing trial balance is a listing of such accounts, along with their account balances.

2. d (LO 6) Of the choices given, this is the only sequence that it is possible to complete in order.

3. b (SO 8) For a reversing entry to accomplish its goal (for it to "work"), it must be the opposite of the related adjusting entry.

4. a (SO 9) The amount used to balance the Income Statement columns of the work sheet and the Balance Sheet columns of the work sheet is the net income or loss. When the amount that is required to bring the Balance Sheet columns into balance on the work sheet is an entry to the credit column, there must have been a net income. The corresponding amount to bring the Income Statement columns into balance will be to the debit column.

5. a (LO 6) Of the accounts listed, Unearned Commissions is the only choice that is not involved in the closing process. Unearned Commissions is a permanent balance sheet account and will remain open from one period to the next if it contains a balance.

6. b (LO 6) When, in the closing process (after revenues and expenses have been closed), Income Summary has a debit balance (expenses have exceeded revenues), the account will be closed by a credit entry equal to the debit balance. The corresponding debit will be an entry to Retained Earnings, reducing the balance of that account by an amount equal to the net loss for the period.

7. c (LO 6) The closing entries are prepared after the adjusting entries, during the end-of-period steps in the accounting cycle. The purpose of the adjusting entries is to update the revenue and expense accounts.

8. a (SO 10) All the components of a statement of retained earnings have been provided, except for net income or loss. A net income figure of $55,000 will correctly answer the question.

9. c (LO 6) Temporary accounts are those that appear on the income statement. They also are referred to as *nominal accounts.*

10. c (LO 1) In designing a firm's accounting system, potential changes (i.e., growth) need to be anticipated. This accommodation for potential change is known as the *flexibility principle.*

11. a (LO 5) Bulletin boards are an excellent means of exchanging information and posting questions over the Internet.

Exercises

1. (LO 6)

	General Journal			
Date		**Description**	**Debit**	**Credit**
July	31	Revenue from Services	4,700	
		Income Summary		4,700
		To close the revenue account		
	31	Income Summary	700	
		Rent Expense		500
		Telephone Expense		50
		Utilities Expense		150
		To close the expense accounts		
	31	Income Summary	4,000	
		Retained Earnings		4,000
		To close the Income Summary account		
	31	Retained Earnings	2,500	
		Dividends		2,500
		To close the dividends account		

2. (SO 10)

Karen's Fix-It Services, Inc.
Statement of Retained Earnings
For the Month Ended July 31, 20xx

Retained Earnings, July 1, 20xx	$3,000
Net Income	4,000
Subtotal	$7,000
Less Dividends	2,500
Retained Earnings, July 31, 20xx	$4,500

3. (SO 9)

Dillon's Maintenance, Inc.
Work Sheet
For the Year Ended December 31, 20xx

Account Name	Trial Balance Debit	Trial Balance Credit	Adjustments Debit	Adjustments Credit	Adjusted Trial Balance Debit	Adjusted Trial Balance Credit	Income Statement Debit	Income Statement Credit	Balance Sheet Debit	Balance Sheet Credit
Cash	2,560				2,560				2,560	
Accounts Receivable	880		(e) 50		930				930	
Prepaid Rent	750			(a) 550	200				200	
Lawn Supplies	250			(c) 150	100				100	
Lawn Equipment	10,000				10,000				10,000	
Accum. Deprec., Lawn Equipment		2,000		(b) 1,500		3,500				3,500
Accounts Payable		630				630				630
Unearned Landscaping Fees		300	(f) 120			180				180
Common Stock		5,000				5,000				5,000
Retained Earnings		1,000				1,000				1,000
Dividends	6,050				6,050				6,050	
Grass-Cutting Fees		15,000		(e) 50		15,050		15,050		
Wages Expense	3,300		(d) 280		3,580		3,580			
Gasoline Expense	140				140		140			
	23,930	23,930								
Rent Expense			(a) 550		550		550			
Depreciation Expense, Lawn Equipment			(b) 1,500		1,500		1,500			
Lawn Supplies Expense			(c) 150		150		150			
Landscaping Fees Earned				(f) 120		120		120		
Wages Payable				(d) 280		280				280
Income Taxes Expense			(g) 1,570		1,570		1,570			
Income Taxes Payable				(g) 1,570		1,570				1,570
			4,220	4,220	27,330	27,330	7,490	15,170	19,840	12,160
Net Income							7,680			7,680
							15,170	15,170	19,840	19,840

4. (SO 8)

		General Journal		
Date		**Description**	**Debit**	**Credit**
Dec.	1	Cash	20,000	
		Notes Payable		20,000
		To record 90-day bank note		
	31	Interest Expense	200	
		Interest Payable		200
		To record accrued interest on note		
	31	Income Summary	200	
		Interest Expense		200
		To close interest expense account		
Jan.	1	Interest Payable	200	
		Interest Expense		200
		To reverse adjusting entry for interest expense		
Mar.	1	Notes Payable	20,000	
		Interest Expense	600	
		Cash		20,600
		To record payment of note plus interest		

Chapter 5

Self-Test

1. c	(LO 5)	**6.** b	(LO 5)
2. b	(LO 2)	**7.** a	(LO 6)
3. a	(LO 3)	**8.** c	(LO 7)
4. c	(LO 4)	**9.** c	(LO 7)
5. b	(LO 5)	**10.** d	(LO 5)

Matching

1. e	**6.** q	**10.** f	**14.** a
2. l	**7.** k	**11.** o	**15.** h
3. p	**8.** b	**12.** j	**16.** n
4. c	**9.** m	**13.** i	**17.** d
5. g			

Short Answer

1. (LO 5)

Business Organization	Name for Owners' Equity Section
Sole Proprietorship	Owner's Equity
Partnership	Partners' Equity
Corporation	Stockholders' Equity

2. (LO 7) *Profit margin*—Shows net income in relation to net sales.

Asset turnover—Shows how efficiently assets are used to produce sales.

Return on assets—Shows net income in relation to average total assets.

Return on equity—Shows net income in relation to average owners' investment.

Debt to equity—Shows the proportion of a business financed by creditors and that financed by owners.

3. (LO 7) *Working capital*—Current assets minus current liabilities.

Current ratio—Current assets divided by current liabilities.

4. (LO 3) *Consistency and comparability*—Applying the same accounting procedures from one period to the next.

Materiality—The relative importance of an item or event.

Cost-benefit—The cost of providing additional accounting information should not exceed the benefits gained from it.

Conservatism—Choosing the accounting procedure that will be least likely to overstate assets and income.

Full disclosure—Showing all relevant information in the financial statements or in the notes.

1. F (LO 5) They are considered current assets if collection is expected within the normal operating cycle, even if that cycle is more than one year.
2. T (LO 6)
3. T (LO 6)
4. F (LO 6) Operating expenses are made up of selling expenses and general and administrative expenses only.
5. T (LO 2)
6. T (LO 7)
7. F (LO 5) Short-term investments in stock should be included in the current assets section of the balance sheet.
8. F (LO 7) *Liquidity* is what is being defined.
9. F (LO 5) The operating cycle can be less than one year.
10. F (LO 5) Net worth is merely another term for owner's equity, and would rarely equal the market value of net assets.
11. T (LO 6)
12. F (LO 6) The net income figures will be the same, although they are arrived at differently.
13. T (LO 6)
14. F (LO 7) Working capital equals current assets *minus* current liabilities.
15. T (LO 7)
16. F (LO 2) *Reliability* is what is being described.
17. F (LO 6) Earnings per share is a measure of *profitability.*

Multiple Choice

1. c (LO 5) The conversion of inventories to cash is the basis for a firm's operations. This conversion cycle (called the normal operating cycle) is frequently less than 12 months. However, if it is *greater* than 12 months, the inventory by definition is still classified as a current asset.
2. c (LO 6) The single-step income statement does not isolate gross margin from sales. Instead, cost of goods sold is combined with other operating expenses and then subtracted from total revenues to calculate income from operations.
3. b (LO 7) The current ratio gives creditors information about a firm's liquidity. Liquidity is important for anticipation of a company's ability to pay its bills.
4. d (LO 5) The owner's capital account would appear on the balance sheet of a sole proprietorship or partnership only.
5. a (LO 7) The ratio described is profit margin, which describes the relationship between net income and net sales.
6. c (LO 6) "Operating expenses" is a broad term referring to expenses of running a company *other than the cost of goods sold.*
7. c (LO 3) Conservatism requires that losses experienced by a firm should be recognized in the period of the decline. Since inventories are subject to fluctuations in value, losses are recorded to reflect a negative economic impact on a firm from market conditions.
8. d (LO 1) Each choice except **d** describes an objective of FASB *Statement of Financial Accounting Concepts No. 1.* The FASB statement stresses *external* use of financial information, and management consists of internal users.
9. d (LO 7) One calculation of return on assets is profit margin times asset turnover, which in this case equals 12 percent.

Exercises

1. (LO 5)

1. d	**5.** a	**9.** f	**13.** X
2. e	**6.** c	**10.** e	**14.** a
3. c	**7.** a	**11.** d	**15.** e
4. g	**8.** b	**12.** a	

2. (LO 7)

a.	$40,000	**d.**	12.5%
b.	3:1	**e.**	16.67%
c.	10%	**f.**	1.25 times

3. (LO 6)

a.

Corvus Corporation
Income Statement (Multistep)
For the Year Ended December 31, 20xx

Net Sales	$200,000
Less Cost of Goods Sold	150,000
Gross Margin	$ 50,000
Operating Expenses	30,000
Income from Operations	$ 20,000
Other Revenues	
Interest Income	2,000
Income Before Income Taxes	$ 22,000
Income Taxes	5,000
Net Income	$ 17,000
Earnings per share	$4.86

b.

Corvus Corporation
Income Statement (Single-Step)
For the Year Ended December 31, 20xx

Revenues		
Net Sales	$200,000	
Interest Income	2,000	$202,000
Costs and Expenses		
Cost of Goods Sold	$150,000	
Operating Expenses	30,000	180,000
Income Before Income Taxes		$ 22,000
Income Taxes		5,000
Net Income		$ 17,000
Earnings per share		$4.86

Solution to Crossword Puzzle
(Chapters 4 and 5)

```
S E C     U S E F U L N E S ▢ S
    L                   A ▓   I
C L A I M   W   C U R R E N ▓ T
Y ▓ S       A   R       N   G
C O S T O F G O O D S S O L D
L   I       E ▓ S           E
E   F U L L     A S S E T   S
    I           F           T
F R E I G H T   O   O T H E R
A   D           F O R       P
S     Z   F     T ▓   P
B E N E F I T     C L O S E D
    R ▓ X ▓ G     A         E
N O N O P E R A T I N G     B
    D   S       T   N E T
```

Chapter 6

Self-Test

1. a	(LO 1)	**6.** a	(LO 4)
2. d	(LO 3, 4)	**7.** d	(LO 3)
3. b	(LO 3, 4)	**8.** c	(LO 5)
4. a	(LO 4)	**9.** b	(LO 5)
5. c	(SO 8)	**10.** d	(LO 7)

Matching

1. h	**6.** k	**11.** m	**16.** r
2. e	**7.** c	**12.** a	**17.** j
3. q	**8.** g	**13.** f	**18.** o
4. b	**9.** i	**14.** p	
5. l	**10.** d	**15.** n	

Short Answer

1. (LO 5) Required authorization for certain transactions
   Recording of all transactions
   Design and use of adequate documents
   Physical controls
   Periodic checks
   Separation of duties
   Sound personnel procedures
2. (LO 7) (Any six of the following would answer the question)
   Separate the authorization, recordkeeping, and custodianship of cash
   Limit access to cash
   Designate a person to handle cash
   Use banking facilities and minimize cash on hand
   Bond employees with access to cash
   Protect cash on hand with safes, cash registers, etc.
   Conduct surprise audits of cash on hand
   Record all cash receipts promptly
   Deposit all cash receipts promptly
   Make all payments by check
   Have a person who does not authorize, handle, or record cash transactions reconcile the Cash account

3. (LO 7) Purchase order, invoice, and receiving report
4. (LO 4)
   Beginning Merchandise Inventory
   + Net Cost of Purchases
   = Goods Available for Sale
   – Ending Merchandise Inventory
   = Cost of Goods Sold
5. (LO 4)
   (Gross) Purchases
   – Purchases Returns and Allowances
   – Purchases Discounts
   = Net Purchases
   + Freight In
   = Net Cost of Purchases

True-False

1. F (LO 4) *Beginning* inventory is needed.
2. F (LO 2) It means that payment is due 10 days *after* the end of the month.
3. T (LO 1)
4. T (LO 3, 4)
5. T (LO 2)
6. F (SO 8) It is a contra account to *gross sales.*
7. T (LO 4)
8. T (LO 4)
9. T (LO 1)
10. T (LO 4)
11. F (LO 3, 4) It normally has a debit balance.
12. F (LO 4) It requires a debit to Office Supplies, because it is not merchandise.
13. T (LO 3)
14. F (LO 4) It is treated as a selling expense.
15. F (LO 4) Both are done at the end of the period.
16. F (LO 2) 2/10, n/30 is a sales discount, offered for early payment. A trade discount is a percentage off the list or catalogue price.
17. F (LO 2) Title passes at the shipping point.
18. F (LO 5) It increases the probability of accuracy but will not guarantee it.
19. T (LO 6)
20. F (LO 7) This procedure could easily lead to theft.
21. F (LO 7) The supplier is sent a purchase order.
22. F (LO 5) Rotating employees is good internal control because it might uncover theft.
23. T (LO 5)

Multiple Choice

1. d (SO 8) According to the terms, Dew would be entitled to a 2 percent purchases discount of $10. In this example (after allowing for the purchase returns), the discount would be entered as a credit to balance the journal entry, which would also include a debit to Accounts Payable for the balance due ($500) and a credit to Cash for the balance due less the discount ($490).
2. c (LO 4) Purchase Returns and Allowances is a contra account to the Purchases account. Purchases has a normal debit balance. Its corresponding contra accounts have a normal credit balance.
3. b (LO 4) Freight Out Expense is a selling expense. It is not considered to be an element of the cost of goods sold.
4. d (LO 7) The purchase requisition is the initial demand for goods. The purchase requisition is prepared by the individual who ultimately needs the inventory for sale or production. The requisition is then authorized by the appropriate person before the process of purchasing begins.
5. a (LO 7) Proper internal control procedures separate the functions of handling of assets and recordkeeping in hopes of preventing employee theft.
6. c (LO 3) Under the perpetual inventory system, purchases of merchandise are recorded in the Merchandise Inventory, not the Purchases, account.
7. b (LO 1) When operating expenses are paid for has no bearing on the length of the operating cycle.
8. d (LO 4) In addition, Credit Card Discount Expense would be debited for $50, and Sales credited for $1,000.

Exercises

1. (LO 4; SO 8)

		General Journal		
Date		**Description**	**Debit**	**Credit**
May	1	Purchases	500	
		Accounts Payable		500
		Purchased merchandise on credit, terms 2/10, n/60		
	3	Accounts Receivable	500	
		Sales		500
		Sold merchandise on credit, terms 2/10, 1/20, n/30		
	4	Freight In	42	
		Cash		42
		Paid for freight charges		
	5	Office Supplies	100	
		Accounts Payable		100
		Purchased office supplies on credit		
	6	Accounts Payable	20	
		Office Supplies		20
		Returned office supplies from May 5 purchase		
	7	Accounts Payable	50	
		Purchases Returns and Allowances		50
		Returned merchandise from May 1 purchase		
	9	Accounts Receivable	225	
		Sales		225
		Sold merchandise on credit, terms 2/10, 1/15, n/30		
	10	Accounts Payable	450	
		Purchases Discounts		9
		Cash		441
		Paid for purchase of May 1		
	14	Sales Returns and Allowances	25	
		Accounts Receivable		25
		The customer of May 9 returned merchandise		
	22	Cash	198	
		Sales Discounts	2	
		Accounts Receivable		200
		The customer of May 9 paid		
	26	Cash	500	
		Accounts Receivable		500
		The customer of May 3 paid for merchandise		

2. (LO 4; SO 8)

Jordan Merchandising Company		
Partial Income Statement		
For the Year 20xx		
Gross Sales		$100,000
Less: Sales Discounts	$ 300	
Sales Returns and Allowances	200	500
Net Sales		$ 99,500
Less Cost of Goods Sold		
Merchandise Inventory, Jan. 1	$10,000	
Purchases	$50,000	
Less: Purchases Discounts	500	
Purchases Returns and Allowances	500	
Net Purchases	$49,000	
Freight In	2,000	
Net Cost of Purchases	51,000	
Goods Available for Sale	$61,000	
Less Merchandise Inventory, Dec. 31	8,000	
Cost of Goods Sold		53,000
Gross Margin		$ 46,500

Chapter 7

1. b	(LO 1)	**6.** d	(LO 4)
2. c	(LO 2)	**7.** c	(LO 4)
3. a	(LO 3)	**8.** d	(LO 5)
4. a	(LO 4)	**9.** d	(LO 5)
5. c	(LO 4)	**10.** b	(LO 3)

Matching

1. j	**6.** e	**11.** c	**16.** n
2. g	**7.** r	**12.** o	**17.** q
3. f	**8.** l	**13.** s	**18.** a
4. m	**9.** i	**14.** h	**19.** b
5. p	**10.** t	**15.** d	**20.** k

Short Answer

1. (LO 4) Percentage of net sales method, accounts receivable aging method, and direct charge-off method
2. (LO 1) It means that the original payee, who discounts the note receivable, must make good on the note if the maker does not pay at maturity.
3. (LO 4) There would be a debit balance when more accounts are written off (in dollar amounts) than have been provided for in the adjusting entries for estimated uncollectible accounts.
4. (LO 3) Held-to-maturity securities, trading securities, and available-for-sale securities
5. (LO 1) Cash and cash equivalents, short-term investments, accounts receivable, and notes receivable
6. (SO 6) Bank service charges; a customer's NSF check; bank charges for collecting and paying notes, stop payments, and printing checks; and an error in recording a check (only if underrecorded). (Any three would answer the question.)

True-False

1. T (LO 4)
2. F (LO 4) It follows the matching rule.
3. F (LO 4) The balance must be taken into account.
4. T (LO 4)
5. T (LO 4)
6. T (LO 4)
7. F (LO 5) The computation is 700 × 5/100 × 90/360.
8. T (LO 4)
9. F (LO 1) The payee must make good if the maker defaults.
10. F (LO 5) It has a duration of 62 days.
11. T (LO 1)
12. F (LO 4) Total assets remain the same.
13. T (LO 5)
14. F (LO 4) The debit is to Allowance for Uncollectible Accounts.
15. T (LO 5)

16. T (LO 4)

17. F (LO 2) Accounts Receivable are a short-term liquid asset but not a cash equivalent.

18. F (LO 1) Major credit cards involve factoring without recourse.

19. F (LO 1) It equals short-term liquid assets divided by current liabilities.

20. T (SO 6)

21. T (SO 6)

22. F (SO 6) No entries are made for outstanding checks.

23. F (SO 6) It begins with the September 30 balances.

24. T (LO 2)

25. T (LO 3)

26. F (LO 3) They appear at market value.

Multiple Choice

1. a (SO 6) The error would cause the balance per bank to be understated. Therefore, the $900 should be added.

2. b (LO 5) Principal × rate × time for *b* equals $12. Each of the other choices results in $6.

3. c (LO 4) Using the net sales method of calculating adjustments for Allowance for Uncollectible Accounts, the amount of the Uncollectible Accounts Expense is based on the sales during the period. Therefore, it is not netted with an existing balance in the allowance account.

4. a (LO 1) Because the discounting bank has the right to extract funds from a firm's account if a note is dishonored, the firm carries that liability until such time as the note is paid to the bank. Once the note is paid, the contingent liability is eliminated.

5. b (LO 4) Under this method, Uncollectible Accounts Expense equals the amount deemed uncollectible ($850) minus the credit balance in Allowance for Uncollectible Accounts ($300), or $550.

6. c (LO 4) When an allowance account is established to record anticipated uncollectible accounts, the expense is recorded at the time the adjusting entry is made. As a result, when the actual uncollectible account is known and written off, the allowance account is reduced, and Accounts Receivable is reduced by the same amount.

7. a (LO 5) The discount rate is used as an adjustment to the maturity value of a note to calculate the proceeds on discounting that note to the bank. The details of a note would not include the discount rate because it is not known at the time the note is originated. Additionally, whether a note is going to be discounted or not is irrelevant in determining the note arrangements.

8. b (LO 4) The direct charge-off method of handling uncollectible accounts often postpones the uncollectible accounts expense of a given accounting period to subsequent accounting periods. Usually, a significant period of time elapses between a credit sale and the determination that the corresponding receivable is uncollectible.

9. c (LO 1) Inventory is not considered a short-term liquid asset. The ability of a firm to convert its inventory to cash is the basis of the firm's operations. Short-term liquid assets, by definition, are assets that can be converted quickly to cash (or are cash or near cash) to cover operating expenses and immediate cash requirements.

10. b (SO 6) The company presumably already has recorded the deposits in transit. However, it just learned of the bank service charges, the note collected by the bank, and the interest earned when it received its bank statement, and, therefore, must adjust for those items.

11. c (SO 6) Interest earned would be a component of the balance per bank, but it would not yet have been placed on the books. Because it is interest earned, it should be added.

Exercises

1. (LO 4, 5)

General Journal				
Date		**Description**	**Debit**	**Credit**
Dec.	31	Interest Receivable	75	
		Interest Income		75
		To record accrued interest on Notes Receivable		
	31	Uncollectible Accounts Expense	24,000	
		Allowance for Uncollectible Accounts		24,000
		To record estimated bad debts		
Jan.	3	Notes Receivable	10,000	
		Accounts Receivable, Kohn		10,000
		Kohn substituted a 30-day, 6% note for her debt		
	8	Allowance for Uncollectible Accounts	1,000	
		Accounts Receivable, O'Brien		1,000
		To write off O'Brien's account		
	25	Accounts Receivable, O'Brien	600	
		Allowance for Uncollectible Accounts		600
		To reinstate portion of O'Brien's account		
	28	Cash	200	
		Accounts Receivable, O'Brien		200
		Collection from T. O'Brien		

2. (LO 5)
   a. $16.00
   b. $910.00
   c. $43.17
   d. $4.00

3. (LO 3)

General Journal				
Date		**Description**	**Debit**	**Credit**
Nov.	17	Short-Term Investments	60,000	
		Cash		60,000
		Purchased Simpson stock for trading		
Dec.	31	Unrealized Loss on Investments	4,000	
		Allowance to Adjust Short-Term Investments to Market		4,000
		Year-end adjustment for market decline		
Jan.	12	Cash	66,000	
		Short-Term Investments		60,000
		Realized Gain on Investments		6,000
		To record sale of Simpson stock		

4. (SO 6)
  1. d   **3.** b   **5.** a
  2. c   **4.** d   **6.** d

Solution to Crossword Puzzle
(Chapters 6 and 7)

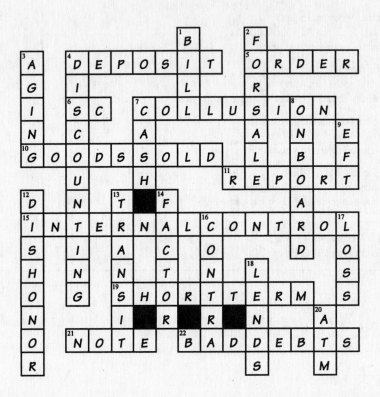

Chapter 8

Self-Test

1.	b	(LO 5)	**6.** d	(LO 1)
2.	a	(LO 2)	**7.** c	(LO 3)
3.	c	(LO 3)	**8.** d	(LO 6)
4.	b	(LO 3)	**9.** d	(SO 7)
5.	d	(LO 3)	**10.** d	(SO 7)

Matching

1. m	**5.** j	**8.** i	**11.** e
2. h	**6.** a	**9.** c	**12.** b
3. d	**7.** f	**10.** l	**13.** k
4. g			

Short Answer

1. (LO 3) Specific identification; average-cost; first-in, first-out; and last-in, first-out
2. (LO 6) Item-by-item and major category methods
3. (SO 7) Retail method and gross profit method
4. (LO 4) The periodic system does not keep detailed records of inventory; the perpetual system does. Under the periodic system, physical inventory taken at the end of each period determines the cost of goods sold.

True-False

1. T (LO 1)
2. T (LO 5)
3. T (LO 5)
4. T (LO 5)
5. F (LO 2) They belong in the buyer's ending inventory if the buyer has title to the goods.
6. T (LO 3)
7. F (LO 3) Not necessarily. The actual flow of goods is not known; the flow of costs is assumed.
8. F (LO 3) It results in the highest income.
9. F (SO 7) Items sold are recorded only at retail.
10. F (SO 7) The cost of goods sold is estimated by subtracting the gross profit percentage of sales from total sales.
11. F (LO 3) Average-cost results in a higher income before income taxes.
12. F (LO 5) The requirement is for LIFO, not FIFO.
13. F (LO 2) The consignee has possession but not title.
14. T (LO 5)

Multiple Choice

1. b (LO 2) The cost to store goods normally is considered too difficult to trace to specific inventory items, so it is expensed when incurred. The other costs listed are more closely related to the acquisition cost of inventory.

2. a (LO 5) Under rising prices, the FIFO inventory method matches current selling prices with the oldest, least expensive costs. Of the inventory methods listed, this method results in the highest income before income taxes.

3. c (LO 5) Forgetting to include in inventory an item in the warehouse results in an understated ending inventory, which, in turn, produces an overstated cost of goods sold. An overstated cost of goods sold produces an understated income before income taxes and, therefore, an understated stockholders' equity.

4. c (LO 3) With low-volume, high-priced goods, it is especially necessary to match the selling price of a particular item with its cost in order to avoid distortion in the financial statements. Only specific identification directly matches cost and selling price.

5. b (SO 7) In performing the retail inventory calculation, freight in is incorporated at cost, not at retail. The other choices provided are included as stated.

6. a (LO 1) The matching rule states that a cost must be expensed in the period in which that cost helps to generate revenue. Therefore, the cost of inventory is expensed in the period in which the inventory is sold.

7. d (LO 2) By definition, inventory should appear on the balance sheet of the company that has title to the goods (although not necessarily possession of them).

8. d (SO 7) The gross profit method is a simple way to estimate the amount of inventory lost or destroyed by fire, theft, etc. It assumes a relatively consistent gross profit ratio over time.

Exercises

1. (LO 3)
   a. $6,600; $8,800
   b. $7,200; $8,200
   c. $6,820; $8,580

2. (SO 7)

	Cost	Retail
Beginning Inventory	$ 70,000	$125,000
Net Purchases	48,000	75,000
Freight In	2,000	—
Cost/Retail	$120,000 ÷	$200,000 = 60%
Less Sales		156,000
Estimated Ending Inventory at Retail		$ 44,000
		× 60%
Estimated Cost of Ending Inventory		$ 26,400

3. (SO 7)

Beginning Inventory at Cost	$150,000
Purchases at Cost	120,000
Cost of Goods Available for Sale	$270,000
Less Estimated Cost of Goods Sold	
($300,000 × 80%)	240,000
Estimated Cost of Ending Inventory	$ 30,000

4. (LO 4)

May 1	Inventory	100 units @ $10		$1,000
4	Purchase	60 units @ $12		720
8	Sale	50 units @ $12		(600)
8	Balance	100 units @ $10	$1,000	
		10 units @ $12	120	$1,120
17	Purchase	70 units @ $11		770
25	Sale	70 units @ $11	($770)	
		10 units @ $12	(120)	
		20 units @ $10	(200)	(1,090)
25	Balance	80 units @ $10		$ 800

Cost of Goods Sold = $600 + $1,090 $1,690

Chapter 9

Self-Test

1. b	(LO 1)	**6.** c	(LO 2)
2. b	(LO 2)	**7.** d	(LO 4)
3. a	(LO 2)	**8.** a	(LO 5)
4. c	(LO 2)	**9.** d	(LO 6)
5. c	(LO 3)	**10.** a	(LO 7)

Matching

1. n	**5.** l	**9.** c	**13.** e
2. k	**6.** m	**10.** j	**14.** i
3. f	**7.** o	**11.** h	**15.** b
4. d	**8.** g	**12.** a	

Short Answer

1. (LO 2) Definitely determinable liabilities, estimated liabilities
2. (LO 3) Some examples of contingent liabilities are pending lawsuits, tax disputes, discounted notes receivable, the guarantee of another company's debt, and failure to follow government regulations.
3. (LO 2) Some examples of estimated liabilities are income taxes payable, property taxes payable, estimated warranty expense, and vacation pay.
4. (LO 2) Some examples of definitely determinable liabilities are trade accounts payable, short-term notes payable, dividends payable, sales tax payable, excise tax payable, current portion of long-term debt, accrued liabilities, payroll liabilities, and deferred revenues.
5. (LO 2) Social security taxes, Medicare taxes, federal income taxes, and state income taxes
6. (LO 2) Social security taxes, Medicare taxes, federal unemployment taxes, and state unemployment taxes

True-False

1. F (LO 2) Unearned Revenue is a liability on the balance sheet representing an obligation to deliver goods or services.
2. T (LO 2)
3. T (LO 1)
4. T (LO 2)
5. F (LO 2) Sales Tax Payable is a definitely determinable liability.
6. F (LO 2) A warranty is an estimated liability.
7. T (LO 6)
8. F (LO 5) Payments associated with an ordinary annuity are made at the *end* of each period.
9. F (LO 6) The higher the interest rate, the *lower* the present value.
10. T (LO 3)
11. F (LO 2) The account is associated with notes whose interest is included in the face amount.
12. F (LO 2) An estimate should be recorded for Product Warranty Expense in year 1, the year of the sale.
13. F (LO 2) Wages Payable is credited for net (take-home) pay.
14. T (LO 2)
15. T (LO 2)
16. T (LO 1)

Multiple Choice

1. c (LO 2) Property tax bills are not available to a firm until months after the liability actually exists. Therefore, the accountant must estimate the property taxes due for the accounting period, and enter that estimate onto the books as a liability. Upon receipt of the actual tax bill, adjustments will be made. This method is required by the matching rule, which allows for estimates when perfect information is not available, to match expenses of a period to that accounting period.

2. d (LO 2) Pending lawsuits, and the settlement thereof, would be recorded as contingent liabilities, but only if the outcome against the company can be estimated and is probable.

3. c (LO 2) Under the matching rule, estimated liabilities for vacation pay as a result of current employee status must be recorded as an expense of the current period. Therefore, by the time the employee exercises the right to a paid vacation, the expense has been recorded by the use of a liability account, Estimated Liability for Vacation Pay. As the liability expires, it is reduced by a debit entry. The credit entry is to Cash for the disbursement of pay to the employee.

4. d (LO 2) The entry to record payment in advance of the property tax bill would be a debit to the Prepaid Property Tax account and a credit to Cash. Then, as each monthly share of the prepaid amount expires, the entry would be a debit to Property Tax Expense and a reduction (credit entry) to the Prepaid Property Tax account.

5. b (LO 5) When interest is calculated on a semiannual basis, the annual interest rate is cut in half, but the number of years must be doubled to arrive at the correct number of semiannual periods.

6. d (LO 6) To calculate the present value of a single sum due in the future, one must multiply the future amount by the present value of a single sum factor, using the assumed discount rate and number of periods.

7. c (LO 5) To calculate the future value of a single sum, multiply the amount invested today by the future value of a single sum factor, in this case for two periods at 12 percent.

8. a (LO 7) Even though the problem states that there is no interest borne by the note, a rate must be applied. The method for doing so would be to record the note, discounted at an appropriate rate. The principal of the note less the discount is the actual "cost" of the equipment to Blue Water, Inc.

9. b (LO 2) With the passage of time, Discount on Notes Payable will be changed into Interest Expense, in accordance with the matching rule.

Exercise

1. (LO 2)

General Journal				
Date		Description	Debit	Credit
20x1 Dec.	31	Product Warranty Expense	525	
		Estimated Product Warranty Liability		525
		To record estimated warranty expense for washing machines		
20x2 Apr.	9	Estimated Product Warranty Liability	48	
		Parts, Wages Payable, etc.		48
		To record the repair of a washing machine		

2. (LO 2)

		General Journal		
Date		**Description**	**Debit**	**Credit**
May	11	Office Wages Expense	260.00	
		Social Security Tax Payable		16.12
		Medicare Tax Payable		3.77
		Union Dues Payable		5.00
		Employees' State Income Taxes Payable		8.00
		Employees' Federal Income Taxes Payable		52.00
		Wages Payable		175.11
		To record payroll liabilities and wages expense for Sue Diamond		
	11	Payroll Taxes and Benefits Expense	36.01	
		Social Security Tax Payable		16.12
		Medicare Tax Payable		3.77
		Federal Unemployment Tax Payable		2.08
		State Unemployment Tax Payable		14.04
		To record payroll taxes on Diamond's earnings		

3. (LO 5, 6)
- **a.** $747 ($1,000 × .747)
- **b.** $4,122 ($1,000 × 4.122)
- **c.** $1,126 ($1,000 × 1.126)
- **d.** $1,745.81 ($100,000/57.28)

4. (LO 7)

Present value = $2,000 × 4.494 = $8,988

The purchase should not be made because the present value of the future cash savings is less than the initial cost of the equipment.

5. (LO 7)

		General Journal		
Date		**Description**	**Debit**	**Credit**
(a) 20x1 Jan.	1	Equipment ($10,000 × .826)	8,260	
		Discount on Notes Payable	1,740	
		Notes Payable		10,000
(b) 20x2 Jan.	1	Interest Expense ($8,260 × .1)	826	
		Discount on Notes Payable		826
(c) 20x3 Jan.	1	Interest Expense ($1,740 – $826)	914	
		Notes Payable	10,000	
		Discount on Notes Payable		914
		Cash		10,000

6. (LO 1)
- **a.** $60,000 ($100,000 − $40,000)
- **b.** 11 times

$$\left[(\$290{,}000 - \$15{,}000) \div \left(\frac{\$30{,}000 + \$20{,}000}{2}\right)\right]$$

- **c.** 33.2 days (365 ÷ 11)

Solution to Crossword Puzzle
(Chapters 8 and 9)

¹S		²C	O	N	³S	I	G	N	M	E	N	T		⁴P
A		O			P									R
⁵L	C	M		⁶M	E	R	C	H	⁷A	N	D	⁸I	S	E
A		M			C				V			T		S
R		⁹E	S	T	I	M	A	T	E	D		E		E
I		R			F				R			M		N
E		C		¹⁰F	I	F	¹¹O		¹²A	P	B			T
S		I			C		R		G		¹³L			
	¹⁴W	A	G	E		¹⁵I	D	L	E		¹⁶L	I	F	O
¹⁷V		L					I		¹⁸I		N			
A		P		¹⁹C	O	N	T	I	N	G	E	N	²⁰T	
²¹L	O	A	N	²²S		A			T				A	
U		P		²³O	P	E	R	A	T	I	N	G	X	
E		E		L		Y			M					
		R		²⁴D	U	E			²⁵R	E	T	A	I	L

Chapter 10

Self-Test

1. b	(LO 1)	**6.** b	(LO 6)
2. a	(LO 2)	**7.** c	(LO 7)
3. a	(LO 3)	**8.** a	(LO 8)
4. a	(LO 4)	**9.** d	(LO 8)
5. b	(LO 5)	**10.** c	(SO 9)

Matching

1. e	**7.** r	**13.** u	**18.** a
2. f	**8.** h	**14.** c	**19.** i
3. n	**9.** v	**15.** k	**20.** d
4. s	**10.** j	**16.** m	**21.** p
5. l	**11.** b	**17.** g	**22.** q
6. t	**12.** o		

Short Answer

1. (SO 9) Additions, such as a new building wing, add to the physical layout. Betterments, such as a new air-conditioning system, simply improve the existing layout.
2. (LO 5) When the cash received equals the carrying value of the asset sold
3. (LO 7) The cost of the well, the estimated residual value of the well, the estimated barrels to be extracted over the life of the well, and the actual barrels extracted and sold during the year
4. (SO 9) Ordinary repairs (a paint job, a tune-up) merely maintain the asset in good operating condition. Extraordinary repairs—for example, a complete overhaul—increase the asset's estimated residual value or useful life.
5. (LO 1) Amortization, depreciation, and depletion
6. (LO 3) Physical deterioration and obsolescence

True-False

1. T (LO 1)
2. T (LO 5)
3. T (LO 1)
4. F (LO 3) Depreciation is a process of allocation, not valuation.
5. F (LO 3) The physical deterioration of a machine is irrelevant in computing depreciation.
6. T (LO 2)
7. T (LO 3)
8. T (LO 4)
9. F (LO 4) Depreciation expense will be $1,000 in the second year also.
10. T (SO 9)
11. T (LO 6)
12. F (LO 4) It results in more net income.
13. F (LO 3) Depreciable cost equals cost minus residual value.
14. T (SO 9)
15. F (LO 8) A trademark is a name or symbol that can be used only by its owner.

16. T (LO 2)
17. F (SO 9) A betterment is a capital expenditure.
18. F (SO 9) The carrying value increases because the accumulated depreciation account is decreased (debited).
19. F (LO 5) The Accumulated Depreciation account always is debited when a depreciable asset is sold.
20. F (LO 2) *Capital expenditure* refers to the purchase of an asset; *expense* refers to the expiration of asset cost through the use or depreciation of an asset.

21. T (LO 6)
22. F (LO 5) Depreciation expense should be brought up to date before the sale is recorded.
23. T (LO 8)
24. T (LO 4)
25. T (LO 8)
26. F (LO 8) Research and development costs normally are charged as expenses in the year incurred.
27. T (LO 7)
28. T (LO 1)

Multiple Choice

1. c (LO 2) Because the relative values of the lump-sum purchase are known, a ratio can be determined and applied to the purchase price of both assets. The total appraised value of the land and building is $80,000. Of that $80,000, $20,000, or 25%, is apportioned to the land. So 25% of the purchase price for both assets, $16,500, would be allocated to land.

2. a (LO 3) The expired cost of an asset is its total accumulated depreciation to date. Depreciation is the allocation of the cost of an asset over its useful life.

3. d (LO 4) The declining-balance method would probably produce the greatest depreciation charge in the first year, although it is possible that the production method could be greater. Therefore, more information is needed to answer the question.

4. c (SO 9) The change requires an adjustment to the depreciation schedule of the asset. The remaining depreciable cost would be spread over the remaining (new) estimated useful life of the machine.

5. c (LO 8) Although the life of an intangible asset can be difficult to estimate, GAAP set a "reasonable" limit on how long a firm can amortize the costs associated with intangible assets.

6. b (LO 2) Although land is not a depreciable asset, improvements to land (buildings, street lights, pavement, etc.) are. Each improvement has an estimated useful life over which the costs will be allocated.

7. d (LO 5) In order to eliminate the asset from the company's accounting records, existing ac-counts pertaining to the asset must be removed from the books as part of the transaction. Because the book value of the machine was $2,000 and the original cost was $9,000, accumulated depreciation must have been $7,000 (credit balance). To eliminate that account, a debit of $7,000 should be recorded to Accumulated Depreciation.

8. b (LO 2) A new roof has an economic life of more than a year. Therefore, the expenditure for a new roof is considered a capital expenditure.

9. d (LO 2) Understatement of net income results from expensing a capital expenditure. By definition, capital expenditures should be spread over the useful life of the acquisition (more than one period). If the entire cost is put into one period, expenses for that period will be overstated.

10. b (LO 7) Depletion costs assigned to a given period are the result of calculations based on expected total output over the life of an asset. Total costs divided by total expected units of output equal the depletion cost per unit. If the expected units of output are overestimated, the unit cost will be underestimated.

11. a (LO 8) Up to a point at which the software is technologically feasible, its costs are treated as research and development and, therefore, must be expensed.

12. d (LO 8) Research and development costs are considered revenue expenditures and are recognized in the period incurred. It is difficult to estimate the useful life of research and development.

Exercises

1. (LO 4)

	Depreciation Expense for 20x2	Accumulated Depreciation as of 12/31/x2	Carrying Value as of 12/31/x2
a.	$4,800	$ 9,600	$16,400
b.	$6,240	$16,640	$ 9,360

2. (LO 4)

$$\$2,250 = \left(\frac{\$35,000 - \$5,000}{100,000 \text{ toys}} \times 7,500 \text{ toys} \right)$$

3. (LO 2)

a. C	d. C	f. R	h. C
b. R	e. C	g. C	i. R
c. R			

4. (LO 6)

General Journal				
Date		**Description**	**Debit**	**Credit**
Jan.	2	Machinery (new)	23,000	
		Accumulated Depreciation, Machinery	17,000	
		Loss on Exchange of Machinery	500	
		Cash		15,500
		Machinery (old)		25,000
		To record exchange of machine, following GAAP		
	2	Machinery (new)	23,500	
		Accumulated Depreciation, Machinery	17,000	
		Cash		15,500
		Machinery (old)		25,000
		To record exchange of machine, following income tax rulings*		

*For income tax purposes, neither gains nor losses are recognized on the exchange of similar assets.

5. (LO 7)

General Journal				
Date		**Description**	**Debit**	**Credit**
Dec.	31	Depletion Expense, Coal Deposits	40,000	
		Accumulated Depletion, Coal Deposits		40,000
		To record depletion of coal mine for 20xx		

Chapter 11

Self-Test

1. a (LO 1)		**6.** d (LO 5)
2. c (LO 2)		**7.** c (LO 5)
3. b (LO 3)		**8.** b (LO 6)
4. d (LO 4)		**9.** d (LO 7)
5. b (LO 5)		**10.** c (LO 8)

Matching

1. i	**7.** j	**12.** l	**17.** p
2. u	**8.** f	**13.** b	**18.** h
3. q	**9.** c	**14.** g	**19.** k
4. a	**10.** e	**15.** r	**20.** t
5. o	**11.** m	**16.** n	**21.** d
6. s			

Short Answer

1. (LO 2) A debenture bond is an unsecured bond, whereas a bond indenture is the contract between the bondholder and the corporation.
2. (LO 3) A premium would probably be received when the bond's interest rate is higher than the market interest rate for similar bonds at the time of the issue.
3. (LO 3) Interest = Principal × Rate × Time
4. (LO 4) The present value of periodic interest payments and the present value of the face value at maturity
5. (LO 1) Stockholders retain their level of control; interest is tax deductible; increased earnings accrue to stockholders (financial leverage).

True-False

1. F (LO 2) They are creditors.
2. T (LO 1)
3. F (LO 2) Bond interest must be paid on each interest date. It is not declared by the board of directors.
4. T (LO 3)
5. F (LO 5) It will be less than the cash paid.
6. T (LO 5)
7. F (LO 6) Bond Interest Expense is credited.
8. T (LO 5)
9. F (LO 5) It equals interest payments *plus* the bond discount.
10. T (LO 7)
11. F (LO 5) The premium amortized increases each year.
12. T (LO 5)
13. F (LO 8) The statement describes capital leases.
14. T (LO 8)
15. F (LO 7) No gain or loss is recorded.
16. T (LO 3)
17. T (LO 8)
18. T (LO 1)
19. F (LO 1) It would indicate a high risk of default.

Multiple Choice

1. **d** (LO 6) When bonds are issued between interest dates, the amount the investor pays for the bond includes the accrued interest as of the date of issue. On the interest date, the full interest due for the entire period is paid out to each bondholder, including those who have held a bond for only a partial period. The issuing firm maintains the abnormal balance in the Bond Interest Expense account until the interest is paid to the bondholders.

2. **a** (LO 8) Interest expense on a mortgage is based on the unpaid balance. Over time, as the principal of the mortgage is reduced, the interest portion of a fixed payment becomes less. Therefore, the portion of the payment applied to the reduction of the unpaid balance increases.

3. **d** (LO 3) Bonds issued at a premium have a carrying value above the face value. The Unamortized Bond Premium should be shown on the balance sheet under Long-Term Liabilities after the Bonds Payable line with the two items being totaled.

4. **c** (LO 6) Interest expense for the period must be recorded as an adjustment at year end. In recording interest expense for bonds that were sold at a discount, the calculation includes a reduction in Unamortized Bond Discount, which has a normal debit balance.

5. **b** (LO 5) Using the effective interest method, the calculation of interest expense is based on the current carrying value of the bonds. As the bond discount is amortized, that carrying value increases. As a result, the interest expense per period also increases.

6. **b** (LO 8) The lease described in **b** does not meet the requirements for a capital lease. The arrangement does not resemble a sale. It is, therefore, an operating lease.

7. **c** (LO 7) Early retirement of bonds is considered an extraordinary occurrence. Therefore, when a gain or loss results from the transaction, the results are presented on the income statement as an extraordinary item. In the transaction described, the company paid $204,000 ($200,000 × 102%) for bonds outstanding with a carrying value of $195,000. The difference between the carrying value and the amount paid ($9,000) is a loss.

8. **c** (LO 7) The carrying value of the bonds is $612,000. If one-third of the bonds are converted, the carrying value of the bonds payable will be reduced by $204,000 ($612,000/3).

Exercises

1. (LO 3, 5)
  a. $9,000 ($600,000 − $591,000)
  b. $21,000 ($600,000 × 7% × ½)
  c. $21,450 $\left(\$21,000 + \dfrac{\$9,000}{20}\right)$
  d. $593,700 ($600,000 − $6,300)

2. (LO 3, 5)
  a. $550,000 ($500,000 × 110%)
  b. $17,500 ($500,000 × 7% × ½)
  c. $16,500 ($550,000 × 6% × ½)
  d. $1,000 ($17,500 − $16,500)
  e. $549,000 ($550,000 − $1,000)

3. (LO 5)

Interest payments ($600,000 × 8% × 10)	$480,000	
Premium on bonds payable ($600,000 × 6%)	36,000	
Total interest cost	$444,000	($44,400/year)

4. (LO 8)

General Journal					
Date		**Description**	**Debit**	**Credit**
20x1 Dec.	31	Cash	50,000	
		Notes Payable		50,000
		Borrowed $50,000 at 10% on 5-year note		
20x2 Dec.	31	Notes Payable	10,000	
		Interest Expense	5,000	
		Cash		15,000
		Made first installment payment		
20x3 Dec.	31	Notes Payable	10,000	
		Interest Expense	4,000	
		Cash		14,000
		Made second installment payment		

5. (LO 8)

General Journal					
Date		**Description**	**Debit**	**Credit**
20x1 Dec.	31	Cash	50,000	
		Notes Payable		50,000
		Borrowed $50,000 at 10% on 5-year note		
20x2 Dec.	31	Notes Payable	8,190	
		Interest Expense	5,000	
		Cash		13,190
		Made first installment payment		
20x3 Dec.	31	Notes Payable	9,009	
		Interest Expense	4,181	
		Cash		13,190
		Made second installment payment		

Solution to Crossword Puzzle
(Chapters 10 and 11)

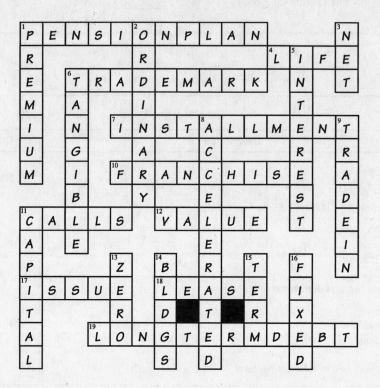

Chapter 12

1. a	(LO 1)	**6.** c	(LO 5)
2. c	(LO 2)	**7.** a	(LO 6)
3. c	(LO 3)	**8.** b	(LO 6)
4. b	(LO 4)	**9.** a	(LO 7)
5. b	(LO 4)	**10.** a	(LO 8)

Matching

1. f	**6.** m	**11.** d	**16.** q
2. k	**7.** g	**12.** h	**17.** i
3. p	**8.** a	**13.** c	**18.** r
4. l	**9.** o	**14.** s	**19.** j
5. e	**10.** n	**15.** t	**20.** b

Short Answer

1. (LO 1) Separate legal entity, limited liability, ease of capital generation, ease of transfer of ownership, lack of mutual agency, continuous existence, centralized authority and responsibility, and professional management
2. (LO 1) Government regulation, double taxation, limited liability, and separation of ownership and control
3. (LO 3) Contributed capital and retained earnings
4. (LO 5) When dividends are declared and when a corporation liquidates
5. (LO 3, 7) When a corporation has bought back some of its issued stock. Treasury stock is stock that has been issued but is no longer outstanding.
6. (LO 7) Treasury stock is stock that has been issued and later repurchased by the corporation. Unissued stock has never been issued.

True-False

1. T (LO 1)
2. F (LO 1, 6) It was established to protect the *creditors.*
3. T (LO 1)
4. T (LO 2)
5. T (LO 3)
6. T (LO 1)
7. F (LO 5) It may be both.
8. T (LO 5)
9. F (LO 1) Par value does not necessarily relate to market value (worth).
10. T (LO 7)
11. F (LO 5) No stockholders are ever guaranteed dividends.
12. F (LO 3) Common stock is considered the residual equity of a corporation.
13. F (LO 8) The amount of compensation is measured on the date of grant.
14. F (LO 4) Total assets and total liabilities decrease.
15. F (LO 5) Dividends in arrears are not a liability until declared. Any arrearage normally appears in a note to the financial statements.
16. F (LO 7) Treasury Stock is listed in the stockholders' equity section as a deduction.

17. T (LO 1)

18. F (LO 7) Paid-in Capital, Treasury Stock is credited for the excess of the sales price over the cost.

19. T (LO 1)

20. F (LO 1, 7) Return on equity will increase.

21. T (LO 1)

Multiple Choice

1. d (LO 7) When a company is dealing in its own stock, losses never are recognized. What would otherwise be considered a loss is recorded as a reduction in stockholders' equity. The exact nature of the transaction in this case is unknown because of the lack of detail.

2. b (LO 7) Treasury stock is stock that has been issued. For the purpose of cash dividends, however, treasury stock is not considered to be outstanding.

3. c (LO 1, 3) The number of authorized shares is the maximum number of shares a corporation can issue. Until such time as shares are issued, they are considered unissued. Outstanding shares are those shares that are issued and in the hands of stockholders (as opposed to in the treasury of the corporation). Treasury stock is considered to be issued.

4. d (LO 5) Because the preferred stock is noncumulative, there are no dividends in arrears. The current dividend declared will be distributed to preferred stockholders based on 7% of the par value of $100. Of the declaration, therefore, $7,000 will be distributed to the preferred stockholders (.07 × $100 × 1,000 shares). The remaining $33,000 will be distributed, pro rata, to the common stockholders.

5. d (LO 1) The stockholders of a corporation are protected from unlimited liability. Under most circumstances, their liability (or potential for loss) is limited to the amount of their investment.

6. d (LO 4) The declaration of a cash dividend requires a journal entry to record the liability and to reduce retained earnings by the amount of the declared dividend. On the date of payment of the dividend, a journal entry is required to record the elimination of the liability created on the date of declaration and the reduction in cash as a result of the payment. The date of record is the data-gathering date, and no journal entry is required.

7. b (LO 4) If stock is purchased after the date of record, the new owner has no rights to the dividends not yet distributed.

8. d (LO 5) The call feature on stock specifies an amount for which the corporation can buy back the stock. It is binding to the stockholder and to the issuing corporation in spite of possible differences between the call price and the market value at the time the stock is called.

Exercises

1. (LO 2, 4, 6, 8)

		General Journal		
Date		**Description**	**Debit**	**Credit**
Jan.	1	Start up and Organization Expense	8,000	
		Cash		8,000
		Paid legal and incorporation fees		
Feb.	9	Cash	575,000	
		Common Stock		500,000
		Paid-in Capital in Excess of Par Value, Common		75,000
		Issued 5,000 shares of $100 par value common stock for $115 per share		
Apr.	12	Buildings	240,000	
		Preferred Stock		200,000
		Paid-in Capital in Excess of Stated Value, Preferred		40,000
		Issued 2,000 shares of preferred stock in exchange for a building		
June	23	Cash Dividends Declared	8,000	
		Cash Dividends Payable		8,000
		Declared a cash dividend on preferred stock		
July	8	Cash Dividends Payable	8,000	
		Cash		8,000
		Paid cash dividend declared on June 23		
Dec.	20	Cash	22,000	
		Common Stock		20,000
		Paid-in Capital in Excess of Par Value, Common		2,000
		To record exercise of stock option by president		

2. (LO 7)

<table>
<tr><td colspan="4" align="center">**General Journal**</td></tr>
<tr><td colspan="2" align="center">**Date**</td><td align="center">**Description**</td><td align="center">**Debit**</td><td align="center">**Credit**</td></tr>
<tr><td>Jan.</td><td>12</td><td>Treasury Stock, Common
    Cash
        To record purchase of treasury stock</td><td>300,000</td><td>
300,000</td></tr>
<tr><td></td><td>20</td><td>Cash
    Treasury Stock, Common
    Paid-in Capital, Treasury Stock
        To record reissue of treasury stock</td><td>130,000</td><td>
120,000
10,000</td></tr>
<tr><td></td><td>27</td><td>Cash
Paid-in Capital, Treasury Stock
    Treasury Stock, Common
        To record reissue of treasury stock</td><td>116,000
4,000</td><td>

120,000</td></tr>
<tr><td></td><td>31</td><td>Common Stock
Paid-in Capital in Excess of Par Value, Common
Retained Earnings
    Treasury Stock, Common
        To record retirement of treasury stock</td><td>10,000
40,000
10,000</td><td>

60,000</td></tr>
</table>

3. (LO 5)
    a. $18,000 (1,000 × $100 × 6% × 3 years)
    b. $33,000 ($51,000 − $18,000)

4. (LO 5)
    a. $6,000 (1,000 × $100 × 6%)
    b. $45,000 ($51,000 − $6,000)

Chapter 13

Self-Test

1. b	(LO 6)	**6.** d	(LO 8)
2. a	(LO 7)	**7.** b	(LO 2)
3. a	(LO 7)	**8.** c	(LO 3)
4. d	(LO 6)	**9.** a	(LO 4)
5. a	(LO 6)	**10.** b	(LO 5)

Matching

1. j	**6.** b	**10.** l	**14.** a
2. c	**7.** n	**11.** p	**15.** k
3. e	**8.** g	**12.** d	**16.** h
4. o	**9.** i	**13.** q	**17.** f
5. m			

Short Answer

1. (LO 6, 7) Net loss from operations, cash dividend declaration, and stock dividend declaration are the three instances discussed in this chapter. (Certain treasury stock transactions, discussed in Chapter 12, will also reduce retained earnings.)

2. (LO 7) A stock split changes the par or stated value of the stock; a stock dividend does not. Also, a stock dividend transfers retained earnings to contributed capital; a stock split does not.

3. (LO 4) It must be unusual in nature, and it must occur infrequently.

4. (LO 2, 4) Correct order: 5, 1, 4, 6, 3, 2

True-False

1. F (LO 3, 4) The net of taxes amount is less than $20,000.

2. F (LO 6) Restricted Retained Earnings is not a cash account.

3. T (LO 8)

4. F (LO 7) Each stockholder owns the same percentage as before.

5. F (LO 7) The market value of the stock is needed to calculate the dollar amount for the journal entry.

6. F (LO 7) Its main purpose is to increase marketability by causing a decrease in the market price. The decrease in par value is a by-product of a stock split.

7. F (LO 4) It does not because it is not an unusual and infrequently occurring event.

8. F (LO 4) Extraordinary items appear on the income statement.

9. T (LO 4)

10. F (LO 7) It is part of contributed capital.

11. T (LO 5)

12. T (LO 3)

13. T (LO 1)

14. F (LO 5) They are included in diluted, not basic, earnings per share calculations.

15. T (LO 7)

Multiple Choice

1. a (LO 7) A stock split simply requires replacing the number of shares outstanding before the split with the number of shares outstanding after the split. There is no adjustment to retained earnings (but the par or stated value is reduced proportionately).

2. c (LO 7) The firm distributed a stock dividend of 1,000 shares (10% of 10,000 shares). The 11,000 shares outstanding after the stock dividend then were split into 4 shares for each 1 share (11,000 × 4), resulting in total shares outstanding of 44,000.

3. d (LO 6) The restriction on retained earnings is simply an indication of the intended use of the balance. The restricted amount remains in the stockholders' equity section of the balance sheet but should be identified separately to identify the amount that is not available for dividends.

4. c (LO 7) On the date of distribution of a stock dividend, Common Stock is credited and Common Stock Distributable is debited. Retained Earnings will be reduced at the end of the accounting period when Stock Dividends Declared is closed to Retained Earnings.

5. a (LO 4) The cumulative effect of an accounting change should appear on the income statement, after extraordinary items and before net income or loss.

6. c (LO 5) For earnings per share calculations, 40,000 shares were outstanding for the entire year. An additional 20,000 shares were out-

standing for 9/12 of the year. 20,000 × 9/12 = 15,000 shares. 40,000 shares + 15,000 shares is 55,000 weighted-average shares outstanding for the year.

7. b (LO 6) There was a $30,000 increase in retained earnings during the year, even after a $15,000 cash dividend. Therefore, net income for the year must have been $45,000 ($30,000 + $15,000).

8. c (LO 4, 6) Discontinued operations are shown on the income statement.

9. b (LO 8) If a corporation has just one type of stock, it would be common stock. Book value per share would be calculated by dividing total stockholders' equity (retained earnings and contributed capital) by the number of shares issued. The current year's dividends already would have reduced total stockholders' equity. Dividend information would be irrelevant to finding book value per share.

10. c (LO 6) Retained earnings accumulate over time as a result of undistributed income. Each accounting period that earnings are not entirely distributed to the stockholders through dividends, retained earnings increase. Accounting periods in which losses occur result in a reduction in retained earnings. Dividends declared and transfers to contributed capital are taken from retained earnings.

11. d (LO 1) The quality of earnings would be affected by the accounting methods and estimates chosen, and by the nature of nonoperating items.

Exercises

1. (LO 7)

		General Journal		
Date		**Description**	**Debit**	**Credit**
Sept.	1	Cash	1,200,000	
		Common Stock		1,000,000
		Paid-in Capital in Excess of Par Value, Common		200,000
		To record issuance of stock		
Mar.	7	Stock Dividends Declared	65,000	
		Common Stock Distributable		50,000
		Paid-in Capital in Excess of Par Value, Common		15,000
		To record declaration of stock dividend		
	30	No entry		
Apr.	13	Common Stock Distributable	50,000	
		Common Stock		50,000
		To record distribution of stock dividend		

2. (LO 3, 4)

Operating Income Before Taxes		$100,000
Less Income Taxes Expense		40,000
Income Before Extraordinary Item		$ 60,000
Extraordinary Lightning Loss	$30,000	
Less Applicable Taxes	12,000	18,000
Net Income		$ 42,000

3. (LO 3)

		General Journal		
Date		**Description**	**Debit**	**Credit**
20x1		Income Taxes Expense	24,000	
		Income Taxes Payable		16,000
		Deferred Income Taxes		8,000
		To record income taxes for 20x1		
20x2		Income Taxes Expense	12,000	
		Deferred Income Taxes	4,000	
		Income Taxes Payable		16,000
		To record income taxes for 20x2		
20x3		Income Taxes Expense	28,000	
		Deferred Income Taxes	4,000	
		Income Taxes Payable		32,000
		To record income taxes for 20x3		

4. (LO 8)

Total stockholders' equity		$680,000
Less:		
Par value of outstanding preferred stock	$200,000	
Dividends in arrears	28,000	
Equity allocated to preferred shareholders		228,000
Equity pertaining to common shareholders		$452,000

Book value per share:

Preferred stock = $228,000/4,000 shares = $57.00 per share

Common stock = $452,000/30,000 shares = $15.07 per share

5. (LO 5) Basic earnings per share $= \dfrac{\$50,000 - \$20,000}{10,000 \text{ shares}} = \$3.00$ per share

Solution to Crossword Puzzle
(Chapters 12 and 13)

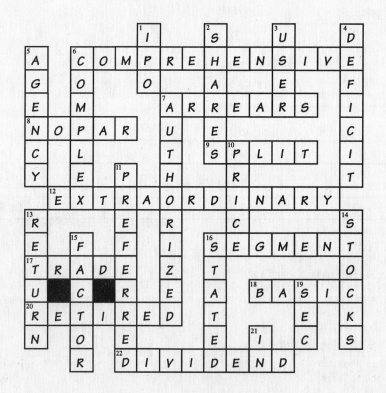

Chapter 14

Self-Test

1. a	(LO 1)	**6.** a	(LO 6)
2. d	(LO 2)	**7.** c	(LO 1)
3. c	(LO 3)	**8.** b	(LO 4)
4. c	(LO 5)	**9.** d	(SO 8)
5. d	(LO 6)	**10.** c	(SO 9)

Matching

1. f	**4.** g	**7.** h	**10.** b
2. j	**5.** e	**8.** c	
3. i	**6.** a	**9.** d	

Short Answer

1. (LO 3) Issuing capital stock to retire long-term debt and purchasing a long-term asset by incurring long-term debt
2. (LO 5) Because they represent noncash expenses that have been legitimately deducted in arriving at net income. Adding them back effectively cancels out the deduction.
3. (LO 6, 7; SO 9) Cash Flows from Investing Activities, Cash Flows from Financing Activities, and Schedule of Noncash Investing and Financing Transactions
4. (LO 1) Money market accounts, commercial paper (short-term notes), and U.S. Treasury bills

True-False

1. T (LO 1)
2. F (LO 3) It is considered an operating activity.
3. T (LO 6)
4. T (SO 9)
5. T (LO 5)
6. F (LO 3, 5) Depreciation, depletion, and amortization would be found in the operating activities section.
7. F (SO 8) The reverse is true.
8. T (SO 8)
9. F (LO 4) It implies that the business is generally contracting.
10. T (LO 6)
11. F (LO 5) It would be added to net income.
12. F (SO 9) Depreciation must be *deducted* from operating expenses in this case.
13. T (LO 6)
14. T (LO 3, 6)
15. F (LO 7; SO 9) Both methods produce the same net-change-in-cash figure.
16. F (LO 4) Dividends are deducted because in the long run they must be paid to retain stockholder interest.

Multiple Choice

1. a (LO 5) Cash receipts from sales, interest, and dividends are used to calculate cash inflows from operating activities. Under the indirect method, they are simply components of the net income figure presented.

2. b (LO 5) Net income in the operating activities section of the statement of cash flows includes the gain on sale of investments. That amount needs to be backed out of the operating activities section to avoid duplication of cash inflow data.

3. a (LO 5) An increase in accounts payable indicates an increase in cash available to the firm. To reflect the absence of that cash outflow, the amount by which the payables have increased is added to the Cash Flows from Operating Activities section under the indirect method of preparing a statement of cash flows.

4. e (LO 3) The purchase of a building by incurring a mortgage payable does not involve any cash inflow or outflow. The investing and financing activity is disclosed in the schedule of noncash investing and financing transactions.

5. d (LO 6) The payment of dividends is a cash outflow and would be disclosed in the financing activities section of the statement of cash flows. Investments in a corporation by its stockholders through the purchase of stock are considered a source of financing by the corporation.

6. b (LO 5) The increase in inventory represents a cash outflow and would be deducted from net income in the operating activities section of the statement of cash flows. The counter-entry is the adjustment for changing levels of accounts payable.

7. c (LO 6) Cash receipts from the issuance of stock are a cash inflow from financing activities. No adjustment to net income is required because the sale of stock is not recorded as a revenue and is not presented on the income statement.

8. d (SO 8) In the analysis of transactions for the preparation of the statement of cash flows, each operating, investing, and financing activity of the period is reconstructed. Net income results in an increase in Retained Earnings, and the analysis begins with a credit entry to that account.

9. b (SO 9) Total sales were $100,000. Of that amount, $14,000 is accounted for by an increase in accounts receivable. $100,000 less $14,000 equals $86,000 in cash receipts from cash sales and accounts receivable.

10. c (LO 4) The numerator for all three calculations is net cash flows from operating activities.

Exercises

1. (SO 9)

a. $57,000 ($70,000 operating expenses + $1,000 increase in Prepaid Expenses + $6,000 decrease in Accrued Liabilities – $20,000 in Depreciation Expense)

b. $360,000 ($350,000 Sales + $10,000 decrease in Accounts Receivable)

c. $31,000 ($33,000 Income Taxes Expense – $2,000 increase in Income Taxes Payable)

d. $221,000 ($240,000 Cost of Goods Sold – $12,000 decrease in Inventory – $7,000 increase in Accounts Payable)

e. $51,000 (**b** – **d** – **a** – **c** above)

2. (LO 4)

a. 2.0 times

b. 13.3%

c. 15%

d. $55,000

3. (SO 8)

<table>
<tr><td colspan="6" align="center">Connector Corporation
Work Sheet for the Statement of Cash Flows
For the Year Ended December 31, 20x9</td></tr>
<tr><td rowspan="2"></td><td rowspan="2">Account
Balances
12/31/x8</td><td colspan="4" align="center">Analysis of Transactions
for 20x9</td><td rowspan="2">Account
Balance
12/31/x9</td></tr>
<tr><td colspan="2">Debit</td><td colspan="2">Credit</td></tr>
<tr><td>Debits</td><td></td><td></td><td></td><td></td><td></td><td></td></tr>
<tr><td>Cash</td><td>35,000</td><td></td><td></td><td>(x)</td><td>6,000</td><td>29,000</td></tr>
<tr><td>Accounts Receivable</td><td>18,000</td><td>(b)</td><td>3,000</td><td></td><td></td><td>21,000</td></tr>
<tr><td>Inventory</td><td>83,000</td><td></td><td></td><td>(c)</td><td>11,000</td><td>72,000</td></tr>
<tr><td>Plant Assets</td><td>200,000</td><td>(f)</td><td>62,000</td><td>(e)</td><td>30,000</td><td>232,000</td></tr>
<tr><td>Total Debits</td><td>336,000</td><td></td><td></td><td></td><td></td><td>354,000</td></tr>
<tr><td>Credits</td><td></td><td></td><td></td><td></td><td></td><td></td></tr>
<tr><td>Accumulated Depreciation</td><td>40,000</td><td>(e)</td><td>10,000</td><td>(g)</td><td>26,000</td><td>56,000</td></tr>
<tr><td>Accounts Payable</td><td>27,000</td><td>(d)</td><td>8,000</td><td></td><td></td><td>19,000</td></tr>
<tr><td>Bonds Payable</td><td>100,000</td><td>(h)</td><td>10,000</td><td></td><td></td><td>90,000</td></tr>
<tr><td>Common Stock</td><td>150,000</td><td></td><td></td><td>(h)</td><td>10,000</td><td>160,000</td></tr>
<tr><td>Retained Earnings</td><td>19,000</td><td>(i)</td><td>12,000</td><td>(a)</td><td>22,000</td><td>29,000</td></tr>
<tr><td>Total Credits</td><td>336,000</td><td></td><td>105,000</td><td></td><td>105,000</td><td>354,000</td></tr>
<tr><td>Cash Flows from Operating Activities</td><td></td><td></td><td></td><td></td><td></td><td></td></tr>
<tr><td>Net Income</td><td></td><td>(a)</td><td>22,000</td><td></td><td></td><td></td></tr>
<tr><td>Income in Accounts Receivable</td><td></td><td></td><td></td><td>(b)</td><td>3,000</td><td></td></tr>
<tr><td>Decrease in Inventory</td><td></td><td>(c)</td><td>11,000</td><td></td><td></td><td></td></tr>
<tr><td>Decrease in Accounts Payable</td><td></td><td></td><td></td><td>(d)</td><td>8,000</td><td></td></tr>
<tr><td>Gain on Sale of Plant Assets</td><td></td><td></td><td></td><td>(e)</td><td>4,000</td><td></td></tr>
<tr><td>Depreciation Expense</td><td></td><td>(g)</td><td>26,000</td><td></td><td></td><td></td></tr>
<tr><td>Cash Flows from Investing Activities</td><td></td><td></td><td></td><td></td><td></td><td></td></tr>
<tr><td>Sale of Plant Assets</td><td></td><td>(e)</td><td>24,000</td><td></td><td></td><td></td></tr>
<tr><td>Purchase of Plant Assets</td><td></td><td></td><td></td><td>(f)</td><td>62,000</td><td></td></tr>
<tr><td>Cash Flows from Financing Activities</td><td></td><td></td><td></td><td></td><td></td><td></td></tr>
<tr><td>Dividends Paid</td><td></td><td></td><td></td><td>(i)</td><td>12,000</td><td></td></tr>
<tr><td></td><td></td><td></td><td>83,000</td><td></td><td>89,000</td><td></td></tr>
<tr><td>Net Decrease in Cash</td><td></td><td>(x)</td><td>6,000</td><td></td><td></td><td></td></tr>
<tr><td></td><td></td><td></td><td>89,000</td><td></td><td>89,000</td><td></td></tr>
</table>

Chapter 15

Self-Test

1. a	(LO 1)	**6.** d	(LO 4)
2. d	(LO 2)	**7.** c	(LO 4)
3. a	(LO 3)	**8.** c	(LO 5)
4. b	(LO 5)	**9.** a	(LO 5)
5. c	(LO 4)	**10.** c	(LO 5)

Matching

1. g	**4.** e	**7.** h	**10.** d
2. b	**5.** j	**8.** i	**11.** c
3. l	**6.** f	**9.** k	**12.** a

Short Answer

1. (LO 5) Profit margin, asset turnover, return on assets, and return on equity
2. (LO 4) Horizontal analysis presents absolute and percentage changes in specific financial statement items from one year to the next. Vertical analysis, on the other hand, presents the percentage relationship of individual items on the statement to a total within the statement.
3. (LO 2) Rule-of-thumb measures, analysis of past performance of the company, and comparison with industry norms
4. (LO 1) The risk of total loss is far less with several investments than with one investment because only a rare set of economic circumstances could cause several different investments to suffer large losses all at once.
5. (LO 5) Cash flow yield, cash flows to sales, cash flows to assets, and free cash flow

True-False

1. T (LO 4)
2. F (LO 4) Common-size financial statements show relationships between items in terms of percentages, not dollars.
3. F (LO 5) The current ratio will increase.
4. T (LO 5)
5. F (LO 5) It equals the cost of goods sold divided by average inventory.
6. F (LO 5) The reverse is true because the price/ earnings ratio depends on the earnings per share amount.
7. F (LO 5) Interest is not added back.
8. T (LO 5)
9. F (LO 5) The higher the debt to equity ratio, the greater the risk.
10. F (LO 5) Receivable turnover measures how many times, on average, the receivables were converted into cash during the period.
11. T (LO 5)
12. T (LO 5)
13. F (LO 5) It is a market strength ratio.
14. F (LO 4) Sales would be labeled 100 percent.
15. T (LO 3)
16. T (LO 3)
17. T (LO 5)
18. F (LO 5) A higher payables turnover will produce a *shorter* average days' payable.

Multiple Choice

1. b (LO 5) Interest coverage is a measure of security that a creditor can use to gauge a company's ability to cover interest payments on loans extended to the firm.
2. d (LO 5) The quick ratio measures a company's ability to cover immediate cash requirements for operating expenses and short-term payables.
3. c (LO 5) Asset turnover is calculated using net sales as the numerator and average total assets as the denominator. It is a measure of the efficient use of a company's assets.
4. a (LO 5) A high price/earnings ratio indicates optimism about a company's future. That positive outlook may be due to anticipated increases in earnings and growth of the company.
5. a (LO 4) Index numbers are calculated to reflect percentage changes over consecutive periods of time. The base year is assigned the value of 100%; then changes from that base are assigned a percentage so that subsequent amounts can be compared with base amounts. This method is used to identify trends, eliminating differences resulting from universal changes, such as inflation.

6. b (LO 1) Management uses financial statements to make decisions about the future of the company. Management also uses financial statements to analyze variances between actual results and budgeted results of operations. By using financial statements, management is better able to plan and control major functions of management. Each of the other choices listed is an external user of financial statements.
7. d (LO 2) Each of the factors listed in choices **a** through **c** contributes to the complications of comparing a company with the industry in which it operates.
8. c (LO 5) The turnover of receivables is the number of times receivables are collected in relation to sales in an accounting period. If the number is low, average accounts receivable balances are presumed to be high and credit policy is presumed to be weak.
9. b (LO 4) Net income is given a percentage in relation to sales, as are all other components of the income statement. Sales equal 100%.
10. c (LO 5) The commitments free cash flow allows for are dividends and net capital expenditures.

Exercises

1. (LO 4)

	20x1	20x2	Increase (Decrease) Amount	Increase (Decrease) Percentage
Sales	$200,000	$250,000	$50,000	25.0%
Cost of Goods Sold	120,000	144,000	24,000	20.0
Gross Margin	$ 80,000	$106,000	26,000	32.5
Operating Expenses	50,000	62,000	12,000	24.0
Income Before Income Taxes	$ 30,000	$ 44,000	14,000	46.7
Income Taxes	8,000	16,000	8,000	100.0
Net Income	$ 22,000	$ 28,000	6,000	27.3

2. (LO 5)

    a. 2.0 ($500,000/$250,000)

    b. $13\left(\dfrac{\$500,000 - \$180,000}{\$250,000}\right)$

    c. 1.9 times ($350,000/$180,000)

    d. 192.1 days (365/1.9)

    e. 12.0% ($106,000/$880,000)

    f. 22.1% ($106,000/$480,000)

    g. 6.0 times ($600,000/$100,000)

    h. 60.8 days (365/6.0)

    i. 17.7% ($106,000/$600,000)

    j. 0.7 times ($75,000/$106,000)

    k. 12.5% ($75,000/$600,000)

    l. 8.5% ($75,000/$880,000)

    m. .68 times ($600,000/$880,000)

    n. $8 \text{ times}\left(\dfrac{\$40}{\$106,000/21,200 \text{ shares}}\right)$

    o. 7.0 times ($350,000/$50,000)

    p. 52.1 days (365/7.0)

Chapter 16

Self-Test

1. a	(LO 1)	**6.** c	(LO 5)
2. c	(LO 1)	**7.** d	(LO 6)
3. a	(LO 2)	**8.** c	(LO 7)
4. b	(LO 3)	**9.** b	(LO 7)
5. d	(LO 4)	**10.** c	(LO 7, 8)

Matching

1. b	**5.** j	**9.** l	**13.** e
2. f	**6.** d	**10.** n	**14.** m
3. i	**7.** k	**11.** h	**15.** a
4. g	**8.** p	**12.** o	**16.** c

Short Answer

1. (LO 4)

Classification	Method
Noninfluential and noncontrolling	Cost adjusted to market
Influential but noncontrolling	Equity
Controlling	Consolidate

2. (LO 5) Under the cost adjusted to market method, Dividend Income is recorded when dividends are received. Dividend Income is credited. Under the equity method, the Investment account is credited (decreased).

3. (LO 7) When the cost exceeds the book value of the net assets purchased, any excess that is not assigned to specific assets and liabilities should be recorded as goodwill.

4. (LO 6) Intercompany items are eliminated to avoid presenting misleading consolidated financial statements. For example, if intercompany receivables and payables were (incorrectly) included in consolidated financial statements, that portion would represent the amount that the combined companies owed themselves.

5. (LO 1) When the exchange rate changes between the transaction date and the payment date, and foreign currency is involved, the domestic company would record an exchange gain or loss.

True-False

1. T (LO 4)

2. F (LO 5) The investor would do that under the equity method.

3. F (LO 4) Over 50 percent is the requirement for consolidated financial statements.

4. T (LO 7)

5. F (LO 6) The subsidiary's earnings are included from the date of acquisition only.

6. T (LO 5)

7. F (LO 7) Minority interest should be reported either in stockholders' equity or between long-term liabilities and stockholders' equity.

8. T (LO 7)

9. T (LO 1)

10. T (LO 1)

11. T (LO 1)

12. T (LO 1)

13. F (LO 8) Purchases of goods and services from outsiders should not be eliminated.

14. T (LO 7)

15. F (LO 4) They would be accounted for at cost, adjusted by discount or premium amortization.

Multiple Choice

1. b (LO 5) Under the cost adjusted to market method of accounting for investments, dividends received are recorded as a source of income. The dividends are not used to adjust the value of the investment.

2. d (LO 7) The book value of each long-term asset will be reduced in proportion to the value of each asset relative to the whole. Each asset will maintain its value relative to the other assets, but the total book value will be reduced to the purchase price.

3. a (LO 7) The investment in the subsidiary company will be credited in making eliminations to prepare consolidated financial statements of the parent and subsidiary companies.

4. b (LO 7) Goodwill is used as a balancing figure on the consolidation of the parent and subsidiary companies. Goodwill does not appear on the unconsolidated financial statements of the parent company.

5. d (LO 7, 8) Profit on goods sold by the subsidiary to outsiders is an income item that is part of the total income of the parent and subsidiary upon consolidation. It will not be eliminated during consolidation.

6. d (LO 5) The adjustment required to recognize a loss on long-term investments includes a debit to Unrealized Loss on Long-Term Investments and a credit to Allowance to Adjust Long-Term Investments to Market. Since the market value of the investment is $35,000 below the cost, and the allowance account has a credit balance of $10,000, the adjustment for the current period will be an additional $25,000 credit.

7. d (LO 5) So that the users of financial statements will get a fair picture of the value of the company, Unrealized Loss on Long-Term Investments appears as a reduction in stockholders' equity and as a component of other comprehensive income. The corresponding allowance account is a contra-asset account and is used to revalue the investment account to market. Upon disposal of the long-term investment, the unrealized loss may be realized and appear on the income statement.

8. c (LO 1) Since fewer dollars were required to satisfy the payment for the asset, the company has experienced a gain in reporting the transaction in dollars. At the payment date, more francs were received per dollar.

Exercises

1. (LO 7)

Account Debited	Amount	Account Credited	Amount
Common Stock (Trahan)	$60,000	Investment in Trahan Corporation	$165,000
Retained Earnings (Trahan)	90,000	Minority Interest	30,000
Building	10,000		
Goodwill	35,000		

2. (LO 5)

		General Journal		
Date		Description	Debit	Credit
		Cash	12,000	
		Dividend Income		12,000
		To record cash dividend from Tewa*		
		($80,000 × 15%)		
		Cash	15,000	
		Investment in Rorris Company		15,000
		To record cash dividend from Rorris		
		($50,000 × 30%)		
		Investment in Rorris Company	19,500	
		Income, Rorris Company Investment		19,500
		To recognize 30% of income reported by Rorris Company		
		($65,000 × 30%)		

*Tewa's earnings of $110,000 are irrelevant, since Glenn is using the cost adjusted to market method to account for the investment.

3. (LO 1)

		General Journal		
Date		Description	Debit	Credit
		Accounts Receivable, Mexican company	5,000	
		Sales		5,000
		To record sale of merchandise		
		($100,000 × $.05)		
		Cash	4,500	
		Exchange Gain or Loss	500	
		Accounts Receivable, Mexican company		5,000
		To record receipt of payment		
		($100,000 × $.045)		

Solution to Crossword Puzzle
(Chapters 14, 15, and 16)

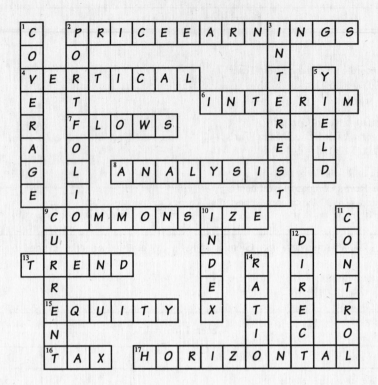

1.

Southwest Mart, Inc.
Work Sheet
For the Month Ended March 31, 20xx

Account Name	Trial Balance Debit	Trial Balance Credit	Adjustments Debit	Adjustments Credit	Adjusted Trial Balance Debit	Adjusted Trial Balance Credit	Income Statement Debit	Income Statement Credit	Balance Sheet Debit	Balance Sheet Credit
Cash	1,000				1,000				1,000	
Accounts Receivable	700				700				700	
Merchandise Inventory	400				400		400	620	620	
Prepaid Rent	750			(a) 250	500				500	
Equipment	4,200				4,200				4,200	
Accounts Payable		900				900				900
Common Stock		3,000				3,000				3,000
Retained Earnings		1,200				1,200				1,200
Sales		9,800				9,800		9,800		
Sales Discounts	300				300		300			
Purchases	3,700				3,700		3,700			
Purchases Returns and Allowances		150				150		150		
Freight In	400				400		400			
Salaries Expense	3,000		(b) 500		3,500		3,500			
Advertising Expense	600				600		600			
	15,050	15,050								
Rent Expense			(a) 250		250		250			
Salaries Payable				(b) 500		500				500
Depreciation Expense			(c) 375		375		375			
Accumulated Depreciation, Equipment				(c) 375		375				375
Income Taxes Expense			(e) 180		180		180			
Income Taxes Payable				(e) 180		180				180
			1,305	1,305	16,105	16,105	9,705	10,570	7,020	6,155
Net Income							865			865
							10,570	10,570	7,020	7,020

2.

		General Journal		

Date		Description	Debit	Credit
		Income Summary	131,900	
		Sales Returns and Allowances		5,300
		Cost of Goods Sold		52,700
		Freight In		3,200
		Selling Expenses		39,400
		General and Administrative Expenses		24,800
		Income Taxes Expense		6,500
		Sales	244,100	
		Income SUmmary		244,100
		Income Summary	112,200	
		Retained Earning		112,200
		Retained Earnings	50,000	
		Dividends		50,000

Matching

1. a **3.** c **5.** b
2. d **4.** e

Exercises

1. a. J **d.** CP **g.** J **j.** CP
   b. CR **e.** S **h.** J **k.** CR
   c. P **f.** CP **i.** J

2.

		Cash Receipts Journal							Page 1
				Debits			**Credits**		
Date		Account Debited/Credited	Post. Ref.	Cash	Sales Disc.	Other Accts.	Accts. Receiv.	Sales	Other Accts.
Feb.	3	Don Morris	✓	490	10		500		
	9	Land	135	8,000					8,000
	14	Common Stock	311	10,000					10,000
	23	Sue O'Neill	✓	150			150		
	28	Sales		25,000				25,000	
				43,640	10		650	25,000	18,000
				(111)	(412)		(114)	(411)	(✓)

3. a. Cash payments journal
   b. The Other Accounts total should have a check mark (not an account number) below it to signify that it is not posted at the end of the month.
   c. May 1 Paid DePasquale Supply Co. for $800 of supplies previously purchased. Paid within the discount period, receiving a $16 discount.
   May 7 Purchased for cash $2,000 of office equipment from Monahan Business Equipment.
   May 13 Paid $350 for ad placed in the *Celestial News.*
   May 19 Paid Denecker Motors for $420 of items previously purchased. Did not pay within the discount period (or no discount allowed).

   d. 1. The amounts in the Accounts Payable column were posted to the accounts payable subsidiary accounts (DePasquale Supply Co. and Denecker Motors).
   2. The amounts in the Other Accounts column were posted to the general ledger accounts (Office Equipment and Advertising Expense).
   3. The 315 is an error, as already explained. The other numbers refer to the account numbers within the general ledger to which the column totals were posted.

Appendix C

Matching

1. e	**5.** b	**8.** h
2. f	**6.** c	**9.** a
3. j	**7.** g	**10.** d
4. i		

Exercises

1. a. A = $14,500 ($10,000 + $3,000 + $1,500)
   B = $13,000 ($10,000 + $2,000 + $1,000)
   C = $13,000 ($10,000 + $2,500 + $500)
   b. A = $7,000 ($10,000 + $3,000 − $6,000)
   B = $8,000 ($10,000 + $2,000 − $4,000)
   C = $10,500 ($10,000 + $2,500 − $2,000)
   c. A = ($8,000) ($10,000 + $3,000 − $21,000)
   B = ($2,000) ($10,000 + $2,000 − $14,000)
   C = $5,500 ($10,000 + $2,500 − $7,000)

2.

	General Journal			
Date		**Description**	**Debit**	**Credit**
a.		Cash	12,000	
		G, Capital	800	
		H, Capital	800	
		I, Capital	400	
		J, Capital		14,000
		To record purchase of one-third interest by J		
b.		Cash	15,000	
		J, Capital		15,000
		To record purchase of one-third interest by J		
c.		Cash	21,000	
		G, Capital		1,600
		H, Capital		1,600
		I, Capital		800
		J, Capital		17,000
		To record purchase of one-third interest by J		